Latina and Latino Voices in Literature for Children and Teenagers

FRANCES ANN DAY

Latina and Latino Voices
in Literature for Children and Teenagers

HEINEMANN ◆ PORTSMOUTH, NH

Heinemann
A division of Reed Elsevier Inc.
361 Hanover Street
Portsmouth, NH 03801-3912

We would like to thank those who have given their permission to include material in this book.

The guidelines listed on page 5 were adapted from *Guidelines for Selecting Bias-Free Textbooks and
Storybooks* by the Council on Interracial Books for Children, 1841 Broadway, New York, NY 10023.

Library of Congress Cataloging-in-Publication Data
Day, Frances Ann.
        Latina and Latino voices in literature for children and teenagers
    / Frances Ann Day.
            p.   cm.
        Includes bibliographical references and indexes.
        ISBN 0-435-07202-1
    1. American literature—Hispanic American authors—Bibliography.   2. Hispanic American litera-
ture (Spanish)—Bibliography.   3. Children's literature, American—Hispanic American authors—
Bibliography.   4. Young adult literature, American—Hispanic American authors—Bibliography.
5. American literature—20th century—Bibliography.   6. Latin American literature—20th century—
Bibliography.   7. Children—United States—Books and reading.   8. Teenagers—United States—
Books and reading.   9. Hispanic Americans—Books and reading.   I. Title.
        Z1229.H57D3   1997
        [PS153.H56]
        016.8109'9283'08968—dc20
                                                                                            96-44895
                                                                                            CIP

Editor: Scott Mahler
Production: Renée Le Verrier
Cover design: Catherine Haukes
Manufacturing: Louise Richardson

Printed in the United States of America on acid-free paper
00   99   EB   2   3   4   5   6

For Amelia

Contents

MORE LATINA AND LATINO VOICES

PART THREE ♦ APPENDICES

PART FOUR ◆ INDEXES

Acknowledgments

A very special thank-you to Roxanna, Sandy, and Isis, who have supported my writing each in her own unique way. I would also like to express my special appreciation of the marvelous authors featured in this book, whose humor, insight, and generosity of spirit made the journey a warm and fascinating one. I am grateful to Arte Público Press and the other publishers who generously responded to requests for review materials, permissions, and other information. And to Yoko Kawashima Watkins, Vivian Sheldon Epstein, Edith King, Joyce Hansen, Sook Nyul Choi, and Mildred Pitts Walter, I extend my heartfelt thanks for their kindness, encouragement, and support. My gratitude to all the educators, librarians, and others who responded so enthusiastically to my first book and encouraged me to embark on this new adventure. The librarians and staff at the Sonoma County Libraries are to be commended for their patience, expertise, and caring responses to countless questions. Best wishes to all the young people who will have the opportunity to hear the voices of these fine writers.

Introduction

Latina and Latino Voices in Literature for Children and Teenagers celebrates the lives and work of twenty-three inspiring authors. Readers of all ages are invited to explore the joys of reading authors as well as books. When was it that we each discovered that books were created by real people? As we fell in love with reading, we were intrigued by that mysterious person behind the words in the book. Who are they? Why are they writers? Why do they choose to write picture books, poetry, fiction, personal narrative, folktales, drama, fantasy, or biography? What experiences shaped their lives and thinking and led them to share their joys, struggles, defeats, and triumphs with their readers?

Come along for a passionate journey where reading is not just reading. It is also developing a relationship with the authors who wrote the books we are enjoying. When we identify with an author, we become much more excited about reading. We develop a unique dialogue with the writer that engages us in an exchange of ideas and perspectives, linking our experiences with those in the book. As our imaginations are expanded, we gain insights into worlds we have not understood or imagined. When the experience is similar to ours, we feel validated, often finding that our awareness of ourselves has been extended and strengthened. We search for the author's next book and the next, learning to read each one within the context of the complete body of work. We become attuned to nuances in style, subtleties in language, and changes in tone, genre, and perspective. We learn to read as writers, watching for the many exciting ways in which words and sentences and paragraphs can be patterned, collaged, and quilted into magical pieces that transport us far beyond our own time, place, and worldview. As we establish stronger connections with the printed word, we find that we are negotiating more sophisticated meaning from our reading and that our writing is becoming richer and more imaginative.

As we look back on the special bonds we have established with books and those unique people who created them, we search for ways to share the joys of these experiences with the young people around us. As educators, parents, and/or librarians, we understand the importance of empowering all youngsters with a sense of positive self-identity and self-esteem. We know that they need literature that reflects their cultural experiences and the history of their people. We recognize each person's need to see themselves in the books they read and to be validated by the images in the literature available to them. We are aware that omission of these images combined with other destructive forms of racism can lead to alienation, loss of cultural identity, self-doubts, and even self-hatred. As we examine the body of children's and young adult literature, we search for good books that celebrate the lives of all the young people we know and cherish. We discover that the field has a history of excluding or distorting the experiences and contributions of Latina/os, African Americans, Native Americans, Asian Americans, and people from other parallel cultures. Although recently there have been significant improvements in publishing the works of diverse authors, the appalling omissions documented by researchers in the field still exist in varying degrees in many schools, libraries, and homes across our country. Knowing that literature has the power to affect the hearts and minds of readers of all ages, we resolve to search for authentic voices from these disenfranchised groups. We are pleased to find many gifted writers from diverse groups who are creating eloquent books for young readers. Wanting all youngsters to feel affirmed, confident, resilient, and capable, we seek ways to spread the word about the vital works of these marvelous authors.

In an earlier book, *Multicultural Voices in Contemporary Literature,* I celebrated the lives and works of thirty-nine authors and illustrators from twenty different cultures. In this book I turn to one of the most dynamic, diverse, fast-growing cultural groups in the United States. The 1990 census counted more than 22 million Latinas and Latinos and projected that that number will increase to 31 million by the year 2000. In *Latino Voices,* Frances R. Aparicio writes that Latinos are not a race but a mixture of Indian, African, and European peoples, making them one of the most racially diverse people in the world. As *mestizos,* they are as diverse in their language as they are in their race, appearance, socioeconomic class, and location in which they live. Many Latinas and Latinos speak Spanish, but very different oral versions of it, with a wide variety of dialects and differing accents and vocabularies. Those who were born in the United States are often bilingual or speak only English or Spanish. Latinas and Latinos have come to the United States from Mexico, Central America, South America, and the Caribbean. The largest groups of Latinas and Latinos are Mexican Americans, Puerto Ricans, and Cuban Americans. They are Catholic, Muslim, Pentacostal, Mormon, Jewish, and many other religions.

Each group of Latinas and Latinos in the United States has a distinct culture due to their separate histories and diverse backgrounds and experiences. Yet there are significant commonalities. And within each group, as within every culture, there are differences as well as commonalities. These differences and similarities have resulted in a vibrant mosaic of rich traditions, experiences, and perspectives. As we examine the writings of Latinas and Latinos, we are struck by the beauty, depth, and power expressed therein. The myth of a singular U.S.-Latina/o experience is shattered by the multiplicity of exciting literary works that are being created. The often patronizing, pastoral, and assimilative images of Latina and Latino characters that pervaded literature for young readers in the past are being replaced by eloquent, authentic, beautifully written and illustrated books. Created by Latinas and Latinos about their perceptions and experiences, these fully dimensional books offer youngsters literary mirrors in which they can see themselves and their people and take pride in their heritage. As they learn about their history and culture, their sense of who they are is clarified and affirmed.

This emergent body of literature is crucial not only to the identities of Latina/o youngsters, but also for young people from other cultures. It is important that all people become aware of and learn to value the myriad ways in which humans explain the world. Without a complete vision of all that it means to be human, we live impoverished and isolated lives. Fortunately, the world of literature for children and teenagers is gradually being transformed to embrace the wondrous complexity, diversity, and depth of the human experience.

In spite of recent changes in the field of literature for young people, however, many educators, librarians, and parents report that these new materials are not yet available to them. Many of the books are being published by small presses and are sometimes difficult to find. Phyllis Tashlik reported in her recent book, *Hispanic, Female and Young,* that her students had gone through nine years of education in the New York City Public Schools and even though the student population is more than a third Latino/a, they had never been introduced to a single novel written by a Latina or Latino author. In a recent interview in the *Albuquerque Journal,* author Pat Mora pointed out that even though 60 percent of the children in the Santa Fe schools are Latina /o, she has yet to come across a children's book with a main character who is Latina or Latino. Similar findings are being reported from Colorado, California, and around the country.

Adults who select and share books with young people are invited to make a commitment to finding the books that speak to each youngster who touches their lives. *Latina and Latino Voices in Literature for Children and Teenagers* was written to help educators, librarians, and parents in this important endeavor. Within the pages of this book, we meet and become acquainted with wonderfully creative Latina and Latino authors. Some of them are well known and have gained a reputation for their fine work in the field of literature for young readers. Others are being introduced here as promising writers who have something very important to share. (Fifteen additional authors are introduced through brief biographical sketches and a summary of one of their books.) Both established and emerging voices are celebrated in the pages that follow. Each chapter features one of these marvelous wordspinners, providing a photograph and biographical information so that adults and youngsters alike can get to know them as real people. The information for the biographical profiles was gathered through personal and telephone interviews, written communication, and/or research of secondary sources. A list of the books written by each author is included along with bibliographic information that will aid in locating them. Most of the books written by the authors are reviewed and accompanied by related works and major themes. Optional activities for ways in which they might be used in library or classroom settings are included in Appendix 2.

A noteworthy section of this book addresses the issues involved in evaluating and selecting books from a pluralistic perspective. "Evaluating Books for Bias" provides helpful guidelines for examining books for racist, sexist, classist, ageist, ableist, and homophobic attitudes. These attitudes—expressed repeatedly in books and other media—gradually distort youngsters' perceptions until stereotypes and myths are accepted as reality. As we search for ways to create a better world, we are learning to challenge the many forms that bias takes. By teaching young people how to detect bias in books, we are helping them break down barriers, both internal and external.

The six appendices at the end of the book:
• Highlight many additional Latina and Latino authors
• Offer suggestions for activities teachers, parents, and librarians might use with the books to extend the literary experience
• List the birthdays of the authors so that each unit might be further personalized
• Supply a calendar of holidays and special days often celebrated by Latinas and Latinos
• Provide information about additional resources for young people such as magazines, videos, and posters
• Provide an extensive bibliography of additional resources for educators, librarians, and parents such as journals, newsletters, catalogs, and organizations.

Four indexes are provided. In addition to the Title Index, Illustrator Index, and Awards and Honors Index, an extensive Subject Index is available to use in planning story sessions and units of study. Themes, curricular areas, genres, and topics are included in this comprehensive index.

As we approach the twenty-first century, we honor the legacy of those trailblazing writers, publishers, educators, and librarians who have demonstrated their commitment to all the diverse people of the world. As we continue the important work of bringing together youngsters and good books, we renew our commitment to "keeping hope alive." We are inspired to instill in young people a love of reading as well as a deeper understanding and appreciation of their own and others' cultures. It is with this empowering spirit that *Latina and Latino Voices in Literature for Children and Teenagers* was created.

Evaluating Books for Bias

Both in school and out, children are exposed to racist, sexist, classist, ageist, ableist, looksist, and homophobic attitudes. These attitudes—expressed repeatedly in books and in other media—gradually distort their perceptions until stereotypes and myths are accepted as reality. It is difficult for an adult to persuade young people to question society's attitudes. *But if a youngster can be shown how to detect bias in a book,* she or he may transfer this awareness to life outside of literature. Although the complexities involved in appraising the intangibles present in the literary arts cannot be encompassed in a checklist, the following guidelines are offered as a starting point in the evaluation of books from a pluralistic perspective.

1. **Omission:** In spite of the fact that many excellent multicultural books are finally being published, omission continues to be one of the biggest problems in literature for young readers today. Exclusion is one of the most insidious and painful forms of bias; a group may be excluded from an entire collection or from the books selected for use in a particular library, school district, school, or classroom. The implicit message is that the group does not exist, is insignificant, or has made no contributions to society. Invisibility is destructive not only to the group(s) involved but to the larger society.

2. **Illustrations:** *Look for stereotypes.* A stereotype is an oversimplified generalization about a particular group that usually carries derogatory implications. Stereotypes may be blatant or subtle. Watch for depictions that demean

or ridicule characters because of their race, gender, age, ability, religion, sexual orientation, socioeconomic class, or native language.

Look for Tokenism. Is one person from the group presented as having admirable qualities while all the others of the group are stereotyped? In illustrations, do people of color look just like whites except for being tinted or colored in? Do all "minority" faces look stereotypically alike or are they depicted as genuine individuals with distinctive features?

Who Is Doing What? Do the illustrations depict people of color in subservient and passive roles or in leadership and action roles? Are males the active doers and females the inactive observers?

3. Check the Story Line: Bias may be expressed in blatant and subtle ways. Watch for the following forms of subtle, covert bias:

Standards for Success. Does it take white male behavior standards for a person of color or a female to "get ahead"? Is "making it" in the dominant white society projected as the only ideal? To gain acceptance and approval, do people of color and females have to exhibit extraordinary qualities?

Resolution of Problems. How are problems conceived, presented, and resolved in the story? Are minority people considered to be "the problem"? Are the conditions facing oppressed groups represented as related to an unjust society? Does the story line encourage passive acceptance or active resistance? Are problems faced by the minority person resolved through the benevolent intervention of a white, able-bodied, middle-class male?

Roles of Females. Are the achievements of girls and women based on their own initiative and work or are they due to their appearances or their relationships with males? Are females presented as problem solvers with a life of their own or is their role in the story only as support to male characters? Is it assumed that female characters will marry and that this is their only or major interest in life? Is there an emphasis on describing the physical appearance of female characters? Are positive female characters portrayed as "beautiful" and negative female characters portrayed as "unattractive"? Are older females portrayed in a negative manner? Are older unmarried females ridiculed and assumed to be bitter and unfulfilled? Are the images of females of all ages prettified? Are they afraid of snakes, spiders, or mice? Do they have to be rescued by a male character?

4. Lifestyles: Are people of color and their setting depicted in such a way that they contrast unfavorably with the unstated norm of white, middle-class suburbia? Watch for inaccuracy and inappropriateness in the depiction of cultures and lifestyles. Are they oversimplified or do they offer genuine insight into the character? Watch for "quaint," "cutesy," or exotic depictions. Check to see if the portrayal of a group is authentic: for example, are all Latinas and Latinos lumped together without acknowledgment of the separate histories and diverse experiences of their groups? Are recent immigrants and people from the same group who were born in the United States portrayed in the same manner?

5. Relationships Between People: Do the males or white characters possess the power, take the leadership, and make the important decisions? Do females, people of color, lesbians, gays, elderly, or disabled people function in essentially supporting, subservient roles?

6. Heroines/Heroes: For many years, books showed only "safe" heroes—those who avoided serious conflict with the white, male, able-bodied, heterosexual establishment. Heroines and heroes should be defined according to the concepts and struggles for justice appropriate to their group. When "minority" heroes/heroines do appear, are they admired for the same qualities that have made establishment heroes famous or because what they have done has benefited the establishment? Whose interest is the hero/heroine serving?

7. Consider the Effects on a Young Person's Self-Image: Are norms established that limit any youngster's aspirations and self-concepts? Consider the effect of the use of the color white as the ultimate in beauty, cleanliness, virtue (*angel* food) and the color black or use of "dark" as evil, dirty, menacing (*devil's* food).

8. Author's or Illustrator's Background: Analyze the biographical data available about the author and illustrator. What qualifies the author or illustrator to deal with the subject? If they are not members of the group they are depicting, is there anything in their background that would specifically recommend them as creators of the book? There has been considerable debate recently regarding what has been termed *cultural borrowing.* It is not ethical for mainstream writers to appropriate the literature of other cultures. Some people believe that it is impossible to write authentically from a perspective one has never experienced personally. People who have been silenced in the past do not take kindly to someone else trying to tell their stories now that those stories are finally being recognized as significant. The publishing industry is still a world filled with scarcity: if an established Euro-American author submits a manuscript for a story representing another culture, will there be room for the emerging writer from that culture to compete? These important issues and related questions are addressed in a special edition on multicultural literature in the March/April 1995 issue of *Horn Book,* as well as in other journals and books.

9. Author's or Illustrator's Perspective: Children's books in the past have often been written by authors who were white, members of the middle class, heterosexual, able-bodied, and Christian, with one result being that a narrow Eurocentric perspective has dominated children's literature in the United States. For example, distorted images frequently portray Latinas and Latinos in assimilative and patronizing ways, often putting such characters in pastoral settings. It is important to watch for books that present multiple perspectives. Does the total collection present many worldviews? Are readers encouraged to look at a situation from several viewpoints?

10. **Loaded Words:** Examples of loaded adjectives are *savage, primitive, conniving, lazy, superstitious, treacherous, wily, crafty, inscrutable, docile, backward, bitter,* and *barren.* Watch for sexist language that excludes or in any way demeans females. The generic use of the words *man* and *he* was accepted in the past but is outmoded today. The following examples show how sexist language can be avoided: *ancestors* instead of *forefathers, humankind* instead of *mankind, firefighters* instead of *firemen, synthetic* instead of *manmade, chair* or *chairperson* instead of *chairman,* and *she or he* instead of *he.*

11. **Copyright Date:** Books on minority themes—often hastily conceived—suddenly began appearing in the mid- and late 1960s. Most of these books were written by white authors, edited by white editors, and published by white publishers. They often reflected a white, middle-class, mainstream point of view. Not until the early 1970s did the children's book world begin to even remotely reflect the realities of a pluralistic society. The copyright date may be *one* clue as to how likely the book is to be overtly biased, although a recent copyright date, of course, is no guarantee of the book's sensitivity. Conversely, *Do not throw out all the books with old copyright dates!* Use these guidelines to examine each one. Also, use the biased books as teaching tools with your children, students, and colleagues.

Alma Flor Ada

Latina of Cuban Roots (1938–)

Birthday: January 3
Address: School of Education
University of San Francisco
San Francisco, CA 94117

"My vocation as a writer started as a young child. I couldn't accept the fact that we had to read such boring textbooks while my wonderful storybooks waited at home. I made a firm commitment while in the fourth grade to devote my life to producing schoolbooks that would be fun—and since then I am having a lot of fun doing just that." (Something About the Author, 4)

Books by Alma Flor Ada

FOR CHILDREN

ABC Campesino. Illustrated by Simon Silva. Lothrop, Lee & Shepard, 1996.

Abecedario de los animales (Animal Alphabet). Illustrated by Vivi Escrivá. Mariuccia Iaconi, 1990. Audiocassette available.

After the Storm. Spanish Edition: *Despues de la tormenta.* Translated from the Spanish by Rosa Zubizarreta. Illustrated by Vivi Escrivá. Santillana, 1993.

A la sombra de un ala (In the Shadow of Wings). Illustrated by Ulises Wensel. Mariuccia Iaconi, no date available.

Barquitos de papel (Paper Boats). Illustraciones de Pablo Torrecilla, Laredo, 1993.

Barreletes (Kites). Illustraciones de Pablo Torrecilla. Laredo, 1995.

Bear's Walk. Hampton-Brown, 1993. Audiocassette available.

Choices and Other Stories from the Caribbean. With Janet Thorne and Philip Wingeier-Rayo. Illustrated by Maria Antonia Ordonez. Friendship Press, 1993.

Dear Peter Rabbit. Spanish Edition: *Querido Pedrín.* Translated into Spanish by Rosalma Zubizarreta. Illustrated by Leslie Tryon. Atheneum, 1994.

Días de circo (Circus Time). Illustraciones de Pablo Torrecilla, Laredo, 1995.

The Empty Piñata. Spanish Edition: *La piñata vacía.* Translated from the Spanish by Rosalma Zubizarreta.

Illustrated by Vivi Escrivá. Santillana, 1993.

Encaje de piedra (Stone Lace). Illustrated by Kitty Lorefice de Passalia. Laredo, no date available.

Friends. Spanish Edition: *Amigos.* Illustrated by Barry Koch. Santillana, 1989.

Giraffe's Sad Tale. Hampton Brown, 1993. Audiocassette available.

The Gold Coin. Spanish Edition: *La moneda de oro.* Translated from the Spanish by Bernice Randall. Illustrated by Neil Waldman. Atheneum, 1991; 1994.

The Golden Cage. Spanish Edition: *La jaula dorada.* Translated by Rosalma Zubizarreta. Illustrated by Vivi Escrivá. Santillana, 1993.

How Happy I Would Be. Spanish Edition: *Me gustaría tener.* Illustrated by Vivi Escrivá. Santillana, 1989.

How the Rainbow Came to Be. Spanish Edition: *Cómo nació el arco iris.* Translated from the Spanish by Bernice Randall. Illustrated by Vivi Escrivá. Santillana, 1991.

I Don't Want to Melt. Spanish Edition: *¡No quiero derretirme!* Translated by Rosalma Zubizarreta. Illustrated by Vivi Escrivá. Santillana, 1993.

I Love Saturdays and Domingos. Illustrated by Michael Bryant. Atheneum, forthcoming.

In the Barrio. Spanish Edition: *En el barrio.* Illustrated by Liliana Wilson Grez. Scholastic, 1994.

In the Cow's Backyard. Spanish Edition: *La hamaca de la vaca.* Translated by Rosalma Zubizarreta. Illustrated by Vivi Escrivá. Santillana, 1991.

It Wasn't Me. Spanish Edition: *No fui yo.* Translated from the Spanish by Rosalma Zubizarreta. Illustrated by Vivi Escrivá. Santillana, 1992.

Jordi's Star. Illustrated by Susan Gaber. G. P. Putnam's Sons, 1996.

The Kite. Spanish Edition: *El papalote.* Translated from the Spanish by Rosalma Zubizarreta. Illustrated by Vivi Escrivá. Santillana, 1992.

Mediopollito/Half-Chicken: A New Version of a Traditional Story. (Bilingual) Translated by Rosalma Zubizarreta. Illustrated by Kim Howard. Doubleday, 1995.

My Name Is María Isabel. Spanish Edition: *Me llamo María Isabel.* Translated by Ana M. Cerro. Illustrated by K. Dyble Thompson. Atheneum, 1993; Aladdin, 1995.

Olmo and the Blue Butterfly. Spanish Edition: *Olmo y la mariposa azul.* Illustrated by Vivi Escrivá. Laredo, 1992; SRA Macmillan/McGraw-Hill, 1995.

El pañuelo de seda (The Silk Scarf). Illustraciones de Vivi Escrivá. Laredo, 1993.

Pín, pín sarabín (Pin, Pin, Sarabin). Illustraciones de Pablo Torrecilla. Laredo, 1993.

Pregones (Vendors' Calls). Illustraciones de Pablo Torrecilla. Laredo, 1993.

El reino de la geometría (The Kingdom of Geometry). Illustrated by José Ramón Sánchez. Laredo, no date available.

The Rooster Who Went to His Uncle's Wedding: A Latin American Folktale. Illustrated by Kathleen Kuchera. Putnam, 1993.

A Rose with Wings. Spanish Edition: *Rosa alada.* Translated from the Spanish by Rosa Zubizarreta. Illustrated by Vivi Escrivá. Santillana, 1993.

Serafina's Birthday. Translated from the Spanish by Ana M. Cerro. Illustrated by Louise Bates Satterfield. Atheneum, 1992.

The Song of the Teeny Tiny Mosquito. Spanish Edition: *La canción del mosquito.* Illustrated by Vivi Escrivá. Santillana, 1989.

Strange Visitors. Spanish Edition: *Una extrana visita.* Translated by Rosalma Zubizarreta. Illustrated by Vivi Escrivá. Santillana, 1989.

A Surprise for Mother Rabbit. Translated from the Spanish by Rosalma Zubizarreta. Illustrated by Vivi Escrivá. Santillana, 1992.

La tataranieta de Cucarachita Martina (Martina's Great-grandaughter). Illustrated by Ana López Escrivá. Laredo, no date available.

Turkey for Thanksgiving Dinner? No, Thanks! Spanish Edition: *¿Pavo para la cena de gracias? ¡No gracias!* Translated from the Spanish by Rosa Zubizarreta. Illustrated by Vivi Escrivá. Santillana, 1993.

The Unicorn of the West. Spanish Edition: *El unicornio del oeste.* Translated by Rosalma Zubizarreta. Illustrated by Abigail Pizer. Atheneum, 1993.

El vuelo de los colibríes (The Flight of the Hummingbirds). Illustrated by Judith Jacobson, Laredo, 1995.

What Are Ghosts Afraid of? Spanish Edition: *El susto de los fantasmas.* Translated from the Spanish by Rosalma Zubizarreta. Illustrated by Vivi Escrivá. Santillana, 1992.

Where the Flame Trees Bloom. Spanish Edition: *Donde florecen los flamboyanes.* Illustrated by Antonio Martorell. Atheneum, 1994.

Who's Hatching Here? Spanish Edition: *¿Quién nacerá aquí?* Illustrated by Vivi Escrivá. Santillana, 1989.

Additional sets of Small Books, Big Books, Early Learning Packs, and Chart Sets by Alma Flor Ada are available from Hampton-Brown, P.O. Box 369, Marina, CA 93933, 1-800-333-3510.

Many of Alma Flor Ada's books, cassettes, videos, etc. are available through Del Sol Books, Inc., 29257 Bassett Rd., Westlake, OH 44145, 1-888-335-7651.

FOR TEACHERS, PARENTS, AND LIBRARIANS

A Chorus of Cultures: Developing Literacy Through Multicultural Poetry. Written with Violet J. Harris and Lee B. Hopkins. Hampton-Brown, 1993.

Culture Through Literature and Music: Cassette Guide (Spanish Elementary Series). Illustrated by Jan Mayer. Addison-Wesley, 1989.

DLM Pre-Kindergarten and Kindergarten Early Childhood Programs. Written with Pam Schiller. McGraw-Hill, 1995.

The Magical Encounter: Spanish Language Children's Literature in the Classroom. Laredo, no date available.

Mariposa Literature Kits: Teacher's Guides for Approximately Sixty Books. Available through Mariuccia Iaconi, 1-800-955-9577.

The Power of Two Languages: Literacy and Biliteracy for Spanish-Speaking Students. Coeditor with Josefina Villamil Tinajero. Macmillan/MacGraw-Hill, 1993.

Whole Language and Literature: A Practical Guide. Addison-Wesley, 1989.

Alma Flor Ada is a renowned author, translator, scholar, educator, storyteller, and advocate for bilingual and multicultural education. She has written many distinguished books for children in Mexico, Argentina, Peru, Spain, and the United States in both English and Spanish. She has also written and edited numerous textbooks, educational materials, and magazine articles and served as editor in chief of the *Journal of the National Association of Bilingual Education*. She is a professor of multicultural education at the University of San Francisco and travels throughout the United States facilitating workshops for educators. She has been the recipient of many awards and grants, including the University of San Francisco Outstanding Teacher Award and the California Parent Teacher Association Yearly Award.

Ada was born in Camagüey, Cuba, in a hacienda on the outskirts of town. She lived there with her parents, Alma Lafuente Ada, a teacher, and Modesto A. Ada, a surveyor and professor, and their extended family. In *Where the Flame Trees Bloom (WFTB),* Ada describes her childhood and provides insight into the experiences that shaped her development. Her grandmother taught her to read before she was three years old by writing the names of plants on the ground with a stick. In this way, reading and nature became closely intertwined for her. Her grandmother was a gifted storyteller, and her father invented stories to explain to her all he knew about the history of the world. As Ada writes about her impressions of the people, events, animals, and plants that surrounded

her for the first eight years of her life, a picture emerges of a beautifully sensitive and loving person. For the first seven years of her life, she was the only child living in the very large, very old house. Ada writes about her special connection with the large trees that surrounded their home. "Though I grew up surrounded by loving people and fascinated by all the life around me, it was to the trees that I told all my sorrows and my joys, and especially my dreams" (*WFTB*, 6). Ada writes about her childhood feelings and questions concerning issues of justice, freedom, and respect for all living beings. Even as a child, she questioned discrimination, poverty, and slavery. "How could anyone dare to think that he could own or control anyone else?" (*WFTB*, 3). Growing up during World War II, she wondered, "How could it be . . . that people could hate one another so much that they would want to fight and kill each other?" (*WFTB*, 65).

When Ada was eight years old, her family moved into the city. She had loved the countryside and open air, and the move was difficult for her. "Like a plant transplanted into too small a pot, lacking sunshine and rain, I withered" (*WFTB*, 74). But with the indomitable spirit characteristic of her ancestors, she gradually adjusted to the change. Because her parents wanted her to have the opportunity to learn English and to be educated bilingually, Ada attended St. Paul's Episcopal School, one of the two American schools in her town. She wore a mustard-colored uniform and was teased mercilessly by the children who attended nearby Catholic schools. An avid reader, Ada

enjoyed the wonderful storybooks she had at home but was dismayed by the lack of imagination in her textbooks. When she was in the fourth grade, she decided to devote her life to remedying this situation by creating schoolbooks that would be fun to read.

After earning her undergraduate degree from Universidad Central de Madrid in Spain in 1959, Ada moved to Peru, where she completed her master's degree and doctorate at Pontificia Universidad Catolica del Peru. She was an instructor and head of the Spanish department at Colegio Alexander von Humboldt in Lima, Peru, before moving to the United States, where she has worked as an associate professor of romance languages at Emory University in Atlanta, and a professor of language and codirector of the Institute for Bilingual Bicultural Services at Mercy College of Detroit. In 1976, Ada moved to California to accept a position with the University of San Francisco, where she is currently a professor of education and director of doctoral studies. She has traveled to a variety of locations as a visiting professor, including Texas, Guam, and Spain. In addition, Ada has been a Fulbright scholar, has served as a board member for *Sesame Street in Spanish,* and has worked as a publishing house consultant as well as chairing numerous seminars and policy conferences on bilingual education. She has been involved with many other projects, activities, and groups including being a founding member and president of the International Association for Children's Literature in Spanish and Portuguese.

As an author and translator, Ada has worked tirelessly to make stimulating textbooks and storybooks available to Spanish-speaking children and speakers of English who are learning Spanish. Her efforts to promote bilingualism have resulted in children's books that are printed in both Spanish and English, enabling youngsters to learn from and appreciate both languages. Drawing upon the inspiration of the great storytellers from her childhood and her own unique gift for writing, Ada has written many memorable books for young readers. She often explores themes of identity and self-discovery in her books. *My Name is María Isabel* is the poignant story about a child's pride in her name and heritage and the challenges she faces in fitting into a new environment. *The Gold Coin* features a thief who sets out in search of gold and discovers the true meaning of wealth. In *The Unicorn of the West,* the main character searches for his identity and finds his mission in life as well. *A Surprise for Mother Rabbit* celebrates the diversity of all the many people of the world. Ada skillfully employs elements from folklore, sometimes retelling traditional Latin American tales. She has a unique way of writing about the wonders hidden within each of her fascinating characters, enabling listeners and readers to connect with their struggles and joys.

Ada's writing has been greatly influenced by her passion for multicultural and bilingual education and her work as a scholar of romance languages. She has also been inspired by her own children, who helped her remember what it was like to be a child. Once when she was writing a scholarly book, her three-year-old daughter complained that she was writing ugly books. This comment instantly took Ada back to her childhood resolution of creating books that were fun to read. Ada notes, "One of my greatest joys is that my daughter collaborates with me" [*Something About the Author (SATA)*, 5]. Her daughter, Rosalma Zubizarreta, has translated many of her books into both Spanish and English.

In her videotape *Writing from the Heart,* Ada talks about her life and writing. As she reads from some of her books, her genuine love for literature and her young readers is apparent. She tells the viewer that writing helps her understand her feelings and gives her great joy. She enthusiastically encourages children to write, saying, "Everyone can be an author. Everyone is special!" This renowned expert in bilingual and multicultural education is making a significant contribution to the field of children's literature, not only by creating so many fine books, but also by inspiring potential writers of all ages to write and by encouraging educators to reform the curriculum to meet the needs of children from diverse populations.

More Information About Alma Flor Ada

Contemporary Authors. Volume 123, pp. 2–3.

Something About the Author. Volume 43, pp. 25–26.

Something About the Author. Volume 84, pp. 1–6.

Where the Flame Trees Bloom by Alma Flor Ada. Spanish Edition: *Donde florecen los flamboyanes.* Illustrated by Antonio Martorell. Atheneum, 1994.

Meeting an Author (videotape). Available through Hampton-Brown, 1-800-333-3510.

Writing from the Heart (videotape). Available through Hampton-Brown.

• Alphabet
• Poetry
• Music
• Sounds

Preschool–Grade 2

Abecedario de los animales

Two delightful poems for each letter of the alphabet and exquisite color illustrations have made this charming book a favorite of children and teachers. The poems about the letters playfully explore sounds, shapes, and words associated with each letter. This large-format book is available with a cassette on which Suni Paz sings the songs for each letter.

RELATED WORK
Cassette available through Mariuccia Iaconi Book Imports, 1-800-955-9577.

After the Storm

After a storm, in the late summer, several seeds fall to the ground. All but one of the seeds is eaten by animals. This little seed, not wanting to be eaten, requests help from the elements. The kindly sun hears the cry of the little seed. As the seasons come and go, the little seed goes through a number of changes. One day, the sun is greeted by what appears to be another sun. "The little seed had become a flower that mirrored the sun's round brightness" (13). This beautiful sunflower, in expressing her connection with the one who helped her grow, follows the sun as it moves across the sky. "And to this day, that is what sunflowers do" (14). This engaging book pays loving tribute to nature and working together. The cooperative efforts of the sun, wind, clouds, and rain enable the seed to grow. As she has done in a number of her other books, Alma Flor Ada has provided a perfect opportunity for teachers to integrate science with literature. She brings alive a basic science lesson featuring the growing cycle of a plant. This brightly illustrated book is a good choice for introducing a unit on plants in which youngsters are invited to plant seeds of their own. It is one of twelve books in the Stories the Year 'Round Series written by Ada and illustrated by Vivi Escrivá. An interesting art extension is to invite youngsters to create a seasonal mural in which elements from all twelve books are featured. As each book in the series is read and shared, the accompanying drawings or paintings might be added to the mural, allowing the borders of each to merge. A number of the books in this lively series also lend themselves beautifully to dramatic and written activities.

- Cooperation
- Growing Cycle
- Plants
- Science
- Seeds
- Seasons

Grades K–3

RELATED WORK
Spanish Edition: *Despues de la tormenta.* Illustrated by Vivi Escrivá. Santillana, 1993.

A la sombra de un ala (In the Shadow of Wings)

This engaging edition of Alma Flor Ada's poetry will inspire children to use their own talents to write poems. It might be used in conjunction with Ada's video *Writing from the Heart,* in which she encourages young people to experience the joy of writing their own books and poems.

- Poetry

Grades K–1

Dear Peter Rabbit

Parents' *Choice Honor Award*

The correspondence among well-known storybook characters is cleverly woven together, providing an engaging tale with a touch of mystery. In the first letter, Pig One invites Peter Rabbit to a housewarming party at his newly built straw house. Peter Rabbit writes back to say he cannot attend because he is in bed with a cold he caught while hiding from Mr. McGregor in a watering can half-full of water. Meanwhile, Baby Bear writes to Goldilocks McGregor, in response to her apology for breaking his chair. In her reply,

- Goldilocks
- The Three Bears
- The Three Little Pigs
- Little Red Riding Hood
- Peter Rabbit
- Communication
- Letter-writing

Goldilocks mentions that her father is very upset about the missing vegetables from their garden. Later, on her way home from a visit to the Bear House in the Woods, Goldilocks meets Little Red Riding Hood. While these and other lively letters are being dispatched, several intriguing behind-the-scenes adventures unfold. The enchanting drama culminates in a birthday party that brings these literary favorites together face-to-face.

As a child, Alma Flor Ada had many imaginary conversations with characters from her storybooks. Many years later, she conceived the ideas for *Dear Peter Rabbit* during the long drives from her mountain home in northern California to the University of San Francisco, where she is a professor of education. Drawing upon her interest in children's literature, she ingeniously combined familiar elements of popular fairy tales to create an enchanting extension of that make-believe world. Each character writes in a unique voice and the letters are printed in individual styles. Leslie Tryon's captivating illustrations, rendered in pen and ink with watercolors, invite the reader back again and again to enjoy the delightful details.

Grades K–Adult

RELATED WORK

Spanish Edition: *Querido Pedrín.* Translated into Spanish by Rosalma Zubizarreta. Illustrated by Leslie Tryon. Atheneum, 1994.

- Cinco de mayo
- Piñatas
- Sharing

The Empty Piñata

When Elena's uncle gives her a beautiful piñata, she empties her piggybank and sets off to buy candy to fill it before she takes it to school. But on the way to the store, she decides to buy some seeds to feed a hungry little bird. Next she finds a lost kitten, then a puppy, and before long she has spent all her money. Alas, she cannot buy the candy to fill the piñata. But her generosity is rewarded and she happily shares her piñata with her classmates at the Cinco de mayo party at school. Cinco de mayo, the fifth of May, is the celebration of the day Benito Juarez and the Mexican army were victorious over the French army in the Battle of Puebla in 1862. Alma Flor Ada was aware of the paucity of books for young children on Cinco de mayo, and dedicated her appealing book to ". . . Eréndira and Marcos Guerrero, and all Mexican-American children, in hopes that they will take full pride in their cultural heritage." Young listeners and readers will be charmed by Elena's generosity, the rhymes and repetitions of the predictable text, and the attractive illustrations by Vivi Escrivá. *The Empty Piñata* is part of the Stories the Year 'Round Series, which includes twelve books, three for each season of the year.

Preschool–Grade 2

RELATED WORKS

Spanish Edition

La piñata vacía. Translated from the Spanish by Rosalma Zubizarreta. Illustraciones de Vivi Escrivá. Santillana, 1993.

Piñatas

The Piñata Maker/El pátero by George Ancona. Harcourt Brace, 1994.

Cinco de mayo

Behrens, June. *Fiesta! Cinco de mayo.* Children's Press, 1986.

Bradley, Mignon L. *Cinco de mayo: An Historical Play.* Luisa Productions, 1981.

Palacios, Argentina. *¡Viva México!: The Story of Benito Juarez and Cinco de mayo.* Steck-Vaughn, 1993.

Riehecky, Janet. *Cinco de mayo.* Children's Press, 1993.

Encaje de piedra (Stone Lace)
Marta Salotti Award (Argentina)

• Mystery

This intriguing mystery story is set in the Middle Ages in Spain. It invites young readers to explore issues of friendship, trust, biculturalism, bilingualism, discrimination, and the value of learning a second language.

Grades 1–6

Friends

• Geometry
• Math
• Friendship
• Overcoming Differences

This clever book features geometrical figures who are segregated until two circles discover the joy of getting to know others. This is an excellent antibias book for introducing the beauty of diversity. Prejudice and tolerance are treated in a sensitive and easy-to-understand manner. It is sure to prompt lively discussions and help promote a feeling of goodwill toward differences.

Grades K–5

RELATED WORKS

Spanish Edition
Amigos. Illustrated by Barry Koch. Santillana, 1989.

Geometry/Differences
The Kingdom of Geometry by Alma Flor Ada. Spanish Edition: *El reino de la geometría.* Translated by Rosalma Zubizarreta. Illustrated by José Ramón Sánchez. Laredo, 1993; 1995. See page 22.

The Gold Coin
Christopher Award
National Council of Social Studies Notable Children's Trade Book

• Self-Discovery
• Healers

Determined to steal an old woman's gold, a thief follows her all around the countryside and in the process learns a very important lesson. As this award-winning book opens, Juan overhears Doña Josefa say to herself, "I must be the richest person in the world," as she holds a gold coin in her hand. He decides to wait until she leaves her hut to steal the coin. Later, he ransacks her house but fails to find the coin. He tracks her from place to place, each time missing her. As he travels, he discovers that Doña Josefa not only heals people but gives them gold coins. How he finds himself digging potatoes, picking corn, squash, and beans, and helping with the coffee harvest is part of the magic of this special book. When he finally catches up with Doña Josefa, he realizes that he, too, has been touched by her goodness. The satisfying ending will touch the hearts of readers of all ages.

Set in an unnamed South American country, this original tale invites readers to consider the nature of true wealth. As Juan rediscovers the joys of a home-cooked meal, the pleasure that comes from sharing it with others, and the beauty of a sunrise, he gradually changes. Neil Walman's lovely watercolors and Ada's inspiring text capture the subtle transformation of a man who had been a thief for many years. The author dedicated this unique fable to her daughter: "To Rosalma, who believed this story should reach all children. . . ."

Grades K–12

RELATED WORK

Spanish Edition: *La moneda de oro.* Available through Mariuccia Iaconi, 1-800-955-9577.

• Birds
• Disabilities
• Freedom
• Humane Treatment of Animals

The Golden Cage

When Nicholas's grandmother returns from the hospital, she is in a wheelchair. She enjoys sitting by the window watching the birds outside in the yard. Nicholas is very concerned about her and wants to think of something to make her happy. One day, he sees a beautiful golden cage in a pet store window. Remembering how much his grandmother likes birds, he saves his money to buy her the cage so she will always have birds nearby. But he learns that his grandmother values freedom too much to keep a bird inside a cage. What can Nicholas do with the beautiful golden cage? Can he find the perfect gift for his beloved grandmother? Nicholas's generosity of spirit is a refreshing contrast to the greed and selfishness we see all around us. Youngsters will enjoy this charming book with its gentle message about freedom for all creatures. Author Alma Flor Ada and artist Vivi Escrivá have teamed up to create twelve engaging books in the Stories the Year 'Round Series, of which *The Golden Cage* is one of three designated for the winter installment. However, it is also fits perfectly into a study that correlates with Be Kind to Animals Week, which is in the spring.

Grades K–3

RELATED WORK

Spanish Edition: *La jaula dorada.* Translated by Rosalma Zubizarreta. Illustraciones de Vivi Escrivá. Santillana, 1993.

• Big Books   • Numbers
• Poetry

Grades K–3

How Happy I Would Be

This charming big book features numbers and animals engaged in various activities through rhyme.

RELATED WORK

Spanish Edition: *Me gustaría tener.* Illustrated by Vivi Escrivá. Santillana, 1989.

How the Rainbow Came to Be

- Artists
- Colors
- The Earth
- Rainbows
- Cooperation

"Listen closely, for I'm going to tell you an old, old story about what the world was like before there was color." So begins this imaginative tale about how Earth became filled with beautiful colors. Long ago, when Earth was all black and white, Red, Blue, and Yellow decided to remedy the situation. However, they were unable to agree on a plan of action, so working independently, they each took a brush and sprinkled their hues around the world. Then they realized that they needed to work together to provide more variety. As they combined their colors, they transformed Earth into a splendiferous place. When they finished, they admired their work. They were pleased with the beauty they had brought to the gray planet and happy with their newfound friendships. Now, when it rains, the colors show their joy by creating an enormous smile in the sky. "And, that is what we call a rainbow" (14). Illustrated in soft hues by Vivi Escrivá, *How the Rainbow Came to Be* fits perfectly into a study of color. Teachers interested in integrating literature, art, science, and "working together" will welcome this enchanting title. It is part of the Stories the Year 'Round Series, which includes twelve books, three for each season. For dramatization and writing extensions, the roles of Red, Blue, and Yellow could be played by girls as well as boys.

Grades K–3

RELATED WORK

Spanish Edition: *Cómo nació el arco iris.* Illustraciones de Vivi Escrivá. Santillana, 1991.

I Don't Want to Melt

- Snowpeople
- Seasons
- Water Cycle

A little round snowperson discovers the joys of existing in each of his forms. The book opens with Alberto, Marcos, and Laura putting the finishing touches on a new snowperson. Later, when the children leave Detroit for a visit with their grandmother in Miami, they admonish the snowperson not to melt. "It was the first time that the snowman had ever heard the word 'melt'" (8). He spends the remainder of the winter gathering information about melting, all the while hoping that he will escape this terrible fate. His animal friends offer a number of helpful suggestions. When March arrives and the children leave for another vacation, it is the animals who plan for the snowperson's return. Sure enough, the following winter finds him back in his favorite spot. This engaging story ends with the snowperson telling his animal friends about his many adventures as he traveled around the world. Part of the Stories the Year 'Round Series, this pleasing book provides an excellent opportunity for teachers to integrate literature, science, and geography. The little snowperson's experiences bring the scientific information to life; after youngsters enjoy the story for its own sake, they will easily remember the stages of the water cycle. Some may be interested in tracing the journey the snowperson took to the Great Lakes and beyond. Escrivá's appealing illustrations are perfect for this satisfying tale. Ada's daughter, Rosalma Zubizarreta, translated the book from the Spanish.

RELATED WORK

Spanish Edition: *¡No quiero derretirme!* Illustraciones de Vivi Escrivá. Santillana, 1993.

• Neighborhoods
• Sense of Community

In the Barrio

Through simple text and engaging illustrations, this groundbreaking little book lovingly brings the barrio alive. A young Latino boy proudly takes the reader on a tour of his neighborhood, pointing out some of his favorite things. We see colorful murals, listen to lively mariachis playing at a birthday party, and touch the red chiles hanging at the vegetable market. We can almost taste the sweet pan dulce, the delicious enchiladas, and the tangy fruit ices. The narrator's grandmother gives him a warm hug and helps him with his schoolwork. The backgrounds of Liliana Wilson Grez's detailed pictures are filled with images of Latino culture such as a star piñata, a calendar featuring a rooster, and curtains and tile decorated with Mexican motifs. The images presented are very positive for the most part, but the fumes from cars and the loud sirens of fire engines are included as well. *In the Barrio* provides a welcome contrast to the negative images some people have of barrios.

Preschool–Grade 2

RELATED WORK

Spanish Edition: *En el barrio*. Illustrado por Liliana Wilson Grez. Scholastic, 1994.

• Hammocks
• Sharing
• Cumulative Tale

In the Cow's Backyard

"My, it feels so nice to be in the shade! The ant is happy lying in the hammock in the cow's backyard." So begins this cumulative tale where there's always room for one more friend. As the ant continues to invite animal after animal to join the cozy group, the hammock becomes fuller and fuller and sags lower and lower. The test of the ant's generosity comes when an elephant saunters by. Is there room? The animals wait in anticipation. This is a good point to pause and brainstorm solutions to the ways in which "there's always a way for one more friend to squeeze in and play." Young readers and listeners will be charmed by this cheerful tale of goodwill and friendship. They will enjoy chiming in on the predictable lines and delight in the playful illustrations. *In the Cow's Backyard* is part of the Stories the Year 'Round Series written by Alma Flor Ada and illustrated by Vivi Escrivá. Art lovers will enjoy studying the illustrations in each book in the series within the context of the complete set of books. An interesting mural might be created with all the characters from all twelve books joining together for a giant frolic through the seasons.

Preschool–Grade 2

RELATED WORK

Spanish Edition: *La hamaca de la vaca*. Translated by Rosalma Zubizarreta. Illustrated by Vivi Escrivá. Santillana, 1991.

It Wasn't Me

• Mystery

Who trampled the flowers? Who wiped their dirty hands on the clean laundry hanging on the clothesline? Who tracked mud onto the porch? Who spilled the flour? These and other mysteries are waiting to be solved by the curious ears and sharp eyes of young listeners and readers. Perhaps some of these young detectives will have stories about accidents that happened at their house that were difficult to explain. Maybe they were blamed for something they didn't do. Or maybe they blamed someone else for something they did. Was it the dog's fault? Who will clean up these messes? These and other questions will intrigue young sleuths as they try to find the culprit. *It Wasn't Me* is one of twelve books in the Stories the Year 'Round Series.

Preschool–K

RELATED WORKS

Spanish Edition

No fui yo. Illustrated by Vivi Escrivá. Santillana, 1992.

Mystery

Jimmy Lee Did It by Pat Cummings. Lothrop, Lee & Shepard, 1985.

The Kite

• Kite-Making
• Problem-Solving

Using the captivating good news–bad news motif, Ada has written a warm tale about kindness, ingenuity, and perseverance. The story begins when Mama announces she will make the children a kite like the ones her father made when she was little. When she realizes that making a kite is more difficult than it appears, she decides to teach herself this new skill. She doesn't give up, and finally the beautiful new kite is ready. The family patiently waits for a nice day. At last, they are off to the country to fly the kite. Unfortunately, the string breaks and the kite sails off into the sky. They search everywhere, but the kite seems to have disappeared forever. But there is good news waiting for them where they least expect it. Vivi Escrivá's colorful illustrations enhance this installment in the Stories the Year 'Round Series. This book features a woman whose example says, "Don't give up!", "Try new ideas!", and "Books are important." Children will enjoy the upbeat message combined with the surprise ending. They may have a few kite stories of their own to share, possibly adopting the good news–bad news format.

Preschool–Grade 2

RELATED WORKS

Spanish Edition

El papalote. Translated from the Spanish by Rosalma Zubizarreta. Illustraciones de Vivi Escrivá. Santillana, 1992.

Kites

Barreletes (Kites) by Alma Flor Ada. Illustraciones de Pablo Torrecilla. Laredo, 1995.

- Bilingual
- Folklore
- Chickens
- Weather Vanes

Mediopollito/Half-Chicken: A New Version of a Traditional Story

Mediopollito/Half-Chicken is a traditional folktale that has traveled from Spain to various Latin American countries. As a child in Cuba, Ada heard it told by her grandmother. Since then, she has encountered the story many times in two distinct versions. In this book, she has chosen to retell her grandmother's version, in which a helpful chicken is rewarded for his good deeds. The story begins when a very special chick is hatched into the world with only one wing, one leg, one eye, and half as many feathers as other chicks. Named Half-Chicken, he finds himself the center of attention among all the barnyard animals who live on the ranch in Mexico. When he sets out to visit the court of the viceroy in Mexico City, he encounters first water, then fire, and last, wind. After he generously helps them with their problems, he proceeds on his way. But he is not prepared for the trouble that awaits him in the city. Will someone rescue Half-Chicken?

Gifted storyteller Alma Flor Ada has created an engaging adaptation of the folktale explaining the origin of rooster weather vanes. Accompanied by Kim Howard's dynamic illustrations, the predictable and repetitive nature of the tale makes it an appealing read-aloud choice. This story is unique because it celebrates Half-Chicken's differences instead of using them as a reason to reject him.

Preschool–Grade 2

RELATED WORK

The Rooster Who Went to His Uncle's Wedding: A Latin American Folktale by Alma Flor Ada. Illustrated by Kathleen Kuchera. Putnam, 1993. See page 23.

- Newcomers
- Schools
- Identity

My Name Is María Isabel

Third grader María Isabel, born in Puerto Rico and now living in the United States, faces a challenge at her new school. There are two other Marías in the class, so her teacher decides to call her Mary. María Isabel's name is very special to her because she was named after her beloved grandmothers. When the teacher calls on her she doesn't answer because she doesn't realize the teacher is talking to her. As the teacher becomes increasingly irritated with her, María Isabel finds herself excluded from the school's Winter Pageant. How can she reclaim her name? How can she explain to her parents why she isn't singing her favorite holiday song? And how can she find the courage to explain her dilemma to an impatient teacher?

This poignant story beautifully elucidates the integral connection between an individual's name and her sense of self. As a newcomer to the school and to the mainland, María Isabel faces a number of uncertainties and challenges. The issue with her name adds to her discomfort. Alma Flor Ada's gentle story utilizes understatement: María Isabel finds friends, does well in math, and feels comfortable at home. Yet the name change and the resulting problems overshadow everything else. Ada does a beautiful job of juxtaposing María Isabel's thoughts about her predicament with the insights she gains from reading a book. As she ponders the issues in *Charlotte's Web,* she is able to make connections with events in her own life. As the story ends, María Isabel has learned some important lessons about herself and those around her. Another important aspect of the book is the way in which Ada portrays María Isabel's teacher. She is able to admit to herself that she made a mistake and proceed to make amends. Her character, as well as the others in the book, is carefully drawn and avoids stereotypes.

My Name is María Isabel is an engaging story that combines the efforts of a Puerto Rican family to adjust to a new life with a shared sense of pride in their heritage. Augmented by K. Dyble Thompson's realistic black-and-white drawings, the story reads aloud well and could be used along with the related works listed below to explore the issues faced by many newcomers.

Grades 2–5

RELATED WORKS

Spanish Edition:
Me llamo María Isabel. Atheneum, 1994.

Newcomer Books for Children:
Aekyung's Dream by Min Paek. Children's Book Press, 1978.

Angel Child, Dragon Child by Michele Maria Surat. Scholastic, 1983.

The Magic Shell by Nicholasa Mohr. Scholastic, 1995. Illustrated by Rudy Gutierrez. *El regalo mágico,* Spanish edition, 1996. See page 118.

Making a New Home in America by Maxine Rosenberg. Photographs by George Ancona. Lothrop, Lee and Shepard, 1986.

Molly's Pilgrim by Barbara Cohen. Lothrop, Lee and Shepard, 1983.

My Two Worlds by Ginger Gordon. Clarion, 1993.

Over Here It's Different: Carolina's Story by Mildred Leinweber Dawson. Photographs by George Ancona. Macmillan, 1993.

For Older Students:
How the Garcia Girls Lost Their Accents by Julia Alvarez. Algonquin Books, 1991; Dutton, 1992. See pages 40–41.

For Educators, Parents, and Librarians
The Inner World of the Immigrant Child by Cristina Igoa. St. Martin's Press, 1995. See page 209.

Olmo and the Blue Butterfly

- Butterflies
- Transportation

Olmo wakes up one morning to find a beautiful blue butterfly fluttering near his bed. He quickly dresses, jumps out his window, and follows the butterfly through his neighborhood, through the city, across the bay, into the sky. He travels by scooter, skateboard, bicycle, motorcycle, cable car, boat, airplane, helicopter, and finally, spaceship. Alma Flor Ada and Vivi Escrivá have collaborated again to create a delightful book. The colorful scenes are reminiscent of San Francisco, where the author lives and works. This participatory story, complemented by detailed illustrations, will be enjoyed by young listeners and readers. Adults and youngsters alike will be relieved that the butterfly is not subjected to the fate imposed by most butterfly collectors. This book provides an opportunity to discuss the importance of kindness to animals great and small, as well as the various forms of transportation available today.

Preschool–Grade 2

RELATED WORKS

Spanish Edition

Olmo y la mariposa azul. Illustraciones de Vivi Escrivá. Laredo, 1992; SRA Macmillan/McGraw-Hill, 1995.

Butterflies

A Rose with Wings by Alma Flor Ada. Translated from the Spanish by Rosa Zubizarreta. Spanish Edition: *Rosa alada.* Illustrated by Vivi Escrivá. Santillana, 1993. See page 23.

La Mariposa Bailarina by Carlos Ruvalcaba. Illustrated by Francisco X. Mora. Santillana, 1995.

- Birds
- Cranes
- Wildlife Rescue
- Kindness to Animals

Grades 2–6

El pañuelo de seda (The Silk Scarf)

A young girl discovers the true meaning of compassion when she sacrifices her favorite possession in order to save the life of a wounded crane. This is an inspiring story about wildlife preservation, ecology, and clarifying what is of true value. Listeners and readers of all ages will want to discuss the importance of kindness to animals of all species. Perhaps some will volunteer to share personal experiences related to rescuing animals. Engaging illustrations grace the pages of this very special book.

RELATED WORK

Animal Rescue

Subway Sparrow, written and illustrated by Leyla Torres. Farrar, Straus, & Giroux, 1993. See page 168.

- Geometry
- Math
- Hierarchies

Grades 3–6

El reino de la geometría

In the Kingdom of Geometry, all the geometrical figures live in harmony until King Square decides that squares are superior. This clever book is an effective tool for discussing discrimination, injustice, and oppression.

RELATED WORK

Friends by Alma Flor Ada. Spanish Edition: *Amigos.* Illustrated by Barry Koch. Santillana, 1989. See page 15.

The Rooster Who Went to His Uncle's Wedding: A Latin American Folktale

- Folklore
- Cumulative Tales
- Chickens

In this cumulative folktale from Latin America, a perfectly groomed rooster sets out early one morning for his uncle's wedding. But before long his stomach begins to growl and he realizes that he forgot to eat breakfast. When he spies a tantalizing kernel of corn lying in a puddle of mud next to the road, his hunger overcomes him and he gobbles it down. Alas, his previously spotless beak is now covered with mud. What can he do? When the velvety grass refuses to help, the rooster appeals to a woolly lamb to eat the grass that won't clean his beak so he can go to his uncle's wedding. The list of recalcitrant characters grows with each brightly colored page. Will anyone help poor rooster?

This engaging cumulative tale has roots in many Spanish-speaking countries around the world. Alma Flor Ada's first memories of the story are of hearing it as a little girl in Cuba from her grandmother. Her lively adaptation, using harmonious repetition and economical language, will delight young listeners and readers. The rooster is a universal folk character humanized in many cultures. Kathleen Kuchera's brilliant geometric prints complement the story vividly.

Preschool–Grade 2

RELATED WORKS

The Bossy Gallito/El Gallo de Bodas: A Traditional Cuban Folktale retold by Lucía M. Gonzales. Illustrated by Lulu Delacre. Scholastic, 1994. See page 96.

Mediopollito/Half-Chicken: A New Version of a Traditional Story by Alma Flor Ada. Translated by Rosalma Zubizarreta. Illustrated by Kim Howard. Doubleday, 1995. See page 20.

A Rose with Wings

- Animals
- Worms
- Metamorphosis
- Science
- Schools

"If your teacher said, 'Choose any animal,' which one would you think is the most wonderful?" The children busily work on their animal projects: reading, drawing, and sharing. Gabriel chooses an unusual little creature—a tiny worm. He creates a comfortable habitat for his new friend. As the others talk about their spectacular animals, Gabriel quietly observes the mild little worm. Then one day, as the children debate which animal is the most exceptional, Gabriel discovers a chrysalis on the branch where he last saw the worm. Later, the caterpillar awakens and is transformed into one of the most special creatures of all. This engaging story of metamorphosis brings a basic science lesson alive, providing a perfect opportunity to integrate literature with science. Vivi Escrivá's delightful illustrations feature a multicultural group of children including a child in a wheelchair, a refreshing rare image in children's books. Gabriel, as a divergent thinker, is accepted and respected by his classmates and teacher. *A Rose with Wings* is one of twelve enchanting books, written by Ada and illustrated by Escrivá, in the Stories the Year 'Round Series.

Preschool–Grade 2

RELATED WORKS

Spanish Edition

Rosa alada. Illustrated by Vivi Escrivá. Santillana, 1993.

Butterflies

Olmo and the Blue Butterfly by Alma Flor Ada. Spanish Edition: *Olmo y la mariposa azul.* Illustrated by Vivi Escrivá. Laredo, 1992; SRA Macmillan/McGraw-Hill, 1995. See pages 21–22.

- Big Book
- Food Chain
- Science
- Cumulative Tale

Grades K–5

The Song of the Teeny Tiny Mosquito

This enchanting tale introduces the concept of the food chain through text and pictures. Excellent for integrating science and literature.

RELATED WORK

Spanish Edition: *La cancíon del mosquito.* Illustrated by Vivi Escrivá. Santillana, 1989.

- Easter
- Eggs
- Rabbits
- Differences

A Surprise for Mother Rabbit

Each year around Easter time, Mother Rabbit has too much work to do, gathering and painting so many eggs. So this year, her eight children plan to surprise her by gathering the eggs themselves. Each little bunny rabbit meets a different kind of bird and requests an egg. Each time the response is the same: "All my eggs are hatched. All my eggs are gone. But since it's for you, I'll lay a new one." Mother Rabbit is very pleased with the collection of eggs her children gather. Just like people, their differences make them special. This charming book ends with an eloquent tribute to the diversity of humankind: we learn something from each person: "When we love and understand . . . There's no need to choose the best. Each one is special, And different from the rest" (23–24). Vivi Escrivá's lively paintings portray each adorable little rabbit as an individual. The uniqueness and beauty of the birds is lovingly depicted through words and illustration. Youngsters will be enchanted by the rhythm and repetition of the predictable text combined with the inventive approach to a holiday theme. *A Surprise for Mother Rabbit* is part of the Stories the Year 'Round Series, which features twelve books, three for each season of the year.

Preschool–Grade 3

- Cockroaches
- Mice
- Folktales

Grades K–5

La tataranieta de Cucarachita Martina

Alma Flor Ada has taken the classic tale of Cucarachita Martina and Ratón Perez and provided a whimsical retelling set in modern times.

RELATED WORK

Perez and Martina: A Puerto Rican Folktale by Pura Belpré. Illustrated by Carlos Sanchez. Frederick Warne, 1932; Spanish Edition: *Perez y Martina,* Viking, 1991. See page 178.

Turkey for Thanksgiving Dinner? No Thanks!

- Thanksgiving
- Vegetarianism
- Problem-Solving
- Spiders

When a turkey overhears a conversation about plans to cook him for Thanksgiving, he is understandably very upset. As he contemplates his situation, he is befriended by a descendant of Charlotte, the spider, who saved Wilbur, the pig, many years earlier. But unlike Charlotte, this little spider has never had the opportunity to go to school and cannot write. Will she be able to follow the legacy of her great-grandmother's great-grandmother and save the turkey? As she puts her problem-solving skills to work, the turkey finds himself learning new skills and breaking out of the patterns set by generations of ancestors. Youngsters will be enchanted by the ingenuity of the wise little spider and cheer for the plucky turkey. As she did in *Dear Peter Rabbit,* Ada here combines familiar themes from a popular tale to create an engaging sequel, providing numerous options for extensions. Perhaps an older child would enjoy telling younger ones the classic story of *Charlotte's Web.* Gifted young readers will want to read it for themselves and perhaps share highlights with classmates. *Turkey for Thanksgiving Dinner? No Thanks!* is one of twelve books in the series Stories the Year 'Round.

Grades K–5

RELATED WORKS
Spanish Edition: *¿Pavo para la cena de gracias? ¡No gracias!* Illustrated by Vivi Escrivá. Santillana, 1993.

Charlotte's Web by E. B. White. Harper & Row, 1952.

The Unicorn of the West

- Identity
- Unicorns

In this gentle tale, a mysterious animal searches for his identity. He has never before met anyone like himself, or for that matter, any other creatures at all. Now, each season brings a new friend: a spring robin, a summer butterfly, and an autumn squirrel. Each promises to try to "find someone just like you, so I can tell you who you are." With winter comes a new sound, an enchanting melody that beckons the beautiful white animal to a meeting with three others like himself. They introduce themselves as the Unicorns of the North, East, and South and explain that he is the Unicorn of the West. Every seven years on the first full moon after the winter solstice, the unicorns gather to ensure that beautiful dreams live on and that there is enough love for all in the world. Reassured, the Unicorn of the West returns to his home in the forest. There he is reunited with the robin, butterfly, and squirrel, who have traveled to the other three corners of the world and brought back news of the other unicorns. This satisfying story ends with the promise of enduring friendship as well as universal well-being.

Abigail Pizer's lovely watercolors perfectly capture the magical mood of this original fable. It will appeal not only to young children, who will enjoy listening as it is read aloud, but to many fourth and fifth graders, who are also often captivated by the allure of unicorns.

Grades 1–5

- Immigration

Grades 4–8

El vuelo de los colibríes (The Flight of the Hummingbirds)

A grandmother recounts the tale of how her family left the countryside in Mexico and moved to California. This lovely book eloquently describes this story of migration as experienced by one family.

- Halloween
- Mystery

Preschool–Grade 2

What Are Ghosts Afraid of?

When Carmen, Roberto, and Francisco stay up late on Halloween, they encounter a number of images that look suspiciously like ghosts. The ghost reclining on the living room couch turns out to be the costume their mother wore to her office party. The white shape in the hall window is only the curtain. And the billowing images in the backyard are the sheets their mother hung out to dry. As each of these mysteries is solved, Carmen bravely proclaims, "There's no such thing as a real ghost!" At this point two new characters enter the scene: Ghostie and Ghoster. Where can they go to escape the approaching storm? How do ghosts stay dry when it rains? Will Carmen, Roberto, and Francisco notice the new white blankets on their bed?

Vivi Escrivá's enchanting illustrations enhance the delicious suspense of this delightful mystery. She mischievously adds little touches of humor along the way, making the story all the more intriguing.

In spite of the growing awareness of the need for change, books for young readers often depict girls as timid followers. Thus, it is significant that Ada chose to portray Carmen as the brave leader of the trio.

RELATED WORK

Spanish Edition: *El susto de los fantasmas.* Illustrated by Vivi Escrivá. Santillana, 1992.

- Autobiographical Short Stories
- Cuba
- Authorship

Where the Flame Trees Bloom

This warm collection of eleven short stories provides insight into the childhood of renowned author Alma Flor Ada. As she reminisces about her first eight years growing up in rural Cuba, Ada paints a loving portrait of family and home. Beginning with an introduction to her homeland, Ada writes about the people, events, and experiences that greatly shaped her development. Two stories feature her great-grandmother, Mina, who never went to school and could not read or write but remembered the birthdates and exact ages of all her children, grandchildren, and great grandchildren. Even after she lost her sight, she continued to make rag dolls for the children of the village. Another story is about Ada's maternal grandmother, Delores, who filled her granddaughter's early years with fascinating stories and outdoor adventures. Both an intellectual and a very practical person, Delores was a principal of two schools: an elementary public school during the day and a school for working women in the evenings. The lessons she taught her students included the grammar of the heart as well as the mathematics of the mind. Ada writes about her grandfather, who left Spain for Cuba when he was twelve years old. Years later, he refused to leave his dying wife's side to travel to Havana to save the family fortune. Throughout the collection, Ada's love and reverence for all living beings is apparent. When her father amputated the gangrenous leg of a stray dog, she respectfully kept him company while he recuperated. She writes lovingly of her strong connections with the ancient flame trees, fruit trees, and bamboo trees that surrounded the family hacienda. She recognized the racism in the comic books distributed to the students at her school. Provided as propaganda during World War II, the books portrayed the Japanese people in an extremely negative way. After she arrived at her house, the young student, feeling great sadness and shame, tore the books into pieces.

The subtle black-and-white illustrations in this book are by Antonio Martorell, a Puerto Rican artist who frequently shuttles between his workshops in Ponce and New York.

Grades 3–8

Who's Hatching Here?

- Big Book   • Birds
- Science   • Poetry

The reader is invited to guess, from the poems and illustrations, what animals will hatch from the eggs pictured on every other page. This captivating book offers an intriguing integration of science with poetry.

Grades K–3

RELATED WORKS

Spanish Edition

¿Quién nacerá aquí? Illustrated by Vivi Escrivá. Santillana, 1989.

Birds and Eggs

A Surprise for Mother Rabbit by Alma Flor Ada. Translated from the Spanish by Rosalma Zubizarreta. Illustrated by Vivi Escrivá. Santillana, 1992. See page 24.

Isabel Allende

Chilean (1942–)

Birthday: August 2

"I have had a tormented and long life, and many things are hidden in the secret compartments of my heart and my mind. Sometimes, I don't even know that they are there, but I have the pain—I can feel the pain; I can feel this load of stories that I am carrying around. And then one day I write a story, and I realize that I have delivered something, that a demon has come out and has been exorcised."
(Iftekharuddin interview)

"I believe that one writes because one cannot avoid doing so. The need to do it is an overwhelming passion. If I don't write, words accumulate in my chest, grow and multiply like carnivorous flowers, threatening to choke me if they don't find a way out."
(World Authors, *19*)

"Writing for me is the possibility of creating and recreating the world according to my own rules, fulfilling in those pages all my dreams and exorcising some of my demons."
(Dictionary of Literary Biography, *40*)

Books by Isabel Allende

Eva Luna. Translated from Spanish by Margaret Sayers Peden. Alfred A. Knopf, 1988; Bantam, 1989; HarperCollins, 1995.

The House of the Spirits. Translated from Spanish by Magda Bogin. Alfred A. Knopf, 1985; Bantam, 1986.

The Infinite Plan. Translated from Spanish by Margaret Sayers Peden. HarperCollins, 1993.

Of Love and Shadows. Translated from Spanish by Margaret Sayers Peden. Alfred A. Knopf, 1987; Bantam, 1988.

Paula. Translated from Spanish by Margaret Sayers Peden. HarperCollins, 1994.

The Stories of Eva Luna. Translated from Spanish by Margaret Sayers Peden. Macmillan, 1991.

Isabel Allende is the best known and most widely read woman writer from Latin America. She has mesmerized readers throughout the world with her own blend of magical realism, political and social issues, and fascinating characters. Highly praised for her powerful writing, her books have been translated into numerous languages and many have become best-sellers.

Allende was born in Lima, Peru, the eldest child of Francisca Llona Barros and Chilean diplomat Tomás Allende. Her father was a first cousin of Salvador Allende, president of Chile, with whom the family maintained a close relationship. Her parents separated when she was three years old, and she returned with her mother and two younger brothers to Santiago, Chile. She grew up in the home of her maternal grandparents, Isabela and Augustine Llona, who exerted a strong influence on her imagination and development. Her grandmother was an extraordinary woman with a wonderful sense of humor and compassion. A magical storyteller, she left a deep imprint on her granddaughter. Allende writes that she was detached from earthly matters, spiritual, and that she could speak with the dead. "I grew up in that extravagant home, surrounded by benevolent ghosts" (*World Authors,* 19). "Our family home, a delight when she was presiding over it with her gathering of intellectuals, Bohemians, and lunatics, became at her death a cheerless and empty place populated only by currents of air" (*Paula,* 25). Allende writes that the character she loves most in all her books is Clara from *The House of the Spirits,* who was inspired by her beloved grandmother.

Allende's mother, who was the most important person in her childhood, also told her stories. She created an imaginary world where they were all happy, where the ruthless laws of nature and human vices did not exist. "That was where my passion for stories was born, and I call upon those memories when I sit down to write" (*Paula,* 33). Allende invented tales of suspense for her brothers that filled their heads with fears during the night. She writes that nobody thought her storytelling inclinations could be useful. "I was a girl and therefore my education was not directed toward creativity" (*World Authors,* 19). Nevertheless, her love for storytelling did not vanish with menstruation, as her Nani predicted it would, but instead expanded, and years later her children would suffer the "same ordeal that my poor brothers did" (*World Authors,* 19). She loved books, often reading under the covers at night with a flashlight. She discovered a trunk of books in the cellar of the house and spent long hours voraciously gobbling them down. When she was nine, she dove into the complete works of Shakespeare and later developed a devotion to science fiction. Allende writes that she was a lonely and angry child. "I always believed I was different; as long as I can remember I have felt like an outcast, as if I didn't really belong to my family, or to my surroundings, or to any group" (*Paula,* 50).

When her mother remarried, again to a diplomat, the family left Santiago to follow him on his assignments. Allende's mother gave her a notebook, saying, "Here, write what's in your heart" (*Paula,* 56). The ten-year-old girl left the complex mural she had painted on her bedroom wall, "in which were registered my desires, fears, rages, childhood doubts, and growing pains" (*Paula,* 55), and moved to Bolivia, where she lived with her family for several years. Because she was Chilean, she was the victim of offensive schoolyard pranks in the new country. She sought refuge in the family garden, where she found private places to read and secret places to hide her notebook with the story of her life. From Bolivia the family moved to Lebanon, where Allende learned French. When she was fifteen they returned to Chile, where she finished high school and began working as a secretary for the Food and Agricultural Organization of the United Nations. She was interested in writing and soon entered the field of journalism and communications. She wrote a column for a women's magazine and edited a leading magazine for children titled *Mampato.* She also wrote short stories for children and wrote and produced plays. In 1972, she married Miguel Frías, with whom she had two children, Paula and Nicolás.

On September 13, 1973, a military coup in Chile led to the assassination of President Salvador Allende. This event and its aftermath of repression and violence have had a profound impact on Isabel Allende and her writing. Risking her life, she stayed in Chile for fifteen months, helping her compatriots escape military persecution and providing food and aid to the families of the victims of the regime. "Because of my work as a journalist I knew exactly what was happening in my country, I lived through it, and the dead, the tortured, the widows and orphans, left an unforgettable impression on my memory" (*Dictionary of Literary Biography [DLB],* 34). Allende was forced to flee her beloved homeland in 1975. She settled with her family in Caracas, Venezuela, where she worked as a teacher and school administrator and later wrote satirical articles for one of the leading newspapers in the country.

Suffering from the pain of exile and concerned about her grandfather, who was dying in Chile, Allende sat down on January 8, 1981, to write him one last letter. That momentous letter turned into the manuscript for her first book, *The House of the Spirits*. Allende describes the experience: "From the first lines I wrote, other wills took control of my letter, leading me far away from the uncertain story of the family to explore the more secure world of fiction. . . . I wrote without effort, without thinking, because my clairvoyant grandmother was dictating to me" (*Paula*, 275). Allende had spent more than twenty years on the periphery of literature—journalism, television scripts, theater, short stories—but it took three books before she wrote "writer" as her profession when she filled out a form. *The House of the Spirits* was translated into fifteen languages and became an overnight best-seller wherever it appeared. Since then Allende has written five additional books, and has joined the ranks of the most distinguished writers in contemporary literature.

The enormous appeal of Allende's writing is often attributed to the nature of her style: a dynamic combination of characters and events structured around a fast-paced narrative. Her work has been described as "enthralling," "richly imaginative," "a genuine rarity," "moving and compelling," and "a unique achievement." Allende writes to improve the world, bearing witness to social and political injustices. She believes, "All of us who write and are fortunate enough to be published ought to assume the responsibility of serving the cause of freedom and justice" (*DLB*, 40). Throughout her work, women's issues are central, and often the protagonist is endowed with a gift for writing. Even her minor characters have a defined personality, a complete biography, and an individual voice.

Partly out of superstition but also for reasons of discipline, Allende has begun all of her books on a January 8. Because she is more creative in the mornings, she gets up very early and writes until mid-afternoon, when she sorts her mail, answers letters, reads and researches. Allende's first book initiated her "into the ineradicable vice of telling stories. That book saved my life. Writing is a long process of introspection; it is a voyage toward the darkest caverns of consciousness, a long, slow process" (*Paula*, 9). Allende's mother, who has always been one of her best friends, is her personal editor, the one who corrects her books.

Until she wrote *Paula*, Allende had never shared her past. Her fiction was loosely autobiographical, but Allende did not reveal the details of her personal life. But when her daughter fell into a coma, Allende started a letter to her which told the story of their family. Just as her first book started with a letter, so did this letter turn into a book, this time an autobiography. For Allende, writing is a search for answers. As she sat by her dying daughter's bedside, she created a soul-baring memoir that will give her readers insight into her life and her work.

After her divorce from her first husband, Allende met William Gordon, an attorney, while on a lecture tour in the United States. They were married in 1988 and settled in Marin County, north of San Francisco, California. Her publisher was concerned that the new location might stifle her imagination, but Allende's recent books attest to her ability to draw inspiration wherever she finds herself. She has taught literature at several institutions including the University of California at Berkeley. She has won numerous awards and honors from around the world, among them doctorates of letters from Bates College, Dominican College, and New York State University. She was selected to the Women's Hall of Fame in Marin, California, and won the Feminist of the Year Award presented by the Feminist Majority Foundation in 1994. Her books have been translated into approximately twenty-seven languages, and two of them have been made into movies.

More Information About Isabel Allende

Dictionary of Literary Biography, Volume 145, 33–41.

510: East Bay Arts and Culture Magazine, Issue 3, 18–19, 48–50.

"Interview with Isabel Allende" by Farhat Iftekharuddin (unpublished interview, University of Texas, June 1994).

¡Latinas! Women of Achievement. Visible Ink, 1996.

Paula, by Isabel Allende. Translated from Spanish by Margaret Sayers Peden. HarperCollins, 1994.

San Francisco Focus, January 1996, 43.

World Authors. H. W. Wilson Company, 1991, 18–22.

Eva Luna

American Book Award

- Storytelling
- Authorship

Isabel Allende's third novel is basically a Bildungsroman about a twentieth-century Scheherazade who learned early to "barter words for goods" and to use her imagination to survive as a female from the poverty class in an unnamed, politically unstable Latin American country. Consuela, Eva's mother, sowed in her mind "the idea that reality is not only what we see on the surface; it has a magical dimension as well and, if we so desire, it is legitimate to enhance it and color it to make our journey through life less trying" (22). Eva's mother dies when she is six years old but remains with her in spirit throughout her life. The young orphan is buffeted from one servant position to another, at times living on the street, all the while buoyed by her rebellious nature and her inventiveness in turning carrots into princesses and paintings into voyages. Along the way she senses that her life will "be one long series of farewells" (70) as she encounters an assortment of fascinating characters and learns to appreciate the diversity of each. About the kind Turkish emigré shopkeeper with a cleft palate who befriends her, she "thought of his imperfection as a gift of birth, something that made him different from others—unique in this world" (153). When he arranges for her to learn to read and write, she is euphoric and discovers that writing is the best thing that had ever happened to her. She continues to write at night until years later, when she is finally able to make writing the focus of her life. The passages describing her feelings when she first sits down to write are breathtaking. "I believed that that page had been waiting for me for more than twenty years, that I had lived only for that instant . . ." (251). With no fortune but her stories, she becomes a successful writer of a unique new kind of soap opera for television.

Woven into Eva's "autobiography" is the life story of her future lover, Rolf Carlé, starting with his childhood in Nazi Austria to his immigration to South America and his eventual work as a filmmaker. Allende based his character on a story given to her while she was on a lecture tour to Germany. After a lecture in Hamburg, a listener told her about his life and she took notes on a paper napkin. Later, she "just introduced the paper napkin into the computer, and there was Rolf Carlé" (*510 Magazine*, 49). Other multidimensional characters include Huberto Naranjo, a street child who later becomes a leader of the guerrilla forces, and Melesio/Mimi, a talented, caring, transsexual actor who becomes Eva's friend and housemate.

Set in a country that closely resembles Venezuela, the story spans four decades of the twentieth century, with a focus on two dictatorships and the guerrilla movement around 1959 to 1969. The epic tale is filled with fantasy, foreshadowing, and ironic humor. The young Eva snatches the wig off her *patrona's* head, empties a chamberpot on the head of a minister of state, and entertains the servants with her imaginative stories. She later denounces the abuses and cruelty of dictatorships, the corruption that permeates all aspects of government, and the violence of military repression. As with her other books, Allende's canvas is large, including topics such as child abuse, suicide, mummies, concentration camps, murder, class issues, a stillborn birth of a two-headed baby, disappearances of political prisoners, prostitution, infidelities, and sadism. Unlike Allende's first two books, which featured protagonists from upper-class families, Eva Luna's only fortune is her imagination. All three books speak to women's issues, and celebrate writing.

RELATED WORKS

Large type edition: *Eva Luna.* Hall, 1990.

The Stories of Eva Luna by Isabel Allende. Translated from Spanish by Margaret Sayers Peden. Macmillan, 1991. See pages 36–37.

The House of the Spirits

Grand Roman d'Evasion Prize

- Historical Fiction
- Magic Realism

Isabel Allende's first novel traces the experiences of four generations of the del Valle–Trueba family through the first seventy-five years of the twentieth century. Set in an unnamed South American country (similar to Chile), the epic story focuses on the lives of three remarkable women who successively serve as the central characters: Clara, Blanca, and Alba. Interwoven into the 368-page book is the story of Esteban Trueba, who is respectively the husband, father, and grandfather of the female protagonists. The book begins at the turn of the century, in the childhood home of Clara del Valle, who will be the mother and grandmother as well as the spiritual leader of the clan. Endowed with a gift for clairvoyance, Clara can predict the future, communicate with the spirits, read fortunes, and recognize people's intentions. The poisoning of her sister, Rosa, is the "first of many acts of violence that marked the fate of the del Valle family" (29). As the story unfolds against the backdrop of the tragic political history of the country, Allende explores the complex relationships between individual and family, family and country, past and present, and spiritual and political. She makes a significant contribution to our understanding of class and gender issues as well as the history of Chile.

Dedicated "To my mother, my grandmother, and all the other extraordinary women of this story," the book is not strictly autobiographical but is based loosely on Allende's memories and her family's experiences in Chile. Her maternal grandparents provided inspiration for two of the book's central characters: Clara, the warm-hearted, mystical matriarch who, while taking gifts to the poor, advises her daughter, "This is to assuage our conscience, darling. But it doesn't help the poor. They don't need charity; they need justice" (117); and her violent, landowner-politician husband, Esteban.

The House of Spirits pays tribute to the women of Latin America and everywhere. Their strength and creativity in combatting the patriarchal system are inspiring. Clara's mother, one of the first feminists in the country, works for women's right to vote; Clara, ignoring her husband, fills her house with her spiritualist friends, conducts consciousness-raising sessions at the country estate, and concentrates on her visionary tasks; Blanca defies her father and her class by choosing a lifelong relationship with a revolutionary peasant leader who opposes everything her father believes in; Esteban's sister, Férula, becomes his rival for Clara's attentions; and Alba joins the student movement, steals her grandfather's weapons and hides them for the opposition, and falls in love with a guerrilla leader. The peasant women do not fare as well. Esteban, with his characteristic cruelty, rapes all the young women on his country estate, as well as many from neighboring haciendas, and ignores all his children who are born as a result of these violations. In the only passage in the book that bears criticism, Pancha, Esteban's first victim, is portrayed as enjoying sex with him the day after he brutally rapes her. Esteban's violence is extended to animals, his employees, his daughter, and his wife.

In the epilogue, it is revealed that Alba is the major narrator of the book. She uses her grandmother Clara's journals and her own memories to reconstruct the history of her family. Her grandfather, Esteban, is the secondary narrator. By juxtaposing the two voices, Allende contrasts the two perspectives, lending insight into differences in gender and generational interpretation of events. It was her grandmother Clara's spirit who came to Alba during the horrific days of her imprisonment to suggest that she write in her mind a testimony that not only would call attention to the terrible treatment she was enduring, but would occupy her attention and thus save her life. Later, near the end of the book, Alba writes that the days of the perpetrators are numbered because they are unable to destroy the spirits of the women. She resolves to overcome her own terrors, reclaim the past, and break the terrible chain of unending blood and sorrow.

Grades 12–Adult

RELATED WORKS

Spanish Edition

La casa de los espíritus by Isabel Allende. Plaza y Janés, 1982; HarperCollins, 1995.

Movie

The House of the Spirits

Book

One Hundred Years of Solitude by Gabriel García Márquez. HarperCollins, 1970; 1991.

Of Love and Shadows

- Dictatorships
- Journalism
- Historical Fiction

Isabel Allende's second novel tells the story of the disappearance of fifteen people in an unnamed South American country that has fallen under the rule of a military dictatorship. At the center of the novel are Irene Beltrán, a journalist from an upper-class family, and her lover, Francisco Leal, a photographer, the son of political exiles from Spain. When the two set out to research the story of Evangelina Ranquileo, a young woman who appears to have supernatural powers, they find themselves caught up in a series of events that change their lives irretrievably. The story traces Irene's political awakening and self-discovery. As part of the upper class, "she escaped into the orderly, peaceful world of the fashionable neighborhoods, the exclusive beach clubs, the ski slopes, the summers in the country. Irene had been educated to deny any unpleasantness, discounting it as a distortion of the facts" (111). As she works on the case, she develops a social consciousness that compels her to risk her life to uncover the evidence of atrocities committed by military personnel. After she and Francisco discover not only the body of Evangelina but many others in an abandoned mine, their determination to expose these crimes leads to a machine-gun attack on Irene. As soon as she is able to travel, the two flee into exile across the border, pledging to return to their beloved homeland someday.

As she did in her first book, *The House of the Spirits,* Allende bears witness to historical events in Chile. Although the country is unnamed, the fictionalized story is based on a highly publicized incident that occurred in 1978, when the bodies of fifteen people were discovered in an abandoned mine near the village of Lonquén, outside of Santiago. In the epigraph, Allende explains that the story was confided to her and that she carried it in her memory until she could write it down so it would not be "erased by the wind."

Following closely after the phenomenal success of Allende's first book, the second novel has inevitably been held up for comparison. Some reviewers feel that it is better written and more mature, while others find it "smaller, paler, and less magical than the first" (*New Yorker,* August 24, 1987). Both books illuminate class and gender issues and feature individuals struggling against the powerful forces of government and society. *Of Love and Shadows* was a best-seller in Latin America and Europe, and the English translation was nominated for the *Los Angeles Times* Book Prize in 1987.

Allende's analysis of class issues is reason enough to read this book. She writes that "two countries were functioning within the same national boundaries: one for the golden and powerful elite, the other for the excluded and silent masses" (p. 168). She also touches on a number of other significant issues and topics including prostitution, suicide, family rape, religion, marital discord and harmony, resistance movements, hunger strikes, street demonstrations, homosexuality, and the neglect of elderly people.

The major problem in the book is the misleading way in which incest is portrayed. The interactions between Evangelina and her older brother are only described through his voice. Research shows that incest between a young girl and her older brother is the result of an unequal power relationship and that it results in debilitating trauma to the young girl. This is a significant error in the book, one that should not be overlooked during discussions. By discussing this and other issues introduced in the book, readers will become better informed and more equipped to live in a complex, and often, confusing world.

Grades 12–Adult

RELATED WORK
Movie
Of Love and Shadows

Paula

Isabel Allende's sixth book is a soul-baring memoir, which began as a letter to her comatose daughter, Paula. As Allende sat at her cherished daughter's bedside, she wrote this vivid account of her grandparents' and parents' lives, and her remembrance of her own childhood, adolescence, and womanhood. Woven into her life story are poignant passages on her daughter's illness and her unsuccessful efforts to save her life.

"Listen, Paula, I'm going to tell you a story, so that when you wake up you will not feel so lost." With these loving words, Allende begins her memoir, dedicated to her daughter. Twenty-eight-year-old Paula Frias Allende has fallen into a coma caused by porphyria, a rare metabolic disorder. As her mother keeps a desperate vigil in the corridors of the hospital in Madrid, and later in her home in California, Paula edges closer to death. Allende enlists the help of every kind of remedy and therapy, including the services of an acupuncturist, a psychic, a hypnotist, and a number of other healers, but she must finally confront the painful truth: nothing will bring Paula back to the world of the living. Devastated, Allende cries, "I will never again be the person I was" (207). The death of her daughter at such a young age and the military coup in her beloved homeland, Chile, are the two major tragedies of her life. "I plunge into these pages in an irrational attempt to overcome my terror" (9). Even though "the misery of illness makes everyone equal" (78), "sorrow is a solitary road" (110). Allende points out that until the twentieth century—and even now in all but the most privileged families—losing a child was a common experience. As she unburdens her heart, she provides insight into what it takes to bear that loss and gives a rare gift to her readers.

Until this book Allende had never shared her past. Describing her life as a "multilayered and ever-changing fresco" that only she can decipher, she recalls both positive and bitter memories. She writes that her life has been "filled with intense emotion. I have lived the extremes; few things have been easy or smooth for me . . ." (112). "For nearly fifty years I have been a toreador taunting violence and pain with a red cape, secure in the protection of the good luck birthmark on my back—even though in my heart I suspected that one day I would feel the claws of misfortune raking my shoulder" (206–207). Allende traces the lives of her ancestors, reveals personal and family secrets, and recounts the turbulent history of Chile. She records the years of her exile in Venezuela and her recent move to the United States. She investigates her development as a writer after spending "more than twenty years on the periphery of literature—journalism, short stories, theater, television scripts, hundreds of letters" (275).

Paula is a deeply affecting book, written in the magical prose typical of Allende's novels. The author examines the decisions she made as a woman, as a Chilean, and as a writer; reaffirms her reality; and says good-bye to her beloved daughter. This book has been a best-seller in the United States, Latin America, and Europe. It has brought a new audience to Isabel Allende's writing. Both new readers and longtime admirers will embrace this fine autobiography, one of her best works to date.

- Short Stories
- Storytelling

The Stories of Eva Luna

For her fourth book, Isabel Allende chose to write a book of short stories. She had just published *Eva Luna,* which is about a storyteller, and so the next book, naturally, was a book of the stories she tells. *The Stories of Eva Luna* is a collection of twenty-three tales that cover an array of themes and present an abundance of fascinating characters, some of whom appeared in the earlier work. The book opens with a request from her lover for a story that has never been told. And so Eva and her much-celebrated creator begin a series of entertaining tales that combine magic, fantasy, psychological insight, and sharp social satire. The stories nestle into a variety of settings—deserts, convents, jungles, boardinghouses, brothels, taverns, tropical mountain villages, mansions, and palaces. Readers familiar with *Eva Luna* will recognize Agua Santa, Calle República, and La Colonia, as well as Rolf Carlé, Riad Halabí, and Ines, a schoolteacher. Allende weaves a tapestry of themes and topics—euthanasia, revolution, prostitution, greed, revenge, love, exile, illegal organ plunder, murder, calamity, betrayal, and "layers of blood, sweat, and sorrow"—all in a vibrant tribute to storytelling.

One of the most memorable stories, "Two Words," celebrates the power of language. Belisa Crepusculario makes her living selling words—verses, dreams, letters, and "invented insults." Born into a poor family and without a source of income, she discovers that "words make their way in the world without a master" (11). When she writes a political speech for a colonel, he captures the nation's heart and sets out to right the wrongs of history. In "Letters of Betrayed Love," Analia Torres falls in love with the words in the letters sent to her and discovers years later the person behind the beguiling verses. As she does in her novels, Allende again excels in her portrayal of strong women. "The Gold of Tomás Vargas" tells the triumphant story of a wife and a mistress who collaborate to rid themselves of a scoundrel husband/lover. Ines, in "The Schoolteacher's Guest," finds a satisfying way to avenge the murder of her son. And the protagonist in "Clarisa," who possesses a boundless understanding of human weakness and has the hands of a healer, foils a robber with her unique brand of kindness and practicality.

The last story in the book and the most elaborate is "And of Clay Are We Created." Allende and many other viewers saw a report on television in 1985 about a volcanic eruption in Colombia that killed thousands of people and trapped Omaira Sánchez, a young girl, in a mudslide. Allende's heartbreaking story features Rolf Carlé as the newscaster who tries to rescue the young victim. As he keeps her company for several days until she dies, he finally grieves the sorrows of his own tormented past. Eva tells the story as she watches the horrifying drama unfold on television. Allende refers to this event again in a later book, *Paula,* writing that she tried to exorcise Omaira's story from her mind by telling her story, but "she is a dogged angel who will not let me forget her" (*Paula*, 309). When Allende's daughter fell into a coma, the writer remembered Omaira's face. Both Paula and Omaira were trapped. Allende was finally able to decipher the message in Omaira's eyes: "patience, courage, resignation, dignity in the face of death" (*Paula*, 310).

Grades 12–Adult

RELATED WORKS

Large Type Edition
The Stories of Eva Luna. Hall, 1991.

Spanish Edition
Cuentos de Eva Luna. HarperCollins, 1995.

Book
Eva Luna. Translated from Spanish by Margaret Sayers Peden. Alfred A. Knopf, 1988; Bantam, 1989; HarperCollins, 1995. See pages 31–32.

Julia Alvarez

Dominican American (1950–)

Birthday: March 27
Contact: Susan Bergholz
17 West 10th Street, #5
New York, NY 10011

"I think fiction is truth. It uses strategies of storytelling to get you involved, to weave you into the narrative web, in order to tell you some truth of the human heart."

(The Champaign-Urbana News-Gazette, *Dec. 30, 1994, 3*)

Books by Julia Alvarez

Homecoming. Grove Press, 1984; 1986; Dutton, 1995.

The Housekeeping Book. Burlington, 1984.

How the García Girls Lost Their Accents. Algonquin Books, 1991; NAL Dutton, 1992.

In the Time of the Butterflies: A Novel. Algonquin Books, 1994; NAL Plume, 1995.

Old Age Ain't for Sissies. Crane Creek Press, 1979.

The Other Side/El Otro Lado. NAL Plume, 1995.

Yo! Algonquin Books, 1997.

Julia Alvarez has won acclaim for her fiction, which includes *How the García Girls Lost Their Accents* and *In the Time of the Butterflies.* Long before she discovered her novelist's voice, she was writing engaging poetry. In poetry and prose, her eloquent voice speaks about the experience of being an immigrant to the United States. The recipient of numerous awards and honors, her work has been widely anthologized. She has taught English at several universities and is currently professor of English at Middlebury College in Vermont.

Alvarez's father, a doctor, had met her mother while she was attending school in the United States. Alvarez was born in New York City and spent her early years in the Dominican Republic. She lived with her parents and sisters on her mother's family property. Surrounded by her extended family, Alvarez and her sisters were brought up along with their cousins by her mother, aunts, and maids. She was ten years old when her family fled the repressive regime of Rafael Leónidas Trujillo. Her father had been part of an underground resistance movement that was planning the revolutionary overthrow of the tyrannical dictator. The family narrowly escaped from Santo Domingo, then known as Ciudad Trujillo, to New York City, similar to the fictional García family in

Alvarez's first novel. In "Exile," one of her poems, she writes about "the night we fled the country" and the "loss much larger than I understood."

The young immigrant soon experienced homesickness, alienation, and prejudice. She missed her homeland and her large, close-knit family. She responded to the loss by turning inward. The introverted young girl became an avid reader, immersing herself in books.

During her high school years in Catholic schools and Abbot Academy, she encountered teachers who encouraged her in her writing, so that early on in her new language, she wanted to become a writer. For this reason, she chose Middlebury College as a school reputed for its writing program. There she majored in literature and worked at the Bread Loaf Writers' Conference, where she met other young writers and mentors.

Graduating summa cum laude from Middlebury College, the young scholar went on to earn her master's degree in creative writing at Syracuse University. In her writer-in-residence program for the Kentucky Arts Commission, Alvarez served as the visiting writer in elementary schools, high schools, colleges, and communities throughout Kentucky for two years. Her second writer-in-residence program was in Delaware, where she conducted workshops in a bilingual (Spanish/English) creative writing project sponsored by the Delaware Arts Council, culminating in an anthology, *Yo Soy/I Am*. The third writer-in-residence program took Alvarez to North Carolina, where she participated in a pilot project sponsored by the National Endowment for the Arts and the Arts Council of Fayetteville. She conducted poetry

workshops for senior citizens in rest homes and civic and county centers. This fascinating project culminated in an anthology, *Old Age Ain't for Sissies.*

As an English instructor, Alvarez has taught a variety of classes, including poetry, drama, literary analysis, comic theory, and creative writing, as well as courses on women's studies and minority/ethnic literature. In addition to teaching in a number of locations including California, Massachusetts, Vermont, and Illinois, she was selected as a Jenny McKean Moore Visiting Writer at George Washington University in Washington, D.C. During this one-year fellowship awarded after a national competition, she taught creative writing workshops in poetry and fiction for the community as well as autobiographical writing, and a literature course on memoirs by immigrant Americans called Growing Up Ethnic. Now, as a professor in the English department at Middlebury College, her responsibilities include teaching beginning and advanced creative writing workshops as well as a variety of literature courses including a Hispanic American literature course, a Chaucer, Milton, and Shakespeare course, and other courses in interdisciplinary subjects.

In addition to teaching, Alvarez has served as a judge, consultant, panelist, and assistant editor in a variety of capacities. She often gives readings, lectures, and presentations at conferences, bookstores, classes, book fairs, and other locations and has been interviewed on numerous radio and television programs. In 1992, she was interviewed by WNET, Channel 13, New York City, for the Literature and Entertainment portion of the *Vista Report*, a documentary program on the

growing force of the Latino population in the United States. Alvarez has won many prestigious awards and honors, including a National Endowment for the Arts grant for poetry in 1987–88, a PEN Syndicated Fiction Prize in 1987, and an Ingram Merrill Foundation Grant awarded for fiction manuscripts in 1990. In 1988, she was one of five artists selected from an international competition to live and work in an artist colony at Altos de Chavon in the Dominican Republic. Her responsibilities included conducting workshops and giving readings of her own work.

Alvarez's work has been praised for its significance to Latino culture, women's issues, and the immigrant experience. *Library Journal* commented, "Alvarez is a gifted, evocative storyteller of promise." Other critics have described her work as "finely crafted," "delightful," "warm, honest," "simply wonderful," and "invigorating." Her prose and poetry are innovative and unforgettable.

More Information About Julia Alvarez

American Scholar. Winter 1987, 71–85.

Atlanta Journal. August 11, 1991, A13.

The Champaign-Urbana News-Gazette. December 30, 1994, 3.

¡Latinas! Women of Achievement. Visible Ink, 1996.

Library Journal. May 1, 1991, 102.

Los Angeles Times. June 7, 1991, E4.

New York Times Book Review. October 6, 1991.

Notable Hispanic American Women, 14–17. Gale Research, 1993.

Publishers Weekly. April 5, 1991, 133.

How the García Girls Lost Their Accents

PEN Oakland/Josephine Miles Book Award
American Library Association Notable Book

"They will be haunted by what they do and don't remember. But they have spirit in them. They will invent what they need to survive" (223). With these words, Chuchu, one of the maids, bids farewell to the García sisters, who, with their parents, must flee the repressive regime of Rafael Leónidas Trujillo. The lively story of their adjustment to life in the United States is told through a series of interconnected vignettes beginning in adulthood, and moving backward to their childhood as wealthy members of the upper class in the Dominican Republic. Although fictional, Alvarez's celebrated first novel about the four García sisters growing up in New York City sprang from the themes of rootlessness and assimilation she and her sisters experienced. In this engaging chronicle of a family in exile, each person struggles to regain her equilibrium in her own unique way. Their mother, far from the family compound, copes by trying to invent useful items. At one point she proclaims that it is better to be "an independent nobody than a high-class houseslave" (144). For the daughters, the changes are terrifying and exhilarating, liberating and excruciating. Trying to live up to their parents' version of honor while accommodating the expectations of a new culture is confusing and frustrating. The new identities they forge in the land of wild and loose Americans are at odds with the proper island life they remember. As members of the privileged class, they miss the special pampering from the chauffeurs, gardeners, and half-dozen maids and nursemaids of their earlier years.

Experiences at school are among the most notable. Adolescent Carla is harassed by a gang of boys who chase after her, call her names, and pelt her with rocks. On her way home from school one day, she is accosted by an exhibitionist in a car. Later, insensitive questioning by police officers adds to the humiliation. Her younger sister, Yolanda, develops an interest in writing poetry. She had never been interested in school before, "But in New York . . . since the natives were unfriendly, and the country inhospitable, she took root in the language" (141). By the time she enters college, she thinks she is quite Americanized but soon finds herself feeling profoundly out of place. "For the hundredth time, I cursed my immigrant origins" (94).

Readers will be interested in analyzing the internalized racism in Alvarez's characters. "She's going to look just like an angel, pink and blond" (59), a proud grandmother clucks over her new granddaughter. "All the grandfather's Caribbean fondness for a male heir and for fair Nordic looks had surfaced" (26). Sexism is also alive and well in the States as well as on the island. For example, the fact that there are four daughters and no sons is always an unstated issue between the parents. Readers interested in exploring language issues will also find plenty to discuss, as the García sisters attend expensive schools to smooth the accent out of their English (hence the title of the book). Other topics include anorexia, mental illness, pedophilia, marijuana, illegitimate children, and of course, class privilege.

Years later, Yolanda returns to the island hoping to establish the roots she could never find in the States. She reflects on the twenty-nine years since her family was uprooted from their homeland. "She and her sisters have led such turbulent lives—so many husbands, homes, jobs, wrong turns among them" (11). Alvarez's first book of fiction, written with humor and insight, tells the irrepressible stories of how four immigrants came to be at home—and not at home—in the United States.

Grades 11–Adult

RELATED WORKS

For Educators

The Inner World of the Immigrant Child by Cristina Igoa. St. Martin's Press, 1995. See page 209.

For Younger Readers

The Magic Shell by Nicholasa Mohr. Scholastic, 1995. See page 118.

My Two Worlds by Ginger Gordon. Clarion, 1993.

Over Here It's Different: Carolina's Story by Mildred Leinweber Dawson. Macmillan, 1993.

In the Time of the Butterflies: A Novel

National Book Critics Circle Award Finalist in Fiction
American Library Association Notable Book
American Library Association Best Books for Young Adults

- Dominican Republic
- Historical Fiction
- Women Revolutionaries
- Dictatorships

On November 25, 1960, the bodies of three young women were found at the bottom of a cliff on the north coast of the Dominican Republic. Among the leading opponents of the dictatorship of General Rafael Leónidas Trujillo, these women had been instrumental in the formation of an underground resistance movement and had actively worked for the revolutionary overthrow of the oppressive regime. Martyred, the Mirabal sisters have become legendary figures in their country, where they are known as *Las Mariposas*, the Butterflies, from their underground code names.

Now, three decades later, Julia Alvarez has fictionalized their story in a powerful novel that pays tribute to the spirit of the real Mirabals. (Alvarez's family narrowly escaped to the United States four months before the ambush and murder of Minerva, Patria, and María Teresa Mirabal.) Against the historical backdrop of the brutal, thirty-one-year Trujillo regime, Alvarez chronicles the personal lives, political awakening, and revolutionary strategies of each of the sisters. In alternating chapters, each Butterfly speaks in her own voice, beginning with her childhood in the 1940s. The surviving sister, Dede, speaks across the decades, framing the narrative with her own poignant story of loss and dedication to her sisters' memories. The stories of the convent-educated women, members of a wealthy, conservative Catholic family, slowly unfold as they each acquire revolutionary fervor, building to a gripping intensity. Alvarez artfully captures the atmosphere of the police state, in which interminable atrocities terrify and silence the populace. As the sisters endure the arrests of their compatriots, their own imprisonment, and the threatened disintegration of their movement, they respond in individual, complex ways. Yet they continue to risk their lives to save their beloved country. As Alvarez notes in her postscript, they did what "few men—and only a handful of women—had been willing to do" (323).

Few books have been written about Las Mariposas or the Trujillo dictatorship. Alvarez explains that the situation is similar to what happened in the United States after the Vietnam War, when the novels took some time to come out. "There's a way in which a culture has to sit on something for a while and then begin to understand it, and then redeem that time by telling the story."

Alvarez's second novel contains numerous remarkable aspects. One of the many memorable scenes unfolds when Minerva reaches out to her father's mistress and her four daughters. When she insists on meeting them and later helps pay for her half-sisters' educations, she demonstrates her awareness of the connections among the political struggles the country is engaged in and the class and gender struggles within her own family. A strong, admirable woman who studies law at the university, Minerva once dared to publicly slap Trujillo's face. A subtext of the book is the fear engendered by the despot, who often preyed on young women, ruthlessly discarding each for his next young victim. Trujillo's internalized racism is apparent in his refugee program to whiten the race, his elite all-white guard corps, his use of chemicals and makeup to lighten his skin color, and his killing of twenty thousand Haitians in 1937.

The author achieves a beautifully balanced sense of personal as well as historical drama. She writes, "I hope that through this fictionalized story I will bring acquaintance of these famous sisters to English-speaking readers. November 25, the day of their murders, is observed in many Latin American countries as the International Day Against Violence Toward Women. Obviously, these sisters, who fought one tyrant, have served as models for women fighting against injustices of all kinds" (324).

Grades 12–Adult

• Poetry

The Other Side/El Otro Lado

The poems in *The Other Side/El Otro Lado* reveal Julia Alvarez's engaging voice and the full range of her poetic talents. In the opening poem, "Bilingual Sestina," Alvarez reflects on her immigrant experience of leaving the Dominican Republic for a strange country and a new language. "The Gladys Poems" pay tribute to a pantry maid from her childhood, starting with the time her mother interviewed her, through the sweeping, mopping, and polishing, to the day when Gladys disappeared, leaving the young girl feeling forlorn and abandoned. The "Making Up the Past" poems examine the life of exile as experienced by the young Alvarez. It was a "loss much larger than I understood" at the time, as a part of her was set adrift. In one of the many memorable poems in the book, "New World," Alvarez remembers her Tía

Ana and Tía Fofi, who sewed at a factory during the week and sewed for her family on Saturdays. The "old-world seamstresses . . . were dazed with journeys. But their cutting hand was unerring, their stitching strict as a border, their foot steady on the Singer." Alvarez's poems move from childhood memories of "melting into the USA" through college inspirations to write poetry to adult issues. Alvarez speaks of letting go the losses and trying hard to feel luckier than she felt. The book closes with the long, multipart title narrative, set at an artist's colony not far from her childhood home where Alvarez worked on her writing residency. She suffered a writing block, and the first few weeks were torture. Nothing seemed to "roll back the big boulders of silence/and release the voice that would gather the scattered pieces together/and tell me at last the story of this life I had been living." Finally, the cruelty and struggles experienced in the States "melt away," and she begins "writing in earnest." She eloquently expresses self-doubts, fears, and homesickness as she searches for a way to make up her "divided Dominican-American mind." The last poem is a poignant tribute addressed to Estel, a mute Dominican child. Alvarez's lyrical collection is an innovative examination of internal conflict, rootlessness, and self-evolution.

Grades 12–Adult

RELATED WORK
For more poetry, see the Subject Index on page 223.

Rudolfo Anaya

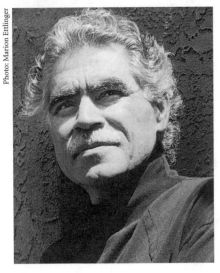

Photo: Marion Ettlinger

Mexican American (1937–)

Birthday: October 30
Contact: Susan Bergholz
17 West 10th Street, #5
New York, NY 10011

"I will not rest until the people of Mexican heritage know the great cultures and civilizations they are heirs to from that country to the south." (Focus on Criticism, *387*)

"Reading is the key to a liberated life. We must take action to wrest our freedom to teach from those forces that still don't acknowledge the existence of the multidimensional and multicultural realities of our country. We must infuse into the study of language and literature the stories of the many communities that compose our country."
(The Anaya Reader, *411*)

Books by Rudolfo Anaya

The Adventures of Juan Chicaspatas. Arte Público Press, 1985.

Alburquerque. University of New Mexico Press, 1992; Warner Books, 1992.

The Anaya Reader. Warner Books, 1995.

Aztlán: Essays on the Chicano Homeland. Coedited with Francisco Lomeli. Bilingual Press, 1984.

Bless Me, Ultima. Quinto Sol, 1972; Warner Books, 1993.

Cuentos Chicanos: A Short Story Anthology. Coedited with Antonio Marquez. University of New Mexico Press, 1984.

Cuentos: Tales from the Hispanic Southwest. Illustrated by Jamie Valdez. The Museum of New Mexico Press, 1980.

Farolitos of Christmas. Illustrated by Edward Gonzales. Hyperion Books for Children, 1995.

Heart of Aztlán. University of New Mexico Press, 1988.

Jalamanta: A Message from the Desert. Warner Books, 1996.

The Legend of la Llorona. Tonatiuh-Quinto Sol, 1984.

Maya's Children. Illustrated by Maria Baca. Hyperion Books for Children, 1996.

Rio Grande Fall. Warner Books, 1996.

The Silence of the Llano. Tonatiuh-Quinto Sol, 1982.

Tierra: Contemporary Fiction of New Mexico. Editor. Bilingual Press, 1989.

Tortuga. University of New Mexico Press, 1988.

Voces: Anthology of New Mexican Writers. Editor. Bilingual Press, no date available.

Zia Summer. Warner Books, 1995.

Rudolfo Anaya, the highly acclaimed author of a number of books, is best known for his classic best-seller, *Bless Me, Ultima*. A retired professor emeritus of English from the University of New Mexico, the legendary writer has recently written a number of new books. His work is recognized for its powerful presentation of Chicano tradition and myth, spirituality and healing, the sacredness of the earth, and the quest for personal, communal, and cultural identity.

Anaya was born in Pastura, a village lying south of Santa Rosa in eastern New Mexico. His mother, Rafaelita Mares, came from a farming family in the village of Puerto de Luna in the Pecos Valley and his father, Martín Anaya, was a *vaquero* from Pastura, a rancher who worked with cattle and sheep. When Anaya was a baby, his parents sat him on a rug on the floor of their house. They placed a variety of items around him including a saddle, a pencil, and some paper. He immediately crawled to the pencil and paper and has continued to follow his interest in writing to this day. Anaya was a very curious child; his mother noticed that he asked a lot of questions, and she knew that he was destined to follow an unfamiliar path. He grew up speaking Spanish at home, so when he started school the transition from a Spanish-speaking world to an English-speaking one resulted in a period of adjustment. Although schoolwork was not difficult for Anaya, he soon learned that he was different and that he had a unique way of perceiving the world.

Anaya's family moved to Santa Rosa when he was a small child and to Albuquerque when he was fifteen. Subsequently, he suffered a spinal injury when he dove into an irrigation ditch and endured an extended stay in a hospital. When he returned home, he was walking with a cane. He later wrote *Tortuga,* a book loosely based on his hospitalization. During his convalescence, he learned to hide his pain, to live within; he learned the true meaning of loneliness. Later, he eloquently expressed this pain and loneliness in his writing.

Anaya attended high school in Albuquerque, where discrimination made life difficult for his people. There were no Mexican American teachers, and the literature and history of his people were not a part of the curriculum. This widespread omission of information about his heritage understandably resulted in feelings of alienation in the young student, as it did in many of his peers. Even during Anaya's undergraduate days at the University of New Mexico, there was no mention of Mexican history or art. Indeed, he was still corrected for allowing his Spanish accent to show. He earned a bachelor's degree in 1963 and an M.A. in 1968 in English and American literature. He married Patricia, a woman from Kansas, to whom he paid tribute in *Tortuga,* which was "Dedicated with love to my wife, Patricia. She walks the path of the sun. She sings the songs of the moon." Also a writer, she believes in Anaya's writing and has become one of his best editors, responding to the strengths and weaknesses of his work.

Anaya wrote poetry and prose to assuage his pain, loneliness, and alienation. As he studied and worked, he struggled for seven years to write his first novel, *Bless Me, Ultima.* He sent the manuscript to dozens of publishers but found no interest among the mainstream presses. Believing in his work, he finally sent it to Quinto Sol Publications in Berkeley, California. The manuscript was accepted immediately and became an instant success. One of the few Chicano best-sellers, the book was awarded the prestigious Premio Quinto Sol Award for the best novel written by a Chicano in 1972. It sold more than 300,000 copies in twenty-one printings, and in 1994 was newly issued in an illustrated, hardcover edition. Anaya has written many other books, poems, plays, articles, and screenplays. His novel *Alburquerque* was awarded the PEN Center West Award for Fiction in 1992.

After teaching junior and senior high school in Albuquerque, Anaya was invited to teach creative writing at the University of New Mexico in 1974. Later, as a full professor of English, he specialized in Chicano literature as well as creative writing. He recently retired from his position as professor emeritus and now devotes his energies to traveling, lecturing, editing, and writing. Today, Rudolfo Anaya is considered one of the leading Latino novelists in the United States. "My writing is ongoing, it fills my life" (*Focus on Criticism,* 388).

More Information About Rudolfo Anaya

BOOKS

The Anaya Reader by Rudolfo Anaya. Warner Books, 1995.

Contemporary Authors: Autobiography Series. Volume 4, 1986, 15–28.

Dictionary of Literary Biography. Volume 82, 24–34.

Rudolfo A. Anaya: Focus on Criticism, edited by Cesar A. Gonzalez. Bilingual Press, Arizona State University, no date available. (602) 965-3867.

MAGAZINES AND NEWSPAPERS

Denver Post. April 7, 1994, 9–10.

Publishers Weekly. June 5, 1995, 41–42.

Alburquerque

PEN Center West Award for Fiction

Against the backdrop of a historic city coming to grips with the complexities of urban growth, a young man searches for his biological father. Abrán González, a former Golden Gloves boxing champion, is unaware that he was adopted until he learns this secret from his birth mother on her deathbed. This revelation sparks a quest that finds him rubbing shoulders with Albuquerque politicians, draws him back into the dreaded boxing ring, and threatens to shake his identity. Meanwhile, a writer struggles to find himself in his stories, a Vietnam War veteran searches for a way to return to his pueblo, and two mayoral candidates develop competing plans for the future of the city.

This far-reaching story introduces a number of interesting characters and provides fascinating information about the history of Albuquerque. Anaya, who has lived in the Albuquerque area all his life, writes "Legend says the Anglo stationmaster couldn't pronounce the first r in Albur, so he dropped it as he painted the station sign for the city. This novel restores the original spelling, Alburquerque." As he writes about his beloved city, Anaya helps readers understand the deep roots and traditions of New Mexico's people. He bares the soul of the city, writing about the conquest of the native territories by the Spanish and Anglos and the appropriation of land, water, and culture by the invaders. He takes a piercing look at racism, anti-Semitism, and class oppression, writing, "they suffered the punishment of the old prejudices, prejudices that still existed. The city was still split. The Anglos lived in the Heights, the Chicanos along the valley. . . . One didn't have to go to El Paso and cross to Juarez to understand the idea of border" (38). Several of the characters are of mixed heritages and, finding themselves living in a hypocritical society that worships racial purity, are struggling to find their identities. On the whole, the book handles these important issues with insight and sensitivity with one exception: the use of the term "Japs." When disparaging remarks are made by racist characters, it is clear that they are wrong. But in this case, the word was uttered by the mayor, an otherwise admirable character.

Followers of Anaya's work will recognize Juan Chicaspatas from *The Adventures of Juan Chicaspatas* and Ben Chávez as Benjie, the son of Adelita and Clemente Chávez in *Heart of Aztlán,* both earlier books. The character of Ben Chávez, a writer, bears some interesting similarities to Rudolfo Anaya himself. Hoping to create a consciousness for his people, Chávez is writing an epic that explores the Mesoamerican mythic elements Chicanos had incorporated into their heritage. Anaya here draws on his trademark magic realism, but adds a touch of madcap adventure and political satire too. Reviewers praised the novel for its intense spirituality, describing it as rich and tempestuous, gentle and fierce, embodying a deep caring for the land and culture of the Southwest. One reviewer wrote, "It is . . . a touching story, one I could not put down once I had started it. Through some passages, I wept copiously. Anaya is that kind of writer—gut-wrenching, tear-jerking, and one who leads you to an examination of your own life" *(World Literature Today).* Both readers who are unfamiliar with "Alburquerque" and those for whom it is an old friend will enjoy this tale of political intrigue and genealogical mystery set in the historic city.

Grades 12–Adult

RELATED WORK
World Literature Today, Winter 1994, 125.

The Anaya Reader

• Collection of short stories, essays, plays, and excerpts from novels

This anthology of mixed-genre pieces is the first collection of writing by a major publishing company wholly focused on a single Chicano writer. Here are excerpts from old favorites such as *Bless Me, Ultima* and *Tortuga* as well as many pieces previously unpublished or available only in small-press editions. *The Anaya Reader* is a tribute to Anaya's versatility as a writer, featuring fiction, short stories, essays, plays, and even a poem. The foreword by César A. González-T. provides insight into Anaya's writing and life. Anaya dedicated this comprehensive 562-page book to his wife, "Patricia, my constant companion and confidante during the long years of birthing these collected pieces, and to a new generation of readers."

The book includes nine short stories which expand on Anaya's vision of life empowered by a love for the earth. One of the most striking stories is "In Search of Epifano," in which an eighty-year-old artist drives her old Jeep south into the desert of Sonora in search of her grandfather. In "The Gift," Jerónimo, carrying a new wooden leg for his father, returns to his childhood home from Cuernavaca in time for the Day of the Dead. "The Silence of the Llano" is a disturbing piece about death, grieving, child neglect, and rape. It ends with a foreboding hint of impending family rape, described in the foreword as "a re-creation of a traditional tale of incest." Other stories feature an oil worker who grew up living and breathing the desert, a writer who explores the meaning of destiny, a deer fenced in by the Los Alamos Atomic Laboratory, and a runner who delivers an urgent message from the Inca.

For readers familiar only with Anaya's fiction, *The Anaya Reader* provides a new glimpse into the mind and writing of the author by including a number of notable essays. Several of these pieces should be required reading for prospective and practicing educators. In "An American Chicano in King Arthur's Court," "On the Education of Hispanic Children," "Take the Tortillas Out of Your Poetry," and "The Censorship of Neglect," Anaya eloquently calls for an end to the omission, censorship, and marginalization of Chicano/a literature, history, and culture. He urges educators and policy makers to incorporate the many voices of literature into the curriculum. He writes, "What we seek now, in our relationship to the broader society, is to eliminate the mindless prejudices that hamper our evolution, and to encourage people of goodwill who do not fear a pluralistic society and who understand that the more a group of people define themselves in positive ways, the greater the contribution they make to humanity" (302). Anaya argues forcefully against censorship, both external and self-imposed. He analyzes the motivation that led to the burning of *Bless Me, Ultima* and other books in 1981 in Bloomfield, New

Mexico: "Censorship is fear clothed in the guise of misguided righteousness" (391). Educators who have been working in the field of multicultural education will be heartened by Anaya's words, and those who are undecided will gain insight into the agenda behind educational systems that routinely exclude the work of some our country's best writers and teach children to be ashamed of their heritage. Anaya writes, "If you are teaching in a Mexican-American community, it is your social responsibility to refuse to use the textbook that doesn't contain stories by Mexican-American authors" (412). He goes on to say that wherever we are teaching, we misrepresent our country and shortchange our students if we don't provide information about all the people who are a part of the population.

Grades 12–Adult

- Career Aspirations
- Death
- Dreams
- *Curanderas*

Bless Me, Ultima

Premio Quinto Sol Literary Award

This best-selling novel depicts the maturation of Antonio Marez, a boy growing up in Guadalupe, a small New Mexico farm village. Seven-year-old Antonio narrates (in flashback form) this story of his relationship with Ultima, a *curandera* (healer) and his spiritual guide. Antonio's parents disagree about his destiny—his mother wants him to be a priest or farmer and his father wants him to follow his *vaquero* (cowboy) ways. Antonio witnesses four deaths during the novel, including three killings and the drowning of a friend. He struggles with spirituality, confused about the teachings of the Catholic Church and about his discovery of a genuine spirituality and legitimate morality outside the Church in nature. His dreams help him sort out these confusions. The book deals with a wide variety of subjects drawn together with intense force. Antonio struggles to understand good and evil, to establish his identity, to conquer childhood fears, and to find his way in his family, school, and community. Throughout the novel, Antonio's trials are balanced against his association with Ultima. She allows him to participate in her life-affirming practices of healing and stabilizing negative forces. Although the novel details only two years in Antonio's life, the reader sees him change and grow in profound ways. The skillful cross-weaving of social, cultural, and psychological levels of action results in a very powerful book.

Grades 9–Adult

RELATED WORK
Spanish Edition: *Bendiceme, Ultima.* Warner Books, 1993.

- Short Stories

Cuentos Chicanos: A Short Story Anthology

The twenty-one short stories in this collection offer highly personalized visions of the world presented in styles that range from oral narratives to experimentation with stream-of-consciousness. From tragic to light-hearted, cynical to exuberant, the stories are distinguished by their diversity and vitality. The collection beautifully captures the dimensions, subtleties, nuances, and paradoxes of Chicano/a life and culture. Rudolfo Anaya's piece, "B.

Traven is Alive and Well in Cuernavaca," features a writer in search of a story. He encounters a number of people, each with a message for him. But it is an illiterate gardener who teaches him the most important lesson of all. Ana Castila's story, "Ghost Talk," is about a woman who confronts the man who abused her mother years ago, resulting in her birth. She writes, "Bigoted North Americans who forget where their grandparents come from say, Why don't you go back to *your* country. I'd be very happy to, thank you, but *your* people have occupied it" (51). Denise Chávez describes her childhood neighborhood in "Willow Game." She remembers a trinity of trees: an Apricot tree, as familiar as their own faces; the Marking-Off tree, a dried-up tree, struggling to live; and a Willow tree, under which they sought refuge. This favorite old friend was later killed by a violent neighbor boy. Chávez eloquently writes, "As children we felt dull leaden aches that were voiceless cries and were incommunicable. The place they sprung from seemed so desolate and uninhabited and did not touch on anything tangible or transferable. . . . A child's sorrow is a place that cannot be visited by others" (62). Marta Salinas's "The Scholarship Jacket" is an important piece about racism and classism that ends happily with the valedictorian eagerly awaiting her well-deserved jacket. Several stories are written in Spanish, including one by Juan Felipe Herrera titled "Para Siempre, Maga." Other contributors are Ron Arias, José Armas, Kathleen M. Baca, Bruce Novoa, Nash Candelaria, Sergio Elizondo, Carlos Nicolás Flores, Lionel G. García, Francisco Jiménez, E. A. Mares, Robert L. Perea, Albert Alvara Riós, Mario Suarez, Jesús Salvador Treviño, Kika Vargas, and Tino Villanueva. The book includes an introduction by Rudolfo Anaya and Antonio Márquez and background information on each of the contributors.

Grades 10–Adult

Cuentos: Tales from the Hispanic Southwest: Bilingual Stories in Spanish and English

- Bilingual
- Folktales
- Southwest
- Storytelling

Twenty-three tales of magic, myth, legend, and the events of everyday life in the Latino/a villages of New Mexico and southern Colorado are based on stories originally collected by Juan B. Rael, selected and adapted in Spanish by Jose Griego y Maestas and then retold in English by Rudolfo Anaya. Rich traditions, values, customs, and wisdom flow through this collection of *cuentos*. Anaya notes in the introduction that "words have the power to weave the multi-colored threads of existence to create a fresh reality" (7). Indeed, these *cuentos* help sustain the creative imagination and stir the heart and mind. Anaya's English versions of the tales retain the inspiration and clarity of the original *cuentos*. So, as he urges, "find a quiet, cozy place and allow the cuentos to weave their spell, or better yet, read them aloud to those you love . . ." (9).

In "The Man Who Knew the Language of the Animals," a young shepherd saves the life of a small snake. Rewarded with the power to understand the languages spoken by the animals, he gains wisdom and fortune. In "Fabiano and Reyes," a young man learns an important lesson about the nature of true beauty. This rare story provides a refreshing contrast to the usual tale in which women are judged by surface attributes and their inner qualities are ignored. "The Dance of the Owls" provides a positive picture of two old women whose magic enables them to change into owls and dance in the moonlight. Other stories feature a parrot who buys firewood, a young man who crosses a river of blood, a boy who protects himself with apples, and a woman who lives with a herd of wild horses. Set along the Santa Fe River and the Sangre de Cristo Mountains, these *cuentos* resound with the calls of crows, cattle, sheep, horses, donkeys, and even a camel. General readers as well as children, educators, folklorists, and historians will enjoy the stories in *Cuentos: Tales from the Hispanic Southwest.* This engaging bilingual book includes a glossary of regional archaic and idiomatic words and is illustrated with visionary black-and-white drawings by Jaime Valdez. This volume is part of an effort by the Museum of New Mexico to preserve the heritage of the Latina/o people of New Mexico.

Grades 4–10

RELATED WORK

Cuentos from My Childhood: Legends and Folktales of Northern New Mexico by Paulette Atencio. Museum of Northern New Mexico Press, 1991. See page 201.

- Tradition and Change
- Christmas
- Grandfathers
- Inventions

The Farolitos of Christmas

Luz's *abuelo* usually makes the traditional *luminarias* for Christmas Eve so the *pastores* can see to perform their annual songs and stories. But this year Luz is worried because Grandfather is too sick to cut the piñon logs needed for the small bonfires. With her father not yet home from the war and her mother too busy with other demands, it is up to Luz to find a way to light the path for the shepherds. Improvising, she tries several plans until she finds one that works. This warm tale of how the Christmas tradition of the *farolitos* came to be radiates with the beauty of the little lanterns that line the driveway, beckoning not only to the Christmas procession but to Luz's wounded father, whose homecoming the family had anxiously awaited. Most of the Spanish words and phrases that are sprinkled throughout the text can be understood through the context of the story, but a glossary is available to help translate words such as *masa, oshá,* and *qué bonita.* The illustrations by Edward Gonzales beautifully capture the setting in the village of San Juan in northern New Mexico. In his first book for children, the accomplished artist depicts the adobe houses, mountainous horizons, and star-filled skies of the Southwest. *The Farolitos of Christmas* presents a very positive image of an admirable Mexican American girl. Luz is a risk-taker and shows ingenuity and leadership skills. Such strong portrayals are important in literature for young readers, and provide inspiration and hope for readers of all ages.

Grades K–4

RELATED WORKS

Carlos, Light the Farolito by Jean Ciavonne. Clarion, 1995.

Too Many Tamales by Gary Soto. Putnam, 1993.

"A New Mexico Christmas" by Rudolfo Anaya. *The Anaya Reader,* Warner Books, 1995.

Heart of Aztlán

- Technology
- Moving
- Newcomers
- Leadership

Rudolfo Anaya's second novel, *Heart of Aztlán* chronicles one momentous year in the lives of Adelita and Clemente Chávez and their children as they move from the rural community of Guadalupe to the barrio of Barelas in Albuquerque, New Mexico. Dedicated to "the good people of Barelas . . . and to people everywhere who have struggled for freedom, dignity, and the right to self-determination," the work is a philosophical novel that draws inspiration from the myth of Aztlán, the mythological place of the Aztecs, said to be located in what is now the southwestern part of the United States. The book opens on moving day for the Chávez family, when they reluctantly sell and leave their beloved land. Anaya eloquently portrays the loss Clemente experiences: "His soul and his heart were in the earth," he writes, and even though he knew they didn't have a choice, "that did not lessen the pain he felt as the roots of his soul pulled away and severed themselves from the earth that had nurtured his life" (3). As they set out in search of a new future for their family, they encounter unforeseen changes that challenge their adaptability, threaten their lives, and shake them to their very core. It is a year of unemployment, alienation, violence, exploitation, and heartbreak as well as a time of transformation, growth, and renewal. Each family member responds individually to the hostile urban environment. Adelita shows tremendous strength and resilience as her family is buffeted by the tides of change. Clemente, struggling to adjust to the harsh realities of their new life, eventually emerges as a leader of his people in their opposition to the insidious powers that shackle and exploit them. His personal odyssey and political awakening are at the heart of the book. With the support of his wife, and Crispín, the barrio sage, he strives to comprehend the roots of poverty and oppression. He realizes, "I cannot let things remain as they are, because then I would not be free. If I refuse to act because I fear the future, then I create a worse enslavement for myself. . . . While my people are not free, I am not free" (142).

Anaya explores a number of important themes and issues in *Heart of Aztlán:* the sacredness of the earth; the enslavement of the people by the giants of technology and industry; a people dispossessed of their heritage and struggling to survive in an alien culture; and the clashes between urban and rural, political and religious, and poverty and wealth. Mythological themes, rich symbolism, and the sense of a shared communal soul combine with an inspiring social message to leave the reader with a feeling of hope.

Grades 9–Adult

RELATED WORK
Benjie Chávez plays a major role in *Alburquerque,* one of Anaya's most recent books.

Tortuga
Before Columbus Foundation American Book Award

- Hospitals
- Paralysis
- Illness
- Autobiographical Fiction
- Euthanasia

Patterned on the mythic journey motif of classical literature, *Tortuga* is the first-person narrative of a paralyzed sixteen-year-old boy's quest for wellness and understanding. The novel takes place in a hospital for young people and traces Tortuga's recovery after a near-fatal accident. Tortuga (turtle), the nickname given the boy by his peers because his body is encased in a shell-like cast, becomes friends with many other young people with disabilities. He meets Salomón, a paralytic, mute patient in an iron lung who communicates with him telepathically and who guides him on his quest to understand his place in the universe.

Tortuga, like many of Anaya's books, has numerous themes and is rich in symbolism. One of the most prominent themes is that physical health is inextricably fused with emotional and spiritual well-being. Tortuga symbolizes the "magic mountain" near the hospital as well as the protagonist's body cast and his psychological shell. Tortuga's literal journey traces his trek from his home across a stretch of New Mexico desert to a hospital that is similar to the Tingley Hospital in Truth or Consequences, where Anaya was treated as a young man for a near-fatal accident like that suffered by Tortuga. During his eighteen-month confinement, the protagonist gradually changes from a withdrawn teenager to a person who discovers his mystical destiny as a singer who will experience the depths of despair and survive to return home with a message of hope voiced through music. The book ends with Tortuga leaving the hospital on crutches to return home, cradling the blue guitar, a bequest from Crispín, the barrio sage who played a prominent role in *Heart of Aztlán*, one of Anayás previous books.

Tortuga is a complex book that contrasts the distress and disease within the hospital with the harmony of nature outside. The hospital serves as a microcosm of a corrupt humanity filled with hate, envy, and greed. But within the hospital environment are forces struggling for good. Salomón is closely associated with butterflies, who emerge after difficult metamorphoses, symbolizing hope, love, and beauty. Like Ultima and Crispín in earlier books, the elderly Filomón provides guidance for the struggling young protagonist.

The critical reception to *Tortuga* was mixed. Some reviewers found it to be a tour de force in which Anaya creates hope amidst suffering. Others were critical of the one-dimensional portrayal of female characters as either idealizations or undesirables. Most recognized the interconnections among the three books in Anaya's New Mexico Trilogy, *Tortuga, Bless Me Ultima,* and *Heart of Aztlán,* including the curative powers of water, the elderly sages, the mythic narratives and themes, the fantastic imagery and symbolism, and the role of dreams and nightmares. Anaya's literary imagination soars in each of these books, repeatedly portraying a powerful struggle that ends in personal harmony and hope.

Grades 10–Adult

RELATED WORK

Tortuga is under contract to a small British independent filmmaking company, Helen Landridge.

Zia Summer

- Mystery
- Albuquerque
- Environmental Issues

Zia Summer is the first book in Rudolfo Anaya's intriguing mystery series featuring Sonny Baca, a private eye who is the great-grandson of the fabled lawyer/detective Elfego Baca. Sonny always carries his forebear's Colt .45, and is both haunted and inspired by the legendary stories surrounding *el Bisabuelo's* exploits. Until now, Sonny has settled for trailing cheating spouses and investigating dubious insurance claims. But when his beloved cousin, Gloria, is murdered, he finds himself embroiled in a case that challenges his resources and endangers his life. Pursuing leads in the sensational murder case with a vengeance, Sonny encounters power-hungry politicians, an international computer entrepreneur, police department corruption, a desperate drug dealer, environmental extremists, an enigmatic psychic, ruthless land developers, cantankerous ranchers, two recently fired employees, several mysterious cult members, and insidious family secrets. Is there a connection between Gloria's death and the cases of cattle mutilations plaguing the area? How many other murder cases have been swept under the rug? And what is the significance of the Zia sun symbol that was etched into the body of the murder victim? Is Sonny in over his head in this bizarre case that leads him into a passionate environmental battle over nuclear waste transport and disposal?

Mystery lovers will enjoy this exciting new tale and look forward to others in the Sonny Baca mystery series. But *Zia Summer* is much more than a mystery. Woven into the story are the illuminating rays of Chicano myth, language, and tradition, the sacredness of the land, the quest for personal and cultural identity, and spirituality and healing. The book is also filled with the history of the Alburquerque area, written by one who has lived there all of his life. (Anaya reminds us that *Alburquerque* was the original spelling of the word.) Anaya's far-reaching work provides insight into a number of contemporary social issues, from the nuclear weapons industry to witchcraft. Anaya clearly distinguishes between the positive work done by many witches and the evil spread by the few engaged in destructive endeavors.

Grades 11–Adult

RELATED WORKS

Latina Mystery for Young Adults

The Girl from Playa Blanca by Ofelia Dumas Lachtman. Arte Público Press, University of Houston, Houston, TX 77204-2090. 1-800-633-ARTE. See page 103.

Chicana Mysteries for Adults

Gloria Damasco Mystery Series by Lucha Corpi. Arte Público Press, University of Houston, Houston, TX 77204-2090. 1-800-633-ARTE.

Gay Latino Mysteries for Adults

Henry Rios Mystery Series by Michael Nava. Alyson Publications, 1-800-5Alyson. See pages 137–140.

Gloria Anzaldúa

Photo: Margaret Randall

Chicana (1942–)

Birthday: September 26
Contact: Aunt Lute Books
P. O. Box 410687
San Francisco, CA 94141

"To write, to be a writer, I have to trust and believe in myself as a speaker, as a voice for the images. I have to believe that I can communicate with images and words and that I can do it well. A lack of belief in my creative self is a lack of belief in my total self and vice versa—I cannot separate my writing from any part of my life. It is all one." (Borderlands, 73)

Books by Gloria Anzaldúa

Borderlands/La frontera: The New Mestiza. Spinsters/Aunt Lute, 1987.

Friends from the Other Side/Amigos del otro lado. Illustrated by Consuelo Méndez. Children's Books Press, 1993.

Making Face, Making Soul/Haciendo caras: Creative and Critical Perspectives by Feminists of Color. Editor. Aunt Lute Foundation, 1990.

Prietita and the Ghost Woman/Prietita y la Llorona. Illustrated by Christina Gonzalez. Children's Book Press, 1995.

This Bridge Called My Back: Writings by Radical Women of Color. Coedited with Cherríe Moraga. Persephone Press, 1981.

Gloria Anzaldúa is a prominent Chicana lesbian feminist, *tejana* patlache poet, and cultural theorist from the Rio Grande Valley of South Texas, now living in Santa Cruz, California. She is one of the most original and powerful voices in feminist literature, known for her groundbreaking work in tackling the difficult and immense task of changing culture and all its oppressive "interlocking machinations." Her prophetic analysis of the intersections of race, gender, class, language, and sexual orientation offers insights into ways diverse cultures might begin to come together and heal the wounds inflicted by centuries of oppression. Her vision invokes new human possibility, providing hope that profound changes are possible.

Born a seventh-generation American on the ranch settlement named Jesus Maria of the Valley of South Texas, Anzaldúa is the daughter of Amalia García Anzaldúa and Urbano Anzaldúa. When Anzaldúa was eleven, the family moved to the small town of Hargill, Texas. Her father died when she was fifteen, and she helped support her family by working in the fields weekends, vacations, and summers until she earned her B.A. from Pan American University in 1969. The experience of working in the fields instilled in her a deep respect for farm laborers. She learned about the hardships of being a migrant worker during the year she traveled with her family from the South Texas valley to the fields of Arkansas. In 1972, she earned her M.A. in English and education from the University of Texas in Austin. She worked as a liaison between migrant camps and public school superintendents, principals, and teachers and was subsequently hired to direct the migrant and bilingual programs for the state. During the ensuing years, she has devoted her energies to writing, speaking, teaching, and leading workshops. She has taught creative writing, Chicano studies, feminist studies, and related classes at the University of Texas, the University of California at Santa Cruz, and Vermont College of Norwich University. She has been a writer-in-residence at The Loft in Minneapolis as well as an artist-in-residence in Chicano studies at Pomona College. She is presently in the doctoral program in literature at the University of California at Santa Cruz.

Writing with admirable candor about her rebellion against the confines of her early home life and women's role, she recounts the struggles of her childhood. She writes about the internalized racism within her own family and how it affected her sense of herself. When she was born, her grandmother inspected her dark skin color. Anzaldúa notes that Mamágrande Locha loved her anyway, because "What I lacked in whiteness, I had in smartness" (*This Bridge Called My Back,* 198). Her struggles with her mother centered around housework—she resisted her mother's orders to scrub and clean and instead spent her time reading, studying, and drawing. From an early age she knew she was different. "I felt

alien, I knew I was alien" (*Borderlands,* 43). She turned to reading—"Books saved my sanity, knowledge opened the locked places in me and taught me how to survive and then how to soar" (*Borderlands,* Preface). The strength of her rebellion enabled her to remain true to herself. She is the only one not only of her family but of the region to pursue a higher education.

The act of reading forever changed her life. But in many of the books she read, her people were portrayed in racist ways, relegated to the roles of villains, servants, or prostitutes. Her teachers were also racist. She remembers being punished with three raps on the knuckles with a sharp ruler for speaking Spanish at recess at school. She writes about being required to take two speech classes to rid her of her accent at Pan American University. In the award-winning book (Before Columbus Foundation American Book Award) *This Bridge Called My Back,* she writes, "The schools we attended or didn't attend did not give us the skills for writing nor the confidence that we were correct in using our class and ethnic languages. I, for one, became adept at, and majored in English to spite, to show up, the arrogant racist teachers who thought all Chicano children were dumb and dirty" (165–166). In the 1960s she read her first Chicano novel, *City of Night,* by John Rechy, a gay Texan. "For days, I walked around in stunned amazement that a Chicano could write and could get published" (*Borderlands,* 59). When she started teaching, she tried to supplement the required reading with works by Chicanos but was repri-

manded and forbidden to do so by her principal. Even in graduate school, she was not allowed to make Chicano literature an area of focus, so she left the Ph.D. program at the University of Texas in 1977.

From the time she was seven years old, Anzaldúa read in bed with a flashlight and told her sister stories to keep her from telling their mother. The stories she created night after night were the beginning of her life's work. She now thinks of writers as shape-changers, creating new ways of perceiving the world, new possibilities. She describes the agonies and ecstasies of writing in *Borderlands.* "Daily, I battle the silence.... Daily, I take my throat in my hands and squeeze until the cries pour out..." (71–72). Ultimately, her writing brings her great joy—it heals her. When she doesn't write for a prolonged period of time, she gets physically sick. She states that being a writer feels very much like being Chicana, or being a lesbian, often coming up against barriers and yet being in a state of limbo where nothing is defined or definite.

With her characteristic strong sense of self, she has broken out of the mold not only in her life but also in her writing. The struggle continues, however. Anzaldúa tells about her mother's reaction to her essay "La Prieta" (The Dark One) in *This Bridge Called My Back,* in which she writes about her childhood and her lesbianism. "My mother told me that if I told the people in my little town that I was a lesbian, she would take a gun and shoot herself" (*Dictionary of Literary Biography,* 9). Her mother refused to welcome her lesbian friends into her home, and Anzaldúa vowed never to go home until she could bring whomever she wanted. After three painful years, her mother relented, realizing that they both had lost. Anzaldúa shows how lesbians and gays are not only ostracized, harassed, and brutalized by the societies in which they live, but often excluded, demeaned, and disowned by their own families.

Going against the tide at home, in her culture, in education, and in society, Anzaldúa transfers the hard-won but valuable lessons to her writing. She has earned a reputation as an innovative writer who utilizes a daring approach, mixing language, modes, and genres. Her work breaks new ground, opening up a fresh space for new inquiry, thought, and vision. A prolific writer, her work appears in myriad journals, anthologies, and alternative presses. Recently, she entered a new writing field—children's literature. Her first book for young readers, *Friends from the Other Side/Amigos del otro lado,* is a bilingual picture book featuring an admirable young Chicana and her new friends who have just crossed the United States–Mexico border in search of a new life. Her second book for children, *Prietita and the Ghost Woman,* tells the story of a young Mexican American girl who becomes lost during her search for an herb to cure her mother and is aided by the legendary *la Llorona.* Anzaldúa is currently working on a short story collection and a book theorizing on the production of writing, knowledge, and identity.

Anzaldúa, who identifies herself as *queer* or *dyke,* often reads her work publicly, gives lectures, and participates in workshops and panel discussions. She serves on editorial boards for various publications nationally and has been a contributing editor of the lesbian press journal *Sinister Wisdom* since 1984 and was a coeditor of the *SIGNS* lesbian issue. In addition to the awards for her books, she received a National Endowment for the Arts Fiction Award, the 1991 Lesbians Rights Award, and the Sappho Award of Distinction in 1992. Although she is involved with many other activities, writing is her first priority. "The Writing is my whole life, my obsession" (*Borderlands,* 75).

More Information About Gloria Anzaldúa

Borderlands/La Frontera: The New Mestiza. Spinsters/Aunt Lute, 1987.

Dictionary of Literary Biography. Volume 122, 8–17.

The Gay and Lesbian Literary Heritage: A Reader's Companion to the Writers and Their Works, from Antiquity to the Present, edited by Claude J. Summers. Henry Holt, 1995.

Making Face, Making Soul/Haciendo caras: Creative and Critical Perspectives by Feminists of Color. Aunt Lute Foundation, 1990.

This Bridge Called My Back: Writings by Radical Women of Color. Persephone Press, 1981.

- Chicana Studies
- Lesbian Studies
- Women's Studies
- Poetry

Borderlands/La Frontera: The New Mestiza

Literary Journal's *One of the 38 Best Books of 1987*

(Note: This book is included as a resource for educators in the hope that its insights into the debilitating nature of racism and other oppressions will provide valuable information to teachers as they plan ways to continue the important work of creating a fair and just society.)

Gloria Anzaldúa explores in prose and poetry the contradictory existence of those living on the border between cultures and languages. In this powerful, multifaceted work which defies conventional notions of genre, she interweaves Spanish and English, poetry, memoir, and historical analysis. Breaking out of traditional forms and employing a remarkable combination of imagination, insight, scholarly research, and poignancy, she has created a unique, illuminating document. It makes a significant contribution to our understanding of how deeply cultural differences cut and how important it is that we learn to regard them as strengths instead of problems.

The book's first half, *"Atravesando Fronteras*/Crossing Borders," is composed of essays that mix theory, prose, poetry, history, anthropology, psychology, literature, and personal and collective experience. The second half of the book is made up of eloquent poetry. The book opens at the border, the steel curtain, "the 1,950 mile-long open wound. . . . This is my home/this thin edge of barb wire" (2). "I have been straddling that *tejas*-Mexican border, and others, all my life." This is a place of contradictions, where cultures clash and economic systems collide.

Anzaldúa's painful, ongoing journey toward mestiza self-retrieval takes her through many barriers and obstacles: the psychological borderlands, the spiritual borderlands, language borderlands, and sexual orientation borderlands. Anzaldúa is an inspiring example of a lesbian of color who is working to create new possibilities, striving to pull the human race into a future free from oppression.

Adults

Friends from the Other Side/Amigos del otro lado

- Bilingual
- *Curanderas*
- Immigration
- Newcomers
- Poverty

An admirable young Mexican American girl befriends a boy who has crossed the Rio Grande from Mexico with his mother to begin a new life in the United States. This bilingual story opens as Prietita meets Joaquín when he comes to her house to sell firewood. As he leaves, some of the neighborhood kids start calling him names and yelling at him to go back where he belongs. Prietita intervenes when one of the boys picks up a rock to throw at Joaquín. As the story unfolds, the friendship between Prietita and Joaquín grows. But what can she do to help him heal the sores on his arms? And how can she protect Joaquín and his mother from the Border Patrol as it cruises up the street?

In her first book for children, Gloria Anzaldúa has tackled what may be considered by some a controversial topic, one that many would rather ignore: poverty. Anzaldúa, known for her groundbreaking work, is to be commended for her honesty and courage in portraying a neglected group in literature for young readers. By introducing the reader to Joaquín and his mother, she has enabled us to see them as real people. And by Prietita's example, the reader learns how to resist peer pressure and take a stand against prejudice and cruelty. How can we overcome the tendency to bully newcomers and those who are perceived to be weaker? Can children's literature impact these deplorable attitudes? Anzaldúa has taken an important step in addressing these issues.

She has also provided us with an exemplary young Latina protagonist, a rare entity in literature for children, and a significant role model capable of instilling pride in children whose heritage is often ignored or marginalized.

Artist Consuelo Mendez uses watercolors with colored pencils, graphite, and collage to create detailed, realistic illustrations that beautifully accompany the text. Children's Book Press has a reputation for publishing exquisitely illustrated books and this one is no exception. Mendez's pictures authentically depict the plants and animals of the region; a fascinating variety of lizards and other creatures inhabit the pages of this commendable book.

Grades 3–Adult

RELATED WORKS

Curanderas

Prietita and the Ghost Woman/Prietita y la Llorona by Gloria Anzaldúa. See pages 59–60.

Bless Me, Ultima by Rudolfo Anaya (for older readers). See page 48.

Illegal Immigration

Across the Great River by Irene Beltrán Hernández (for older readers). See pages 62–63.

Newcomers

The Inner World of the Immigrant Child by Cristina Igoa (for educators). St. Martin's Press, 1995. See page 209.

How the García Girls Lost Their Accents by Julia Alvarez (for older readers). Algonquin Books, 1991; Dutton, 1992. See pages 40–41.

Aekyung's Dream by Min Paek. Children's Book Press, 1978.

Angel Child, Dragon Child by Michele Maria Surat. Scholastic, 1983.

Making a New Home in America by Maxine Rosenberg. Illustrated with photographs by George Ancona. Lothrop, Lee and Shepard, 1986.

Molly's Pilgrim by Barbara Cohen. Lothrop, Lee and Shepard, 1983.

My Two Worlds by Ginger Gordon. Clarion, 1993.

Over Here It's Different: Carolina's Story by Mildred Leinweber Dawson. Photographs by George Ancona. Macmillan, 1993.

- Authorship
- Feminism
- Racism
- Women

Making Face, Making Soul/Haciendo caras: Creative and Critical Perspectives by Feminists of Color

Lambda Literary Best Small Press Book Award

(Note: This book is included as a resource for educators; it makes a significant contribution to our understanding of the complexities and corrosive nature of racism. It is filled with new thought and new dialogue—it is a book that will teach in the most multiple sense of the word.)

This brilliant collection of creative and theoretical pieces includes poetry, essays, letters, and short stories by emerging voices as well as established writers. Representing diverse backgrounds and shattering the "neat boundaries of the half dozen categories of marginality that define us" (xvi), the writers are of mixed Latina, Native, Asian, and African ancestries, both lesbian and heterosexual, and living in a wide variety of places. Many are professors or students at universities as well as writers. Others are involved in a wide variety of fields such as social work, art, carpentry, philosophy, photography, and publishing. The Latinas included in this collection are Norma Alarcon, Gloria Anzaldúa, Judith Francisca Baca, Lorna Dee Cervantes, Sandra Cisneros, Judith Ortiz Cofer, Julia de Burgos, Edna Escamill, Canéla Jaramillo, María C. Lugones, Lynda Marín, Papusa Molina, Pat Mora, Cherríe Moraga, Carmen Morones, Laura Munter-Orabona, Tey Diana Rebolledo, Catalina Ríos, Elba Rosario Sánchez, Chela Sandoval, Helena María Viramontes, Berniece Zamora, and Maxine Baca Zinn.

In her introduction to the book, Anzaldúa notes that she waited for years for someone to compile a book that would continue the work she and Cherríe Moraga started in their groundbreaking book, *This Bridge Called My Back*. This new collection deepens the dialogue, brings more voices to the foreground, and enhances the legacy of the earlier work. The title, *Making Face*, is Anzaldúa's metaphor for constructing one's identity. "In this anthology and in our daily lives, we women of color strip off the *máscaras* others have imposed on us, see through the disguises we hide behind and drop our *personas* so that we may become subjects in our own discourses" (xvi).

Divided into seven sections, this powerful anthology addresses crucial issues such as the corrosive legacy that racism inflicts, strategies for combatting internalized oppression, finding hope through turning the pain around, moving from silence to voice, political art and writing, building solidarity and alliances, and transformation through other modes of consciousness. Varied voices speak of poverty, tokenism, erasure, violence, active and passive devaluation, exclusion, blistering divisions, silencing, exploitation, cultural collisions, abnegation, servitude, classism, homophobia, elitism, and sexism. They explore a full range of concerns, strategies, affirmations, and solutions in over seventy illuminating pieces.

College–Adult

RELATED WORKS

The Ethnic American Woman: Problems, Protests, Lifestyles by Edith Blicksilver. Kendall/Hunt 1989.

This Bridge Called My Back: Writings by Radical Women of Color. Gloria Anzaldúa and Cherríe Moraga, coeditors. Persephone Press, 1981.

Racism in the Lives of Women: Testimony, Theory and Guides to Antiracist Practice by Jeanne Adleman and Gloria Enguídanos. Harrington Park Press, 1995.

For Younger Readers

Coming of Age in America: A Multicultural Anthology, edited by Mary Frosch. New Press, 1994.

Prejudice: Stories About Hate, Ignorance, Revelation and Transformation, edited by Daphne Muse. Hyperion Books for Children, 1995.

Taking a Stand Against Racism and Racial Discrimination by Patricia and Fredrick McKissack. Franklin Watts, 1990.

Prietita and the Ghost Woman/Prietita y la Llorona

- Legendary Characters
- Bilingual
- *Curanderas*

Prietita, a young Mexican American girl, becomes lost while searching for an herb to cure her mother and is aided by the legendary ghost woman. This absorbing story begins when Prietita is at the house of her mentor, *la curandera,* the healer. Prietita's younger sister hurries into the yard with the news that their mother is very ill with the old sickness. When Doña Lola, *la curandera,* discovers that she is out of the herb needed, she draws a picture of it for Prietita. As Prietita searches through the woods for the healing plant, she seeks the help of a white-tail deer, a salamander, a white-wing dove, a jaguarundi, and lightning bugs. As she follows each animal, she journeys deeper into the woods. Several times along the way, she hears a faint crying sound and remembers her grandmother's stories about *la Llorona,* who is said to cry for her lost children and look for other children to steal. Prietita is frightened and lost but she bravely asks the ghost woman for help. *La Llorona* helps her find the herb and then guides her back to the path.

Gloria Anzaldúa writes that her grandmother used to tell her scary stories about *la Llorona.* In fact, the legends surrounding the ghost woman are well known throughout the Southwest and Mexico. Anzaldúa, like other children, was afraid, but even at an early age she wondered if there was another side to the ghost woman. Years later, when she studied the roots of her Chicana/Mexicana culture, she found that there really is a powerful, positive side to the legendary figure, the female and Indian part of her culture. Anzaldúa, in revealing this positive side of *la Llorona,* hopes to encourage youngsters to be critical thinkers. By looking beyond the surface of things, they may discover hidden truths. Anzaldúa is noted for her groundbreaking vision and writing. Just as she has done in her other fine books, she has opened up a fresh space for new inquiry and thought regarding the legendary character of *la Llorona.* By portraying the ghost woman in a positive way, she is breaking out of a mold that constricts the image of females in literature.

Anzaldúa's story is beautifully complemented by colorful paintings rendered by Christina Gonzales, who is a graphic artist, jeweler, and painter. Her portrayal of Doña Lola is particularly striking with her attractive wrinkles and dignified stance. Here is another rarity in children's literature: a middle-aged woman who is portrayed as a wise, stable leader of the community. The engaging illustrations of the animals and plants of the Southwest add to the appeal of this exquisitely designed book.

Grades 3–Adult

RELATED WORK
Friends from the Other Side/Amigos del otro lado by Gloria Anzaldúa. See pages 57–58.

Irene Beltrán-Hernández

Mexican American (1945–)

Birthday: April 4
Address: P.O. Box 190
Satin, Texas 76685

"For myself, to take away my writing is to take away my spirit."
(Something About the Author, *23*)

*"... mend your ideas and try not to class people into categories.
Accept people regardless of skin color or their stations in life."*
(Heartbeat Drumbeat, *71*)

Books by Irene Beltrán-Hernández

Across the Great River. Arte Público Press, 1989.

Heartbeat Drumbeat. Arte Público Press, 1992.

The Secret of Two Brothers. Arte Público Press, 1995.

Irene Beltrán-Hernández is a caseworker in adolescent services for the City of Dallas, Texas. She has also worked as an administrative assistant to the mayor of Dallas, a public information assistant, programming director, and vocational counselor. She has been the recipient of the City of Dallas Service in Excellence Award, San Antonio Writers Festival Award, and a University of Wisconsin Fellowship.

One of eight children, Beltrán-Hernández was born in Waco, Texas, to Isabelle Quinones Beltrán, a nurse, and Emmett Tovar Beltrán, a mechanic. Their life lacked many material comforts, but young Irene found comfort in books. Her mother encouraged her to read, dropping her off on Saturday mornings at the public library, where she checked out a stack of books large enough to last a week. Reading was her escape from the isolation of the country and the routine of the household. However, she remembers that the books that were available did not have "anything with a Mexican slant or Mexican flavor" (*Metropolitan*, 34). She also enjoyed going to visit her beloved grandmother, with whom she lived until she was five. Her first writing experience involved keeping a journal, which she wrote on ordinary notebook paper. She wrote late at night by flashlight; as a teenager, she wrote in shorthand to keep her thoughts and feelings private.

Beltrán-Hernández excelled in her studies at Waco High School. She worked as an assistant in the library, one of her favorite places. "My problem was skin color. I was too white for the Chicano kids and too dark for the Anglos" (*Something About the Author*, 22). Nevertheless, she became friends with three young women; they have continued to be close through their adult years. Beltrán-Hernández remembers a particularly strict English teacher who ignored her all year except for one telling moment. When he returned a paper she had written, he looked her right in the eye and said, "Well, well. Someday, you'll be somebody important. Mark my words." (SATA, 22)

After graduating from high school, she worked at the *Waco News Tribune–Times Herald* as a copy person while attending night school at Baylor University, pursuing a degree in journalism. She later transferred to North Texas State University, where she changed her major to sociology. She was interested in human interest stories, but the journalism teacher repeatedly assigned her to cover business topics. After college she worked as a school counselor where she enjoyed listening to the life stories of her students. A professor at Southern Methodist University invited her to undertake a study dealing with recent illegal immigrants from Mexico. She found the job of interviewing them and compiling the statistics fascinating, but tedious. This experience led her to a series of jobs with the City of Dallas. These positions were demanding and sometimes dangerous. "One's life was on the line every minute of the day, but it was also exciting. I quickly learned how to defend my people as well as to stand my own ground within the city network. . . . I turned to writing as my therapy" (*Something About The Author*, 23). She took a number of creative writing classes, joined a local writers' group, and graduated from the Institute of Children's Literature. She married Gilberto Hernández, a construction superintendent; they have two children, Dominick and Fatima.

Beltrán-Hernández's first book, *Across the Great River,* was rejected numerous times by the major publishing houses. She knew the book was well written and the topic, a family's illegal migration from Mexico to the United States across the Rio Grande, was an important one. She tenaciously searched for a publisher. Eventually the book was published by Arte Público Press and subsequently praised for the contribution it makes to our understanding of immigration issues. Since then, Beltrán-Hernández has written two additional books. When she isn't writing, she takes time to read her work to students in public schools. She plans to continue to write for young readers. "I write basically for the Chicanito. That's the area I want to stay in" (*Metropolitan*, 34).

More Information About Irene Beltrán-Hernández

Metropolitan: The Dallas Morning News (Oct. 13, 1992, 27A, 34A).

Something About the Author, Volume 74, 21–23.

• Illegal Immigration

Across the Great River

In her first novel, Irene Beltrán-Hernández chronicles a Mexican family's illegal entry into the United States. Katarina Campos, a young girl, tells the harrowing story of how she crosses the Rio Grande with her parents and baby brother. The Border Patrol shoots and wounds her mother; her father becomes separated from the others and disappears. The *coyotes* take Kata, her mother and brother to the ranchito of Doña Anita, a gifted healer and seer. Mrs. Campos gradually recovers with the help of Anita and finds work in town as a seamstress. Kata begins learning about herbs as she watches Anita treat numerous ill and injured neighbors. As Kata matures and takes a leadership role in helping her family find its way in a strange land, she meets a number of fascinating characters. Each interaction adds to her awareness of herself and others. The family faces new experiences, challenges, and traumas including violence, illness, and accidents. Finally, they find a way to return to their beloved homeland, where they are reunited with Mr. Campos, who had been jailed by the authorities.

This is a suspenseful novel with well-drawn characters. Against the backdrop of the dangers illegal immigrant families face, we witness the changes in a young girl as she becomes increasingly aware of the world around her. She learns not to judge people by their appearance; for example, she discovers that her first impression of Anita was completely wrong. Anita is fat and unattractive in the traditional sense; she is also a very loving, strong, resourceful person who provides crucial support for the Campos family. Beltrán-Hernández has created a strong Latina protagonist who learns how to solve problems and take care of herself and those she loves; the body of literature for young readers needs more characters like her.

Grades 7–Adult

RELATED WORK
Journey of the Sparrows by Fran Leeper Buss and Daisy Cubias. Dell, 1991.

Heartbeat Drumbeat
Publishers Marketing Association Benjamin Franklin Award

- Navajo/Mexican American Heritage
- Death
- Identity

In her absorbing second novel, Irene Beltrán-Hernández tells the story of Morgana Cruz, the daughter of a Navajo mother and Mexican American father. This is a search for identity; as Morgana says to her mother, "I have a foot in two different cultures and I'm not totally accepted by either race" (89). Heretofore, she has led a sheltered life with her well-to-do parents on a ranch in New Mexico. She speaks Navajo, Spanish, and English, is an accomplished potter, and is confident in any group of people. Early in the book, Isadora, her beloved Navajo mentor, dies. This traumatic loss sets in motion a number of events that quickly change Morgana's life in fundamental ways. She weaves her way through a series of personal, emotional, physical, and cultural challenges. She fights her attraction to Eagle Eyes, an enigmatic Navajo diviner and lawyer, whom Isadora had raised to be her successor. Burial ceremonies, dreams foretelling the future, Rocky Mountain tick fever, herbal medicine, fiestas, a Navajo coming-of-age ceremony, a near-drowning, rape, an attack by a bear, hospitalizations, death, blizzards, loyal horses, wall tapestries, a love triangle, old love letters, and more are all here in this fast-paced, engrossing novel that holds the reader's interest with unexpected twists and turns. This is a well-written book with fine attention to detail. The ending will provide an interesting topic for discussion.

Grades 10–Adult

The Secret of Two Brothers

- Child Abuse
- Family Violence
- Death
- Prison Life

Twenty-one-year-old Francisco "Beaver" Torres is paroled after serving three years in the state penitentiary for being an accomplice in an armed robbery. This solid novel tells the story of his attempt to get back on the right path and to take care of his younger brother, Cande.

The story opens while Beaver is still in prison; the author ably portrays the tension and violence of prison life. When he is released and returns home to the barrio in East Dallas, he finds his brother living alone in their rundown house. After years of being abused by her alcoholic husband, their mother died of a stroke while Beaver was in prison. Their father had abandoned Cande but returns periodically to harass, and Beaver finds out later, to beat his younger son. The brothers are overjoyed to be reunited and Beaver sets out to find a job and to create a decent life for himself and his brother. Beaver is determined to turn his life around, but just when things are starting to improve, a tragedy strikes. Will the two brothers' bond with each other and their growing support system enable them to overcome the barriers they face? What is the secret they guard so anxiously?

This readable novel presents serious problems in a realistic way, giving the reader hope that young people like Beaver and Cande do not have to fall through the cracks of the social service and educational systems. Several stereotype-breaking adult role models are featured, including Beaver's tough-minded but kindhearted probation officer, Ms. Cookie Rodríguez. The rare portrayal of a female character with a well-developed combination of complex qualities in a book for young readers is encouraging. Likewise, the two brothers are admirable in several ways. Their solidarity with each other is unusual; often we read about siblings arguing and competing with each other. Beaver's major goal in life is to serve as his brother's keeper. Cande's interest in and ability to create art combined with the qualities that allowed him to survive years of fending for himself make him a strong character, one that might provide support for male readers being pressured to conform to a macho image. Beltrán-Hernández has tackled important contemporary issues and produced an encouraging book, one that will appeal not only to Latino readers but to a wider audience of teenage readers.

Grades 6–10

Alberto Blanco

Hispanic (1951–)

Birthday: February 18
Address: University of Texas at El Paso
Language and Linguistics
El Paso, TX 79968

"The artist is not a special kind of human being, but each human being is a special kind of artist." (personal communication)

Books by Alberto Blanco

Angel's Kite/La estrella de Angel. Illustrated by Rodolfo Morales. Children's Book Press, 1994.

Dawn of the Senses: Selected Poems of Alberto Blanco. City Lights Books, 1995.

Dos cuentos con alas. Illustrated by Laura Almeida. Colección Botella al Mar, Editorial Grijalvo, Mexico, 1994.

The Desert Mermaid/La sirena del desierto. Illustrated by Patricia Revah. Children's Book Press, 1992.

Mandalas para iluminar. Colección Letra y Color, Ediciones del Ermitaño and SEP, 1984.

Pájaros, pájaros. Illustrated by Patricia Revah. Editorial Trillos, Mexico, 1990.

Un sueño de Navidad. Illustrated by Patricia Revah. Colección Reloj de Cuentos, Number 6, CIDCLI and SEP, Mexico, 1984.

También los insectos son perfectos (poetry). Illustrated by Diana Radaviciute. Colección Reloj de Versos, Number 11, CIDCLI and CONACULTA, Mexico, 1993.

Alberto Blanco is considered one of Mexico's most outstanding poets. The recipient of numerous awards, honors, and scholarships, Blanco is also an artist, art critic, musician, and translator, and has published more than twenty books. A chemist by profession, he has also studied philosophy and has a master's degree in Asian studies with a specialization in Chinese studies. At the present time, he is a full-time professor in the bilingual master of fine arts creative writing program at the University of Texas at El Paso.

Born in Mexico City to parents who were voracious readers, Blanco started writing as a child and has continued writing throughout his life. His father worked in a factory producing pigments and inks, and Blanco's first toys were the little tin caps of the paint tubes. Blanco says, "When I was a teenager, I began to notice that the books I liked to read had some connection to what I was writing, but it was such a subtle connection like some kind of invisible, unworldly connection until I was twenty or twenty-one" (*Rio Grande Review [RGR]*, 38). He goes on to describe attending a literary workshop with a friend where the facilitator, a well-known Mexican writer, encouraged him to have his work published. Blanco realized that he needed to share his work in order to maintain his sense of self. He also knew that he needed to remain true to himself and not let the publishing process distract him from his goals. He has been able to stay in touch with his creativity, and in fact has made it the center of his life.

For Blanco, poetry is at the heart of his writing. He has gradually added many other forms of writing, but poetry remains the sustaining, supporting focus of his literary efforts. He is a prolific writer with ten books of poetry, ten books of translations, seven books for children, and hundreds of works in anthologies, magazines, and newspapers to his credit. One of his many fascinating projects is his translations of the poetry of Emily Dickinson. Her poems were difficult to translate because of the contradictions and sensitivity in her work. He notes, "She's a master of rhymes and rhythms, so what I found was that not each and every poem of Emily Dickinson can be translated into Spanish, but I think I have succeeded in some" (*RGR*, 45). Blanco has also translated the works of other poets such as Kenneth Patchen, Allen Ginsberg, and W. S. Merwin. In addition, he translates other genres such as science books and children's books.

Blanco has been a scholar for the Centro Mexicano de Escritores, the Instituto Nacional de Bellas Artes, and the Fondo Nacional para la Cultura y las Artes. His books of poetry include *Cromos,* which won the Carlos Pellicer Poetry Award, and *Canto a a la sombra de los animales,* which won the José Fuentes Mares National Prize. His poetry can be found in *Dawn of the Senses,* a bilingual poetry anthology edited by Juvenal Acosta. Blanco's poems have been translated into French, German,

Italian, Portuguese, Russian, and of course, English. Recently, Blanco's work has been collected into an American anthology of Mexican poetry, *Light from a Nearby Window.* He recently spent a year as a Fulbright scholar at the University of California at Irvine, where he completed the work on an anthology of American poetry in Spanish, *Antología de Poesía Norteamericana Contemporánea.* The program Blanco is currently involved with at the University of Texas at El Paso is the only master of fine arts in creative writing program in the United States in which students write and study in English, Spanish, or both languages.

In addition to writing, Blanco has performed rock and jazz in the bands Las Plumas Atómicas and La Comuna. As a child, he enjoyed listening to his mother play the piano. Now, he continues to play music on his own but he finds that it isn't the same as being part of a band. So music is gradually appearing with more force in his poems. As he reads his poetry, he sometimes taps his feet and sways to the music of the words. A compact disc has been made featuring some of his poems combined with music.

Another of Blanco's many interests is art. He enjoys painting and has illustrated numerous books and book covers with his collages and designs. He has been writing for many years about Mexican art and artists. He has produced some very interesting books and portfolios in collaboration with Mexican artists such as Rodolfo Morales, Vicente Rojo, and Francisco Toledo. In addition, Blanco often writes essays and catalogues for art museums in Mexico. His wife is tapestry artist Patricia Revah, one of Latin

America's most original illustrators of children's books. Born in Mexico of Greek and Russian heritage, she displays her work in Mexico and Europe and is considered an expert in the art of using color dyes from indigenous Mexican plants.

Several of Blanco's children's books have been illustrated by his wife, including two award-winning books, *Pájaros, pájaros* and *Un sueño de Navidad.* They have collaborated on a bilingual picture book, *The Desert Mermaid,* which was published in the United States by Children's Book Press. In turn, Blanco has illustrated a book written by his wife. Blanco and Revah have two children, Dana and Andrés.

A cultural ambassador, Blanco travels often to Europe and around the United States, teaching, giving lectures, and taking part in conferences and festivals. His interest in philosophy is apparent in a recent interview in which he spoke of paradoxes and contradictions. He also has a great sense of humor, laughing at himself and at life, saying he changes his opinions often: "I have this feeling that sooner or later we're going to be embarrassed by every opinion we've had. . . . I'm pretty serious about the fact that you can't be serious" (*RGR*, 37).

More Information About Alberto Blanco

"Stalking Borders: An Interview with Alberto Blanco." *Rio Grande Review: UT El Paso's Literary Magazine.* Spring 1995.

Fiction International 25. Special Issue: Mexican Fiction by Harold Jaffe. San Diego State University Press, 1994.

First World, ha ha ha!: The Zapatista Challenge, edited by Elaine Katzenberger. City Lights, 1995.

New Writing from Mexico by Reginald Gibbons. TriQuarterly Books, Northwestern University, 1992.

This Same Sky by Naomi Shihab Nye. Four Winds Press, 1992.

The Tree Is Older Than You Are: A Bilingual Gathering of Poems and Stories from Mexico with Paintings by Mexican Artists by Naomi Shihab Nye. Simon and Schuster, 1995.

Angel's Kite/La estrella de Angel

- Bilingual
- Kites
- Bells

Told in English and Spanish, this is the story of how a young kite maker brought back the missing church bell to his beloved town. There are several theories about what happened to the bell, but no one knows where it was. Most people have gotten used to living without it, but Angel, the kite maker, can't forget. So he decides to make the most beautiful kite in the world to take his mind off the missing bell. What special emblem did he include in the magnificent kite? What went wrong when he went out to fly it on a windy day? And why did Angel and his three trusty dogs spend the night on a cold hilltop? Readers will enjoy finding the answers to these questions and others in this heartening story about the magic of hope and hard work.

Rodolfo Morales, the illustrator of this book, is one of Mexico's greatest living artists. The inspiration for this story came from his childhood as a kite maker in Ocotlán, in the state of Oaxaca, Mexico. The exquisitely framed collage pictures are filled with interesting details that readers of all ages will enjoy examining at length. The mystery of the bell will provide an interesting topic for discussion and writing. Drama and art enthusiasts will also be inspired by this beautiful book.

All Ages

RELATED WORK

The Kite by Alma Flor Ada. Spanish Edition: *El papalote.* Translated from the Spanish by Rosalma Zubizarreta. Illustrated by Vivi Escrivá. Santillana, 1992. See page 19.

The Desert Mermaid/La sirena del desierto
Prickly Pear Award for Spanish Language Book

- Bilingual
- Deserts
- Folklore
- Mermaids
- Music

A contemporary folktale told in English and Spanish, this engaging book tells the story of a desert mermaid who seeks to save her people. O'odham Himdag, an Indian poet of the Sonora Desert, provides the theme for this ecological tale: "The only way to bring water to the desert is to know the old songs." When the story begins, the mermaid is living in an oasis. At first she doesn't know that all the oases are gradually disappearing and that she is the only mermaid left in the entire Sonora Desert. With the help of a magic horse named Silver Star, the mermaid bravely sets out on an epic journey to recover the forgotten songs of her ancestors and thus to secure the future of her people. What roles do the songbirds, the swamp alligators, and other animals play in this drama? Where do the three pearls originate and how do they help or hinder the courageous duo? And what amazing sight awaits the mermaid when she arrives at the sea?

These and other questions will be answered as readers of all ages savor this beautifully written and illustrated book. As a child, Alberto Blanco enjoyed spending time in Mexico's beautiful Sonora Desert. Years later, he was inspired by memories to write this original story in the style of a folktale. His wife, Patricia Revah, lovingly illustrated it with fascinating tapestries. *The Desert Mermaid* is a heartwarming tribute to the ecology of the desert and the importance of music in our lives. The stereotype-shattering portrayal of the mermaid as an ingenious, courageous person is encouraging. The ending is particularly refreshing with its celebration of sisterhood—no mention of the damsel being rescued by a prince, and happily, no impending marriage in sight! Like the enchanting songs, this tale has a special rhythm, making it a perfect choice for both reading aloud and reading alone.

All Ages

María Cristina Brusca

Argentine (1950–)

Birthday: May 4
Address: P.O. Box 1221
Port Ewen, NY 12466

"According to my experience, drawing, writing and illustrating books for children can provide a great joy. Of course, there is a lot of work and patience involved, since not always the ideas find their way into images smoothly. But one should always remember that no matter how difficult the work, the search is in itself a reward. My deepest desire is to continue to have the opportunity of working for such a thrilling audience. . . . If my books contribute to a larger understanding of life and different cultures, I will be more than satisfied." (personal communication)

Books by María Cristina Brusca

WRITTEN AND ILLUSTRATED

The Blacksmith and the Devils. Written with Tona Wilson. Henry Holt, 1992. Spanish Edition: *El herrero y el diablo.*

The Cook and the King. Written with Tona Wilson. Henry Holt, 1993.

My Mama's Little Ranch on the Pampas. Henry Holt, 1994.

On the Pampas. Henry Holt, 1991.

Pedro Fools the Gringo and Other Tales of a Latin American Trickster. Retold by María Cristina Brusca and Tona Wilson. Henry Holt, 1995.

Three Friends/Tres Amigos: A Counting Book/Un cuento para contar. Written with Tona Wilson, Henry Holt, 1995.

When Jaguars Ate the Moon and Other Stories About Animals and Plants of the Americas. Written with Tona Wilson, Henry Holt, 1995.

ILLUSTRATED

Mama Went Walking by Christine Berry. Henry Holt, 1990.

The Zebra-Riding Cowboy by Angela Shelf Medearis. Henry Holt, 1992.

María Cristina Brusca is the accomplished author and illustrator of a number of engaging books for children. Her drawings and paintings have been displayed in various exhibitions and collective shows. She has also illustrated numerous book covers and games as well as other projects such as a serial encyclopedia. She currently divides her time between Argentina and the United States.

Born in Buenos Aires, Argentina, Brusca spent as much time as she could at her grandparents' ranch, La Carlota. She enjoyed spending weekends and summers with her cousin at the large *estancia,* riding horses, helping with the chores, and listening to the stories told by the *gauchos.* "I loved the big, flat extensions of the *pampas,* the creatures that lived there, riding horses for hours, talking to the gauchos and learning about their culture, their special way of talking, their clothes, et cetera" (personal communication). Brusca has written two fascinating picture-book memoirs about these childhood experiences, *On the Pampas* and *My Mama's Little Ranch on the Pampas*. "I've hoped to communicate some of these memories, which time and distance make so fragile, and to share some of my experiences with North American children. I've also hoped to show them a little bit of gaucho culture, of the way of life of those who live so close to the land and to nature" (Henry Holt catalogue profile).

It was also at the ranch that Brusca's father taught her how to draw and to paint with watercolors. At thirteen, she began studying art in the city. As she grew older and became more involved in her art studies, she had less time to spend in the country. Her love of art and reading led her to enter a special high school where she studied drawing, painting, graphic design, and book binding.

Brusca graduated from college in 1973 as a professor of graphic design. Between 1973 and 1988, she worked in Buenos Aires designing book covers, illustrating children's books, and collaborating on a number of children's magazines. During that time, she was also drawing and painting her own work and participating in various exhibitions and collective art shows.

In 1988, Brusca moved to the United States and settled in Port Ewen, New York. She gradually established herself as an illustrator and writer of children's books. When her editor suggested that she write a book about her childhood experiences in Argentina, she created *On the Pampas*. This book was received with such enthusiasm that she wrote a sequel, *My Mama's Little Ranch on the Pampas*. The process of creating the books was a very pleasant one for Brusca. "I've had great fun remembering my summers with Susanita—our love of horses, our small adventures, our freedom from being told what to do and what not to do, learning to take care of ourselves. I felt a special emotion drawing my grandmother, the ranch, my friend, Salguero. And going to meet the child that I was" (Henry Holt profile).

From 1992 to the present, Brusca has collaborated with Tona Wilson on a number of enchanting picture books, including one featuring Argentine folktales, a collection of stories about plants and animals indigenous to the Americas, and a bilingual counting book. Brusca notes, "When I met Tona Wilson, I discovered that we had the same enthusiasm for folktales and the same curiosity about the flora and fauna of the Americas" (*Junior Library Guild,* 34). In 1995, two of

these books were published in Spanish by an Argentine publishing house.

The response to Brusca's work has been very enthusiastic. Indeed, the praise for her clear, captivating text and authentic, distinctive watercolors has been widespread. Her work challenges stereotypes of women and girls, showing them actively engaged in the work involved in running a ranch. Brusca's and Wilson's books are noted for their extensive research and loving attention to detail. Together they are making a unique contribution to the field of children's literature.

Brusca concludes, "So far, I have been able to share with American children experiences that come from other parts of the world, particularly the country where I was born. Writing and drawing these books, I had to do a lot of research so I have also learned a lot about myself" (personal communication).

More Information About María Cristina Brusca

Dutchess Magazine. Fall 1994, 74–75.

Henry Holt Catalogue (no info available).

Junior Library Guild. April–September 1995, 34.

Publishers Weekly. March 6, 1995, 70.

School Library Journal. May 1994, 107.

• Blacksmiths
• Folklore
• Argentina

The Blacksmith and the Devils

María Cristina Brusca and Tona Wilson retell this Argentine folktale based on the version told by the famous *gaucho* Don Segundo Sombra in a novel by Ricardo Guiraldes. It is the tale of Juan Pobreza the blacksmith, known in Argentina as "Miseria" and in Spain as "Pedro de Urdemalas" and by other names in other parts of the Americas. Juan Pobreza's "name suited him perfectly since *pobreza* means 'poverty' in Spanish." Although he was poor, he never turned anyone away even if they couldn't pay. On the day he fixes the shoe of a *gaucho's* mule, his life changes in dramatic ways. The *gaucho* claims to be Saint Peter and offers to grant Juan three wishes for his generosity. The story takes an unexpected twist here, leading Juan into a bargain with the Devil that results in a series of hilarious events. As the blacksmith matches wits with the underworld, his antics improve the lives of everyone on the pampas. Well, almost everyone. "A few greedy people, who had gotten rich from other people's troubles, were not pleased." As the tale unwinds, Juan finds himself in an amazing variety of unexpected places and situations.

In the foreword, the authors explain that folktales change a little with each retelling. They invite us to gather around the campfire and listen to this story and then, in the tradition of oral storytelling, to make the story our own by changing it in any way when we tell it to our friends. Readers might enjoy adapting it to their location, time, gender, or worldview. After examining the detailed, humorous illustrations, they might want to create their own pictures to accompany their version of the folktale. Brusca's amusing watercolors are filled with droll details that will elicit many chuckles as readers pore over the double-spread paintings. The facial expressions on the humans as well as the animals are especially comical. The fact that some people were not happy with the peace and harmony on the pampas provides a fascinating topic for critical thinking discussions. Teachers who work in areas where this material might be considered controversial should share the book with their supervisors before introducing it in the classroom.

Grade 3–Adult

RELATED WORKS

Spanish Edition: *El herrero y el diablo.* Henry Holt, 1992.

South American folklore: *The Cook and the King* by the same authors. See below.

The Cook and the King

Nebraska Library Commission's 1993 List of Thirty Best Buys

- Folklore
- South America
- Kings
- Judges
- Culinary Arts

The Cook and the King was inspired by a South American folktale. It is the tale of a wise young woman who teaches a selfish, pompous king an important lesson. The story opens with the annual carnival during which the hardworking people of the kingdom thank their *Pachamama,* Mother Earth, for giving them life. Soon afterward, the king demands that Florinda, famous for her *empanadas,* come cook for him. She wisely agrees only after he promises to grant her one wish whenever she asks for it. From her new vantage point in the palace, Florinda watches as the king makes hasty, foolish, and unfair judgments in settling the disputes among the people. Each time she finds a way to make a subtle but strong objection. But one day she dishes up a lesson that enrages the king and puts her life in danger. Will Florinda be clever enough to save herself? Will the pattern of injustice ever change in this tiny kingdom high up in the mountains of South America?

María Cristina Brusca and Tona Wilson have teamed up to bring us another humorous and insightful folktale from South America, this time featuring a clever young peasant woman outwitting a powerful king and in so doing replacing strife with harmony. They have created an admirable female protagonist that shatters the stereotypes of women as passive conformists. The authors provide additional information about customs and music in a note at the end of the book. Brusca's amusing illustrations add even more gusto to this engaging story. This folktale lends itself nicely to a variety of forms of drama such as pantomime or readers' theater. As the authors note in *The Blacksmith and the Devils,* folktales change a little with each retelling. Storytellers might want to make this story their own by adapting it to their location, time, or interest.

Grades 2–5

RELATED WORKS:

South American folklore: *The Blacksmith and the Devils* by the same authors. See pages 70–71.

Culinary arts: *Roses Sing on New Snow* by Paul Yee. Macmillan, 1991.

• Argentina
• Ranch Life
• Picture Book Memoir

My Mama's Little Ranch on the Pampas

In this captivating sequel to *On the Pampas,* María Cristina Brusca recalls more of her experiences as a young girl in Argentina. This time she chronicles her first year on the small ranch purchased and managed by her mother. She took a very active part in taking care of the farm, opening and closing the windmill, mending fences, caring for the saddles and reins, and riding her horse, Pampero. She helped tend the new cows and their calves and even assisted with the dramatic cesarean delivery of a calf. She celebrated her birthday by driving the sulky into town and dancing the *malambo* at the general store.

Readers of all ages will enjoy this autobiographical reminiscence told through Brusca's authentic voice and distinctive, detailed watercolor illustrations. As she relates "all the funny and scary and wonderful things" that happened that year, the reader experiences them along with her. Brusca's story is refreshingly realistic and includes cow manure, bird droppings, and cattle breeding. The depiction of the emergency cesarean birth of the calf is handled very well, recounting the details of the procedure through text and pictures. Readers from the Northern Hemisphere will be interested in the contrast of the seasons, with spring beginning on September 21. Brusca includes a helpful chart on the seasons in her attractively illustrated glossary, which appears on the inside covers. Regional terms defined in these decorated endpapers and sprinkled throughout the narrative include *pasteles, malambo, rastra,* and *la luz mala.* This is another well-written book with a much-needed strong Latina protagonist, one who is not afraid to get her hands dirty or to try a new adventure. It challenges stereotypes of females, depicting a woman who manages her own ranch and shares all the chores with her daughter. This book provides fascinating reading for youngsters of all backgrounds from the city or the country.

Grades 1–5

RELATED WORK

Prequel: *On the Pampas.* See next page.

On the Pampas

Notable Trade Book in the Field of Social Studies
Parents' Choice *Picture Book Award*

- Argentina
- Ranch Life
- Picture Book Memoir

Based on her experiences as a child, María Cristina Brusca has created a delightful picture book about a girl from Buenos Aires, Argentina, who spends her summers at La Carlota, her grandmother's ranch on the pampas. The pampas are the flat grasslands that stretch for hundreds of miles through central Argentina and Uruguay. The book opens with Cristina's train trip to the *estancia* where she is met by her cousin, Susanita, who knows "everything about horses, cows, and all the animals that live on the *pampas.*" Together the girls ride and groom horses, help with the cattle, read comic books, search for *ñandú* eggs, and listen to the gauchos tell tall tales. Ranch life offers plenty of adventures for these two active and tireless cousins, both of whom embrace every experience wholeheartedly. When the summer ends, Cristina has one last surprise before she returns to the city.

María Cristina Brusca has written an outstanding book, noteworthy for its depiction of girls as adventuresome, courageous, and solvers of problems. *On the Pampas* is also notable for its captivating text and distinctive, detailed watercolors, which capture the excitement of the story. Especially impressive are the faces and figures of the humans, who look like ordinary people and are not at all prettified. Each animal is given an individual face and personality as well. The inside front and back covers provide a fascinating illustrated glossary of terms such as *recado, mate, bombagha,* and *ñandú.* María Cristina Brusca's autobiographical reminiscence is a very special book, one that brings back memories to those of us who grew up in the country and introduces an interesting way of life to those who have always lived in the city. This fine book earned a starred review in *School Library Journal.*

Grades 1–5

RELATED WORKS

Sequel: *My Mama's Little Ranch on the Pampas,* also by María Cristina Brusca.
See page 72.

Spanish Edition: *En la pampa.* Editorial Sudamericana, Buenos Aires, Argentina.

Pedro Fools the Gringo and Other Tales of a Latin American Trickster

- Folklore
- Trickster Tales

Twelve amusing short stories feature Pedro Urdemales, a cunning trickster, who survives by outwitting the rich and powerful. As the authors explain in the introduction, "Some of Pedro's exploits will be familiar from stories about other popular and trickster heroes, such as Coyote and Br'er Rabbit, or the Mayan rabbit Juan Tul." In the first story, a young, poor, homeless Pedro learns to use his wits to keep himself alive. When he finds work with a stingy priest, the lessons he learns about how to get enough to eat prove to be very useful later. As he travels around Chile, Argentina, Mexico, Guatemala, and other parts of Latin America, he escapes a band of vigilantes, outwits a passing gringo with a get-rich scheme, and even tricks the Devil himself. The final story finds him matching wits with San Pedro, trying to find a way to get into heaven.

Trickster stories appeal to people of all ages because they enjoy reading about greedy folks being outwitted by someone who appears to be an ordinary person. The authors inform us that the stories they have selected are just a sampling of the many that have been told in Latin America and the southwestern United States. Slight variations of the same tales are often told in different locations. The book includes a section telling where these stories came from and a bibliography. Black-and-white illustrations accompany each story and add to the fun.

Grades 3–7

- Bilingual
- Counting Book
- Cowgirls and Cowboys

Three Friends/Tres Amigos: A Counting Book/Un cuento para contar

When a cowgirl and cowboy set out to catch some cows, there's no telling what adventures await them. Can they outwit a bevy of armadillos, roadrunners, and coyotes? What other critters are out there in the desert plotting against them? As we count our way through this rollicking story, we have a great time learning about tumbleweeds, saguaro cactus, and other flora and fauna of the area. This humorous book will encourage young readers to learn to count in Spanish and English, and to enjoy the pleasure of being bilingual. People of all ages will savor the playful illustrations, searching out those mischievous little creatures and checking to see what they will be up to next. As the tuckered-out *vaqueros* retire for the night, can they guess what escapades young readers might cook up for tomorrow? Here is an opportunity for great fun combining bilingual counting with drama, writing, science, and art. The inside back cover provides a glossary of related terms such as *botas, lazo, sartén,* and *chaparreras.*

Preschool–Grade 3

RELATED WORK
Uno, Dos, Tres: One, Two, Three by Pat Mora. Clarion, 1996. See pages 130–131.

- Folklore
- Indigenous People
- Animals and Plants
- ABC's

When Jaguars Ate the Moon and Other Stories About Animals and Plants of the Americas
Selection of the Junior Library Guild

Twenty-six tales, featuring an animal or plant for each letter of the alphabet, comprise this fascinating, one-of-a-kind compendium. The authors retell stories about the anteater, iguana, kinkajou, llama, quetzal, tapir, zompopo, and many other fascinating creatures, based on oral traditions, ancient myths, anecdotes, short stories, and parts of longer stories. The people and geographical region where each tale originated are identified. The locations range from all parts of the Americas including Argentina, Paraguay, Guatemala, and Mexico to what is now the United States and Canada. The tales were told by people who have lived on these continents for tens of thousands of years. Some of the stories answer questions such as: How did the Guarani people learn to dance? How did the armadillo get armor? and Why do tapirs eat prickly branches and brambles that no other animal will touch? In the title story, "When Jaguars Ate the Moon," burning bits of the moon fall into the forest. The ensuing pandemonium results in the creation of animals, stars, constellations, and an eerie lunar eclipse.

There are many special features about this book. The authors have lovingly interwoven themes about respect for the interdependence of all the people, animals, and plants of the earth into their engrossing tales. Each story is accompanied by an enchanting illustration and each page is framed with detailed paintings of additional indigenous flora and fauna. The book ends with a map of the Americas identifying the locations of the tales, notes on each of the stories, and an extensive bibliography. Brusca and Wilson are to be commended for the tremendous amount of research that went into creating this beautiful volume. It lends itself perfectly to interdisciplinary studies, combining storytelling, science, social studies, art, and geography. Readers might wish to savor a few pages at a time, stopping periodically for discussion, map study, creative dramatics, or writing.   Grades 2–Adult

Omar Castañeda

Photo: Bleu Castañeda

Guatemalan American (1954–1997)

Birthday: September 6

"I count myself a feminist, an activist for those who are struggling to break the sometimes oppressive weight of history and find just a little space for themselves where they might have dignity and voice."
(Something About the Author, 44)

"Because I am Guatemalan-American and have always lived in non-Hispanic communities in the U.S., I have had to deal with conflicting views of the world. In my writing, I investigate the individual's search for identity in a changing world. My characters glimpse something other than what is sanctioned by their native culture, and at the same time, they uphold many of their society's values."   (personal communication)

"To become proud of differences, we have to write through our family and individual histories."   (personal communication)

Books by Omar Castañeda

Abuela's Weave. Illustrated by Enrique O. Sanchez. Lee and Low, 1993.

Among the Volcanoes. E. P. Dutton/ Lodestar, 1991.

Cunuman. Pineapple Press, 1987.

Dance of the Conquest. Illustrated by Véronique Fontaine. Kane Publishing, 1991.

El Tapiz de Abuela. Lee and Low, 1994. Film version by Spoken Arts, 1994.

Imagining Isabel. Dutton/Lodestar, 1994.

New Visions: Fiction by Florida Writers. Edited by O. Castañeda, C. Blackwell, and J. Harrington. Arbiter Press, 1989.

Omar S. Castañeda, a writer, educator, and lecturer, lived in Bellingham, Washington, and was an associate professor at Western Washington University where he taught creative writing, literature of the Mayas, world literature, and other related courses. He served on numerous educational committees, gave a variety of professional presentations, and organized numerous writing conferences. He often served as a jurist for award and residency programs and was a cofounding editor of *Chiricú.* He was the founder and former director of The Hubless Wheel, a reading series that features minority and ethnic writers. He was committed to broadening the scope of literature for young readers and made an important contribution to the field.

The son of Miriam Mendez Castañeda, a sculptor and homemaker, and Hector Neri Castañeda, a philosopher, Castañeda was born in Guatemala City, Guatemala, and raised in Michigan and Indiana. Although he was hungry for information, he was alienated by the regimentation and punitive nature of the schools he attended. He dropped out of high school for a year and lived on the streets. During this time, he realized the importance of education and returned to school with renewed determination. After high school, Castañeda spent four years in the military. It was during his first creative writing class in college that he immediately knew that he wanted to write. He discovered that writing was a way to work through problems, create possible worlds, and to forge identity. If he went several days without writing, he felt strange, dislocated.

Castañeda was often invited to give readings and workshops. The titles of some of his presentations provide a glimpse into Castañeda's interests and concerns: "The Dubious Immigrant," "Mayan Creation Stories," "Borders and Barriers for a Multicultural Society," "Politics in Publishing Ethnic Difference," "Authenticity in Multicultural Children's Literature," "Issues of Multiculturalism for Teachers," and "Looking Out for the Other."

Castañeda taught in Florida, China, and Indiana. He traveled to South Korea, Hong Kong, Japan, and the Philippines and he worked in Mexico, Guatemala, and China. Several of his short stories have been translated into other languages and used as material for university courses in other countries.

A prolific writer, Castañeda's short fiction has been widely anthologized and appears in numerous journals. He also wrote essays, articles, poetry, and books for adults, young adults, and children. He was the recipient of a number of awards, grants' and fellowships including an Indiana University Ernest Hemingway Fellowship, a Fulbright Senior Central American Research Grant, and the Charles H. and N. Mildred Nilon Award for Excellence in Minority Fiction for one of his books for adults, *Remembering to Say 'Mouth' or 'Face.'* (Other awards for his books for children and young adults are listed with the reviews of the books.)

On professional leave during the 1995–96 academic year, Castañeda was working on a book entitled *Negotiating Values: New Strategies for Fiction Writing Workshops,* which presented not only conventions and techniques of fiction writing, but a critique of those conventions to show their history, social biases, and political implications. Another work in progress was a magic-realist novel about a young woman of mixed Guatemalan and American blood who visits Guatemala to learn more about her heritage. Castañeda was also working on two translation projects: one is of the only book on Maya cosmology written by a Maya group and the other is of an

ongoing publication of *La Liga Maya Internacional.* He finished writing three picture books featuring newly immigrated children to the United States and issues of bilingual education, and two books for adults.

Castañeda's writing is often set in Guatemala or Indiana. He noted, "I write for children out of political interests and artistic challenge; I write for adults for the very same reasons. My writing is characterized by concerns for Guatemala, socio-political upheaval, racism and biculturality in the United States. I often portray cultural conflict, the twin drives of assimilation and confrontation, and reformation of belief under drastic social changes. I show individuals becoming perverse when desiring too much control over people, emotions, even ideas, and, most of all, by not freely inventing their own identity. My experimentation is usually with unreliable narrators and varieties of irreal modes. My writing for children attempts similar objectives, yet in far less experimental ways. My most recent interest has been to capture young Central American immigrant experiences of erasure of language and culture" (personal communication).

Castañeda's bicultural background is central to his writing. He wrote about people experiencing the clash of cultures and how the resulting turmoil contributes to the shaping of identities. His work plays an important role in elucidating the struggles and issues facing people whose existence is often ignored, erased, or marginalized. This theme of developing identity is especially relevant to young people who are struggling with which parts of their traditions they want to keep and what parts of a new worldview fit for them.

While he thought of himself as mostly an adult fiction writer, Castañeda felt that children's literature is also vitally important. His award-winning books for young readers feature admirable Latina protagonists who provide greatly needed strong role models. He found that young people are often the most open to new ideas that might threaten adults. Because children have not yet established such rigid worldviews, they are flexible readers, able to enjoy a wider range of perspectives. He encouraged teachers to be sensitive and open to the forms their students' writing takes. He felt that it is important to honor their complicated emotions and the possible violence and other unpleasant topics that may enter into their writing. Students need an avenue for expression; it is crucial that we do not repress the multiplicity of emotions and variety of plots that emerge in their writing.

More Information About Omar Castañeda

"For the Well-Intentioned Multiculturalist." *Children's Book Council Journal,* Spring/Summer 1995.

Contemporary Authors, Volume 135, 77.

Something About the Author, Volume 71, 43–44.

- Art
- Birthmarks
- Weaving
- Grandmothers

Grades K–4

Abuela's Weave

Consortium of Latin American Studies Programs Honoree
Parents' *Choice Honoree*

This exquisite book tells the story of Esperanza and her grandmother, who live in rural Santa Cruz, Guatemala. The young girl and Abuela work tirelessly on backstrap looms to create handwoven tablecloths, *huipiles* (blouses), skirts, and an exquisite tapestry that blossoms with the images of Guatemala. With Abuela's guidance, Esperanza learns the secrets of making goods that will "pull the wonder right out of people." As they work, Esperanza worries about selling the weavings at the Fiesta de Pueblos in Guate. What if people refuse to buy from Abuela because of her birthmark? What if the shoppers prefer modern, machine-made goods? And will Esperanza have the courage to carry out Abuela's plan? As the story unfolds, a young girl discovers the magic of her grandmother's artistry as well as her own hidden strengths. A woman teaches her granddaughter a lesson about creating from the heart and believing in herself.

Enrique O. Sanchez's brilliantly colored illustrations in this, his first picture book, are rendered in acrylic on canvas. They beautifully complement Castañeda's rich narrative. The text and paintings present a wealth of cultural detail, authentically re-creating images of rural Guatemala. Readers will enjoy discussing Abuela's motivation for hiding her birthmark on this particular day. They will soon realize that since she has been selling her goods for years, she wanted to create a situation where her granddaughter would have to rely on her own wits, and in so doing, develop self-confidence and independence. Thus, she will be prepared to follow her *abuela's* example in the future. This is a gentle, cheerful story of generational sharing and traditional handicrafts.

RELATED WORKS

Spanish Edition: *El Tapiz de Abuela.*

Film: *El Tapiz de Abuela.*

Handicrafts/grandmothers:*The Patchwork Quilt* by Valerie Flournoy. Dial, 1985.

Among the Volcanoes

Child Study Association Book of the Year
New York Public Library Best Books for the Teen Age Award

- Career Aspirations
- Illness
- Tradition and Change
- Gender Roles

This is a poignant story of a young woman's search for a way to break out of the constricting female role and to follow her dream of becoming a teacher. Isabel Pacay lives with her family in the small village of Chuuí Chopaló, Guatemala. She has long dreamed of finishing school and becoming a teacher. However, this seems like an impossible goal in a community that expects females to follow the traditional path of marrying young and self-lessly devoting their lives to their families. Now her mother is ill and as the oldest child in the Mayan family, Isabel is expected to take on the household responsibilities. Her goals seems more unattainable than ever. She struggles with her ambivalent feelings toward her boyfriend, Lucas Choy, knowing that a traditional marriage would end her chances of doing "what she most dearly wanted and could least explain" (6). When a young American arrives in the village to conduct medical research, the family is faced with an apparent life-or-death decision. Should her mother continue to rely on the local healer, the *sanjorín,* whose treatments seem to be ineffective? Or should she defy local tradition and try Western medicine? What is the meaning of the ominous omens left outside the family hut?

With sensitivity and insight, Omar Castañeda has written an exceptional story of a young woman searching for her identity in a world fraught with upheaval and change. The multifaceted characterization of the young protago-nist is remarkably well drawn and memorable. Castañeda's passages about Isabel's hopes for the future are poignant: "As a quetzal . . . she would be elegant and nobler than the life she was born into, and she would wing over the vast wall of volcanoes surrounding the lake and discover the world spreading infi-nitely outward" (8). The conflicts between traditional and Western cultures and the pain of change and loss are presented with depth and insight. Descriptive passages provide a realistic portrait of the complexities of the Mayan culture, the ever-present political unrest of the area, and a strong sense of the natural beauty of the Guatemalan highlands. The betrayal by a best friend, the miscom-munication with and jealousy of a significant other, the inspiration of a respected teacher, the bumbling insights of a newcomer, the needs and demands of family, and, most of all, the belief in and love of self make this a compelling, significant novel. Readers won't want to miss the sequel!

Grades 6–10

RELATED WORKS

Sequel: *Imagining Isabel.* See pages 80–81.

Guatemala: *The Most Beautiful Place in the World* by Ann Cameron. Knopf, 1988.

Women's Career Aspirations

Bitter Herbs and Honey by Barbara Cohen. Lothrop, Lee & Shepard, 1976.

Trouble's Child by Mildred Pitts Walter. Lothrop, Lee & Shepard, 1985.

- Drama
- Guatemala
- History

The Dance of the Conquest: Spotlight on Readers Theatre

This play, written for readers' theater, features the history and culture of Guatemala. Every year the Mayas repeat their history in the Dance of the Conquest, which tells the story of the Mayan defeat by the Spanish invaders in 1524. It celebrates the memory of the heroic men and women who fought to defend their country. The Dance of the Conquest is an important part of annual festivals in which each city in Guatemala honors its patron saint. The dancers act out the terrible events that took place over four hundred years ago.

Omar Castañeda's interesting play is divided into three acts and has eight major parts plus minor roles. The teacher's name is Teacher Pacay. (Castañeda has written Isabel Pacay's story in *Among the Volcanoes* and *Imagining Isabel*.) The easy-to-read play emphasizes cooperation and gender-positive assignment of parts. Participants and audience will learn about history, geography, and culture while enjoying readers' theater, a significant drama form that lends itself well to a variety of interpretations. A pronunciation key is included. Other readers' theater scripts are available from Kane Press, 222 East 46th Street, New York, NY 10017, (212) 986-2240.

Grades 3–5

- Career Aspirations
- Political Awakening
- Gender Roles
- Tradition and Change

Imagining Isabel

New York Public Library Best Books for the Teen Age Award

In this sequel to *Among the Volcanoes,* Isabel Pacay Choy enrolls in a government-run teacher education training program and finds herself involved in the turbulent political and social issues of contemporary Guatemala. Omar Castañeda dedicated this book "To the slain and wounded heroes of the Massacre of Santiago Atitlán, 2 December 1990; and to the more than 220,000 slain or disappeared since the 1954 coup in Guatemala." *Imagining Isabel* begins with sixteen-year-old Isabel's marriage to Lucas and the death of her mother. Her dreams of becoming a teacher seem unattainable until a letter arrives from the National Education Commission inviting her to become a teacher trainee. At first she is filled with doubt and fear. How can she leave her new husband and recently widowed father and both sets of families? Tradition dictates that women lead a selfless life, caring for loved ones. But Isabel has always had a desire to be something other than what she was expected to be. So with her young sister, Marcelina, she attends the eight-week program in the town of Sololá, where she quickly learns more than she ever dreamed possible. As she quietly absorbs the political and philosophical debates between her two very different roommates and observes the people around her, she is at times intimidated and overwhelmed, feeling inadequate, and at times inspired, feeling energized. One day when she goes for a walk, a vaguely familiar figure leads her to the body of a dying man. Terrified, she calls for help and then quietly fades into the background. Aware of the political climate, she wonders if she should tell anyone about the incident. Should she come forward and identify herself as the person who found the body? Should she leave the school and return to the "safety" of her small village? Can she trust anyone at the school, or are they part of the conspiracy? Isabel's political awakening is interwoven with a remarkable story of new friendships, family affection, changing customs, and personal growth.

Readers will not only be inspired by the strong examples of the women in this story but will learn more about Guatemalan history, politics, and culture. Castañeda deftly probed several significant issues in this book including gender roles, the search for truth in a confusing political climate, and Guatemala's struggle to balance tradition with change. Grades 6–10

RELATED WORKS

Prequel: *Among the Volcanoes*. See page 79.

Guatemala: *The Most Beautiful Place in the World* by Ann Cameron. Knopf, 1988.

Women's Career Aspirations

Bitter Herbs and Honey by Barbara Cohen. Lothrop, Lee & Shepard, 1976.

Trouble's Child by Mildred Pitts Walter. Lothrop, Lee & Shepard, 1985.

Sandra Cisneros

Chicana (1954–)

Birthday: December 20
Contact: Susan Bergholz
17 West 10th Street, #5
New York, NY 10011

"I always feel such incredible energy about writing about something that has never been set down on paper, hasn't been documented." (Authors and Artists for Young Adults, *76*)

"When I was 11 years old in Chicago, teachers thought if you were poor and Mexican you didn't have anything to say. Now I think that what I was put on this planet for was to tell these stories."
(Los Angeles Times, *F1*)

Books by Sandra Cisneros

Bad Boys. Mango Press, 1980.

Hairs/Pelitos. Illustrated by Terry Ybañez. Alfred A. Knopf, 1994.

La Casa en Mango Street, translated by Elena Poniatowska. Vintage Books, 1995.

The House on Mango Street. Arte Público Press, 1984; Vintage Books, 1991; Alfred A. Knopf, 1994.

Loose Woman. Alfred A. Knopf, 1994; Vintage Books, 1995.

My Wicked Wicked Ways. Third Woman Press, 1987; Turtle Bay/Alfred A. Knopf, 1992.

Woman Hollering Creek and Other Stories. Random House, 1991; Vintage Books, 1992.

Sandra Cisneros is the highly acclaimed Chicana author of *The House on Mango Street, Woman Hollering Creek,* and several other superb books. The recipient of numerous honors and awards for her poetry and fiction, her books have been translated into ten languages and published internationally. She also writes essays, articles, book reviews, and interviews. A former high school teacher, counselor, college recruiter, and arts administrator, Cisneros has taught writing at practically every level and worked at several colleges and universities as a writer-in-residence. She has lectured extensively at institutions throughout the United States as well as Mexico and Europe. She currently makes her home in San Antonio, Texas.

Born in Chicago, Cisneros is the daughter of Elvira Cordero Anguiano, a Mexican American, and Alfredo Cisneros del Moral, a Mexican. Because he missed his homeland, her father periodically moved the family from Chicago to Mexico City and back. The frequent upheavals were very upsetting to Cisneros and resulted in her becoming introverted and shy. Being the only daughter out of seven children and spending a lot of time by herself added to her shyness. As a result, she became an astute observer of people and the world around her, a trait which later would contribute greatly to her ability to write with insight, compassion, and authenticity: "... that aloneness, that loneliness, was good for a would-be writer—it allowed me time to think and think, to imagine, to read and prepare myself" (*The Mexican American Family Album,* 51).

Cisneros's working-class family moved from place to place, living in poor neighborhoods with empty lots and burned-out buildings. The frequent changing of schools made it difficult for a shy child to make friends. Her early education did not help to build her confidence and self-concept. The Catholic schools she attended stressed discipline and did not individualize instruction or acknowledge the importance of differences. Afraid to volunteer, she learned to blend into the crowd. Being singled out meant being ridiculed and set up as an example. Cisneros described her schooling as a "rather shabby basic education. If I had lived up to my teachers' expectations, I'd still be working in a factory, because my report card was pretty lousy" (*Authors and Artists for Young Adults [AAYA],* 71).

Escaping into books, Cisneros's imagination created a view of life as a story in which she was the main character. Her love of reading came from her mother, who arranged for her daughter to get her first library card before she learned to read. It wasn't until years later that Cisneros realized many people actually buy some of their books in addition to borrowing them from the library. She doesn't remember reading poetry; instead, she checked out mostly works of fiction, with Lewis Carroll being one of her favorite authors. An avid reader, she also wrote secretly at home. She modeled her first poems on the rhythmic passages in her reading texts, letting her ear guide her.

When she was twelve, her parents borrowed the money for a down payment on a two-story house in a Puerto Rican neighborhood on the north side of Chicago. Having her own home and being in a stable environment gave Cisneros friends and neighbors who would later provide inspiration for the unique characters in her highly successful book, *The House on Mango Street,* which has sold over 500,000 copies and is a part of the curriculum at dozens of schools and universities.

It was in high school that Cisneros first found positive recognition for her creativity. When she read poems aloud in class, her feel for what the writer was saying enabled her to interpret them in a very expressive way. Finally when she was a sophomore, a special teacher came along who encouraged the gifted young student to write. As a result, Cisneros gained confidence, became more public with her work, and eventually was selected as editor of the school literary magazine. During her junior year, she was exposed to the works of established American and British writers. Her electives Spanish class introduced her to the works of Latin American poets whose writing deeply impressed the young writer.

After high school, she attended Loyola University, where she majored in English. Believing that college would be a good place for his daughter to find a husband, her father, an upholsterer, supported her efforts. As Cisneros quipped in *Glamour,* "In retrospect, I'm lucky my father believed daughters were meant for husbands. It meant it didn't matter if I majored in something silly like English. After all, I'd find a nice professional eventually, right?" At Loyola she was reintroduced to the Latin American poets via a generation of American poets influenced by the same. One of her teachers encouraged her to enroll in the poetry section of the University of Iowa Writers' Workshop, a program that led to a master's degree.

The two years at the Iowa Writers' Workshop had a major impact on Cisneros's life and writing. At first the experience was extremely painful, and she found herself alienated from her privileged classmates and surroundings. "In graduate school, what I said was looked at as so wacky that you right away shut up.... I became very frightened and terrified that first year.... I discovered my otherness and what it was that made me different from everybody else" (*AAYA,* 72). As she became aware of the class, color, and gender differences between herself and the writers represented in the curriculum, her panic turned to outrage. "It was not until this moment when I separated myself, when I considered myself truly distinct, that my writing acquired a voice. I knew I was a Mexican woman, but I didn't think it had anything to do with why I felt so much imbalance in my life, whereas it had everything to do with it! ...

That's when I decided I would write about something my classmates couldn't write about" (*Publishers Weekly*, 74–75).

After she received her master's degree, Cisneros worked as a teacher of literacy skills with people whose first language was English and second language was Spanish and held a position as a college recruiter. In 1982, she received her first National Endowment of the Arts Fellowship for poetry, and traveled abroad for one and a half years while she finished *The House on Mango Street.* After her fellowship ended she returned to Chicago, where she heard about a job in San Antonio, Texas. She applied and was given the position as arts administrator for a Chicano arts center, a job she left after a year and a half.

As Cisneros was preparing to leave Texas forever, she learned that she had been awarded the Dobie-Paisano fellowship, an award that included a home for six months. This was 1985 and her flight from Texas was deferred. She left Texas several times, but the "final time" was in 1987 because she couldn't find a job teaching. (She later returned to Texas, where she has made San Antonio her home.) Cisneros accepted a position at California State University in Chico, which acknowledged her small press book as a "real" publication. In 1988, Cisneros met her literary agent and, as a result, her books were sold to Random House. *Woman Hollering Creek,* a series of short stories published in 1991, received wide distribution and glowing reviews, thrusting her into the national limelight.

Cisneros has been the recipient of many awards and honors, including a second National Endowment of the Arts Fellowship in 1988, an honorary doctor of letters from the State University of New York at Purchase in 1993, and a MacArthur Fellowship in 1995. (Additional awards are listed below with the reviews of her books.) She has surmounted barriers of gender, class, and race to achieve the success many of her people have been denied. She explains that writers with backgrounds similar to her own have historically been "the illegal aliens of American lit" and "the migrant workers in terms of respect" (*Mother Jones,* 15). But Cisneros, like Esperanza in *The House on Mango Street,* will never forget her roots.

In addition to her writing, Cisneros is an annual volunteer lecturer at schools in the San Antonio area. She is a member and organizer of Mujeres por la Paz, a San Antonio women's peace group. She recently adapted two stories from *Woman Hollering Creek* to the stage—which became *Milagritos,* a show she wrote, directed, and performed. When she gives a reading at a library or school, she frequently passes around her fifth-grade report card, which has mostly C's and D's, to demonstrate that schools often do not recognize the talents of students and that grades are not reliable predictors of a person's future. Cisneros is known as a passionate, electric reader with outspoken views, and her audiences hang on her every word. She often talks with students about the omission of works by Chicanos, asking them, "How many Latino and Latina writers do you see in your books? Why only one?" She adds, "The whole system in their neighborhoods where they are growing up is created to keep them failing. . . . I tell them they have to be very ferocious to beat those odds" (*Boston Globe,* 76).

More Information About Sandra Cisneros

BOOKS

Authors and Artists for Young Adults, Volume 9, 69–76.

Dictionary of Literary Biography, Volume 122, 77–81.

¡Latinas! Women of Achievement, edited by Diane Telgen and Jim Kamp. Visible Ink, 1996.

The Mexican American Family Album, by Dorothy & Thomas Hoobler. Oxford University Press, 1994, 51.

Notable Hispanic Women, edited by Diane Telgen & Jim Kamp. Gale Research, 1993, 99–101.

PERIODICALS

America. July 25, 1992, 39–42.

The Boston Globe. May 17, 1994, 73, 76.

Glamour. November 1990, 256–257.

Library Journal. January 1992, 55.

Los Angeles Times. May 7, 1991, F1.

Los Angeles Times Book Review. April 28, 1991, 3.

Mirabella. April 1991, 46.

Mother Jones. October 1989, 15.

Newsweek. June 3, 1991, 60.

New York Times Book Review. May 26, 1991, 6.

Publishers Weekly. March 29, 1991, 74–75.

San Francisco Examiner. December 22, 1994, A17

VISáVIS. September 1992, 64–65, 121.

Washington Post Book World. June 9, 1991, 3.

Hairs/Pelitos

This endearing bilingual picture book is excerpted from *The House on Mango Street* (see below). The young narrator describes the different types of hair each family member has. The locks vary from stiff hair that stands up in the air, to hair that is thick and straight, to hair that is like fur. And then there is the rebellious hair that refuses to accept hair bands or barrettes. But the most special hair of all smells like fresh bread and symbolizes love, belonging, and security. Vivid illustrations feature the family members on bright backgrounds, each picture framed with playful images of toys, stars, flowers, or birds. Not only do the people have different colors and textures of hair but their faces are of varying hues, providing an intimate portrayal of diversity. Readers of all ages and backgrounds enjoy studying the pictures and reading or listening to the warm, lyrical bilingual text. A natural extension is to discuss (with sensitivity) the similarities and differences in the hair on the heads of the members of the group, whether it be at home, in the library, or in the classroom. After enjoying this exuberant book, readers will want to check out the other stories in *The House on Mango Street*. Hopefully, more of these precious vignettes will find their way into enchanting picture books. The author of this unique book, Sandra Cisneros, notes that she has cropped, straight, shiny black hair.

All Ages

RELATED WORKS
Camille's New Hairdo by Tricia Tusa. Farrar, Straus & Giroux, 1991.
Cornrows by Camille Yarbrough. Coward-McCann, 1979.
An Enchanted Hair Tale by Alexis De Veaux. Harper & Row, 1987.
Hair There and Everywhere by Karin Luisa Badt. Childrens Press, 1994.
Palm Trees by Nancy Cote. Four Winds Press, 1993.

The House on Mango Street
Before Columbus American Book Award

Dedicated "To the Women/A las Mujeres," this stunningly eloquent collection of forty-four short, interrelated vignettes tells the story of Esperanza Cordero, a young girl growing up in the Latino/a section of Chicago. With lyrical power and breathtaking imagery, Cisneros captures the pain of the outsider, the yearning and conflict about belonging and independence, and the poignant search for identity. Esperanza, whose name means hope in English and "too many letters" in Spanish, observes the interactions and happenings in her noisy, crowded neighborhood. As she shares her perceptions of the world around her, she gradually matures and becomes aware of her own strength and beauty. She recounts many touching experiences: the deaths of relatives and neighbors; kids without respect for living things, including themselves; and a humiliating encounter with Sister Superior at school. The lively stories are filled with children jumping rope while making up rhymes, neighbors pitching pennies and playing dominoes, laundry and motorcycles, and coconut and papaya juice. Esperanza describes the girls and women who live on Mango Street: Marin, who is dancing by herself waiting for her life to change; Alicia, who doesn't want to spend her life in a factory or behind a rolling pin; Ruthie, who is a good whistler; Rafaela, whose possessive husband locks her inside their apartment while he plays dominoes; and Sally, who escapes an abusive father into a prison of a marriage. We meet Minerva, who is battered by "her husband who left and keeps leaving," who cries and "writes poems on little pieces of paper that she folds over and over and holds in her hands a long time. . . ."

Cisneros writes that *The House on Mango Street* started out as a memoir but evolved into a collective story based on people from her past and present. She started writing it when she was twenty-two years old and in graduate school. Surrounded by privileged people, studying the works of white writers, she discovered her otherness. She writes that she chose to use a very anti-academic voice in the book: "it's in this rebellious realm of antipoetics that I tried to create a poetic text with the most unofficial language I could find." Thus she created this tender and fierce book about the transformation of a young woman entangled in roots that both enrich and constrain her.

The House on Mango Street was a National Endowment for the Arts Entry in the 1986 Frankfurt and Barcelona International Book Fairs. It has sold over 500,000 copies and is studied in dozens of schools and universities. Rodney D. Smith, a teacher and writer in Piedmont, California, wrote about his experiences using the book in his ninth-grade English class. Before adding the book to the curriculum, he and his colleagues had to overcome criticism from parents, school board members, and coworkers who were concerned that the adoption of the new work would come at the expense of "great literature." They asked what multicultural author could match or excel the works of F. Scott Fitzgerald, Mark Twain, or Shakespeare. Smith responds: "*The House on Mango Street* dispels these criticisms. The book's use of voice, theme, and symbolism, as well as the honesty and clarity of its writing, rival that of the best novels I have ever taught" (*San Francisco Examiner,* A17).

Grades 6–Adult

RELATED WORKS

Spanish Edition: *La Casa en Mango Street.* Random House, 1994.

Audiobook: *Woman Hollering Creek and The House on Mango Street.* Sandra Cisneros reads selections from these two books. Order from Random House Audio Publishing, Dept. JBF (28-2), 201 East 50th Street, New York, NY 10022.

• Short Stories

Woman Hollering Creek and Other Stories

PEN Center West Award for Best Fiction
Anisfield-Wolf Book Award
Lannan Foundation Literary Award
Quality Paperback Book Club New Voices Award

New York Times *Noteworthy Book of the Year*
American Library Journal *Noteworthy Book of the Year*
Los Angeles Times *Best Book of Fiction*

As she drives across the arroyo, Felice "opens her mouth and lets out a yell as loud as any mariachi" (55). Why? Because the name of the creek is Woman Hollering. So every time she crosses the bridge, she hollers. In this evocative collection, Cisneros writes about women's search for independence, for love, for balance. Alternately set in Mexico and the border region of Texas, each story is unique and unforgettable. Cisneros set out to represent her community in an honorable way, stating that she attempted "to populate the book with as many different kinds of Latinos as possible so that mainstream America could see how diverse we are." She continues, "The emotions of almost all the characters are the most autobiographical elements in the stories because I really had to look within myself to make all these characters" (*Authors and Artists for Young Adults [AAYA]*, 74).

In the heartrending story "Eleven," Rachel's birthday is ruined by a cruel teacher. As Rachel burns with humiliation, she thinks, "I wish I was invisible but I'm not . . . I want today to be far away already, far away like a runaway balloon . . ." (9). The old red sweater symbolizes all those other hurts and indignities that Rachel has suffered, the ones that resulted in her being silenced, unable to speak up and say the sweater is not hers. In "Mericans," misogyny rears its ugly head even at an early age when the boys' favorite insult is to call someone "Girl." In "Never Marry a Mexican," the narrator confides, "I'm amphibious. I'm a person who doesn't belong to any class" (71). Some of Cisneros's stories are filled with humor and piercing wit, while others are tender, full of sorrow and so much hurt. These are women who are battered, abandoned, disowned, and shamed and yet they rise up like Ines, Zapata's commonlaw wife who has learned how to abandon her body at will and fly away as an owl. She circles above the village, seeing through the ages, from past to future, watching the fate of her family, of her people. She speaks of "How words can hold their own magic. How a word can charm, and how a word can kill" (105). Cisneros draws on Latin American mythology for some of the stories, but she notes, "I'm very intent on revising mythology because it is male. I'm part of a generation of women that is looking at history in a revisionist manner—in a way that is going to help to empower women to rethink history" (*AAYA*, 75). Another narrator writes a letter in which she says, "those who suffer have a special power, don't they? The power of understanding someone else's pain. And understanding is the beginning of healing" (128). *Woman Hollering Creek* offers much in the way of understanding and healing.

Grades 12–Adult

RELATED WORK

Audiobook: *Woman Hollering Creek and The House on Mango Street.* Sandra Cisneros reads selections from these two books. Order from Random House Audio Publishing, Dept. JBF (28-2), 201 East 50th Street, New York, NY 10022.

Judith Ortiz Cofer

Photo: John Cofer

Puerto Rican American (1952–)

Birthday: February 24
Contact: The Chelsea Forum
420 West 23rd Street, #5D
New York, NY 10011

"My aim as a teacher is to expose students of whatever age to model works of literature that are interesting and accessible, but at the same time I want them to find their own individual voices. My aim is to convince those who want to write that their own lives are the raw material. I show them how they can begin to understand themselves and the world around them by writing about it, as I have done."   (Brochure published by Milledgeville-Baldwin County Allied Arts)

Books by Judith Ortiz Cofer

An Island Like You: Stories of the Barrio. Orchard, 1995.

The Latin Deli: Prose and Poetry. University of Georgia Press, 1993.

The Line of the Sun. University of Georgia Press, 1990.

Peregrina. Riverstone Press, 1986.

Reaching for the Mainland. Bilingual Press, 1987.

Silent Dancing: A Partial Remembrance of a Puerto Rican Childhood. Arte Público Press, 1991.

Terms of Survival. Arte Público Press, 1987.

Judith Ortiz Cofer, an associate professor of English and creative writing at the University of Georgia, is widely recognized for her poetry, fiction, short stories, and essays. Her work has appeared in numerous journals and anthologies. She has won a number of awards for her writing, including the Anisfield Wolf Book Award for *The Latin Deli* and a PEN/Martha Albrand Special Citation for *Silent Dancing*. She has received fellowships from the National Endowment for the Arts, the Witter Bynner Foundation for Poetry, and the Bread Loaf Writers' Conference.

Born in the Puerto Rican town of Hormigueros, Ortiz Cofer was raised in Paterson, New Jersey, and Puerto Rico. Her parents were married when her mother was not quite fifteen years old. Her father joined the United States Army a few months after the wedding and was transferred to Panama, where he stayed for the next two years. Judith was born a year after the wedding and enjoyed the adoration of her mother, grandmother, and aunt for those first few years. Then the family started a pattern that would continue for the remainder of her childhood of moving back and forth between New Jersey and Puerto Rico. The experience of growing up in two worlds was often bewildering, frustrating, and painful. However, this unique heritage has become Ortiz Cofer's literary inspiration: her poetry and prose spring from her experiences as a bicultural and bilingual person. These two parts of herself have contributed substantially to her ability to write poetry and prose that are unique.

Ortiz Cofer's parents, as different as fire and ice, symbolize the dichotomies of her childhood. Her father, quiet and serious, was obsessed with getting out of the barrio and proving that his family was not like other Puerto Ricans. Her mother, earthy and ebullient, reluctantly moved her children back and forth between Puerto Rico and New Jersey, always yearning for her beloved homeland. When they were on the mainland, the children learned to be quiet and inconspicuous and to keep to themselves. Their father was excessively protective and anxious for them to assimilate. Meanwhile, their mother suffered from "*La Tristeza*, the sadness that only place induces and only place cures" (*Silent Dancing*, 61). Ortiz Cofer became an avid watcher of television programs, in which she learned about middle America. She also became an insatiable reader and soon became addicted to fairy tales.

As her family moved from the cold city to the tropical island and back again, Ortiz Cofer became a "cultural chameleon, developing early the ability to blend into a crowd, to sit and read quietly in a fifth story apartment for days and days . . . or, set free, to run wild in Mamá's realm . . ." (*Silent Dancing*, 17). But in either place, she felt like an "oddball." Her peers made fun of her two-way accent: a Spanish accent when she spoke English and when she spoke Spanish, she was told she sounded like a "Gringa." A humiliating experience with a teacher in New Jersey

taught her that language is the only weapon a child has against the power of adults. She quickly began building up her arsenal of words. She served as interpreter and buffer to the world for her mother. Ortiz Cofer was the one who faced store clerks, doctors, and landlords because her mother believed that her exile from Puerto Rico was temporary and therefore did not learn to speak English.

Each time they returned to Puerto Rico, Ortiz Cofer felt "freed . . . like pigeons from a cage" (*Silent Dancing*). Her maternal grandmother was a great storyteller; often her stories were cautionary parables from which her grandchildren were to learn the truth as she saw it. Ortiz Cofer viewed her as her model and liberator. Her grandmother's stories presented contrasting views of women's roles. First, a woman might be like the mythical María Sabida who slept with one eye open, always alert and never a victim. Or she might be like María La Loca, who gave everything up for love and became a victim of her foolish heart. The choices were to get married, become a nun or a prostitute. A woman might become a teacher or nurse until she found a man to marry. But the worst fate of all, according to her grandmother, would be to end up alone.

When Ortiz Cofer was fifteen years old, she went to Puerto Rico for the last time as a child. During her stay there, she realized that she felt smothered by the familial press of her grandmother's home. Resentful at being yanked once again from her life on the mainland, where she felt she was finally beginning to learn the rules, she once again learned a number of valuable lessons from her grandmother. She watched as Mamá

followed a routine of labor and self-sacrifice. She became aware of the new contours and biological changes in her body. During this summer as a *quinceañera*, she thought about the many directions a woman's life might take. Perhaps this is when she decided to pursue her dream of becoming a writer and educator.

Earlier in New Jersey, Ortiz Cofer had entered a high school where she was the only Puerto Rican student. Having gotten into the school after taking a rigorous academic test, she again felt lost. "Everyday I crossed the border of two countries." At the time, she didn't realize that this experience would later provide inspiration for her writing. She learned to depend on knowledge as her main source of security. She loved libraries; they contained the information she needed to survive in two languages and two worlds. She read to escape and also to connect. She notes, "Even now, a visit to the library recharges the batteries in my brain . . . there is no subject I cannot investigate, no world I cannot explore. Everything that is is mine for the asking. Because I can read about it" (*The Latin Deli*, 134).

Her final two and a half years of high school were spent in Augusta, Georgia, where her family moved in search of a more peaceful environment. Her father had retired from the army and relatives in Georgia convinced him that it was a better place to rear teenagers. Ortiz Cofer recalls, "For me it was a shock to the senses, like moving from one planet to another . . ." (*The Latin Deli*, 127). She was the only Puerto Rican in a school of nearly two thousand students. She excelled academically, but her social life was largely uneventful.

She won a scholarship to college and earned a bachelor of arts degree in English from Augusta College in 1971 and a master of arts in English from Florida Atlantic University in 1977. Subsequently, she has been a bilingual teacher, an instructor of both English and Spanish, a lecturer, and has conducted poetry writing workshops. Her many writer-in-residence assignments include Sweet Briar College in Virginia, a women's prison in Georgia, the Guadalupe Cultural Arts Center in San Antonio, and Westchester University in Pennsylvania. She married a native Georgian, Charles John Cofer, in 1971 and has one daughter, Tanya. Currently, she commutes to Athens from her home on the Cofer family farm near Louisville, Georgia.

"I came to writing instinctively, as a dowser finds an underground well. . . . I had found poetry, or it had found me, and it was demanding a place in my life" (*The Latin Deli*, 167). Ortiz Cofer reflects that she felt that something was missing in her life until she started writing. So in order to fit it into her busy schedule, she got up at 5:00 A.M. every day and wrote for two hours. After nearly ten years of writing poetry, she had her first book published. She wrote two pages a day for three and one-half years to complete her first novel, *The Line of the Sun*. This incredible need to write taught her the discipline of art. Painfully aware of the crucial need for social change, she states, "My personal goal in my public life is to try to replace the old pervasive stereotypes and myths about Latinas with a much more interesting set of realities. Every time I give a reading, I hope the stories I tell, the dreams and fears I examine in my work, can achieve some universal truth which will get my audience past the particulars of my skin color, my accent, or my clothes" (*The Latin Deli*, 154).

More Information About Judith Ortiz Cofer

Brochure published by Milledgeville-Baldwin County Allied Arts, Georgia Council for the Arts.

Contemporary Authors. Volume 32, 88–89.

Contemporary Authors. Volume 115, 97–98.

The Latin Deli by Judith Ortiz Cofer. See pages 91–92.

¡Latinas! Women of Achievement, edited by Diane Telgen and Jim Kamp. Visible Ink, 1996.

Notable Hispanic American Women, 103–104. Edited by Diane Telgen and Jim Kamp. Gale Research, 1993.

Silent Dancing: A Partial Remembrance of a Puerto Rican Childhood by Judith Ortiz Cofer. See page 93.

• Short Stories

An Island Like You: Stories of the Barrio

Quick Picks for Reluctant Young Adult Readers
Best Books for Young Adults
Horn Book *Fanfare Award*
Hungry Mind Review *Book of Distinction*

Twelve vibrant stories portray the diverse world of Puerto Rican American teenagers in a New Jersey barrio; these sensitive explorations of adolescence provide insight into the complex experience of growing up in two cultures. Young people of Puerto Rican heritage especially will identify with the challenges and successes depicted in these richly crafted stories; readers of all backgrounds will relate to the universal coming-of-age themes.

Dedicated to the author's family here and on the island, the book opens with a lively poem, "Day in the Barrio." We hear the cinderblock jukebox of El Building blasting salsas, we cross the treacherous bridge of a wino's legs, and we stop at Cheo's bodega for plantains and gossip. We climb the seven flights to the roof where we watch the people below, realizing each one is "an island like you." The interconnected stories introduce likeable, interesting young people. In "Bad Influence," Rita's parents send her to Puerto Rico for a summer with her grandparents to get her away from her boyfriend. Much to her surprise, Rita ends up having one of the best summers of her life. In "Arturo's Flight," the protagonist, ridiculed by his macho classmates for being different, plans to run away. He finds comfort in poetry and the company of an old man who cleans the church. Doris, in "The One Who Watches," feeling scared and invisible, decides she has to start figuring out who she is. She reappears in a later story, "White Balloons," and plays a major role in starting a barrio theater group; she gradually starts feeling fully three-dimensional. "White Balloons" also introduces two gay men, one of whom had grown up in the barrio, escaped to Broadway to become a celebrated actor and returned to start a theater group for young people when he discovered he was HIV-positive.

Written with humor, authenticity, and compassion, the stories in this collection deal with intergenerational issues, eating disorders, peer pressure, death and dying, looksism, sexism, shoplifting, gangs, drugs, mentally challenged people, homosexuality, socioeconomic class, and more. The spirited adolescent characters learn to look closely at people and not to judge them by their age, appearance, disability, gender, language, occupation, or sexual orientation.

Grades 5–10

The Latin Deli: Prose and Poetry

The Anisfield Wolf Book Award

- Short Stories
- Poetry
- Biographical Essays
- Women

By blending fiction, poetry, and autobiographical essays, Judith Ortiz Cofer offers her readers a smorgasbord of the sights, smells, tastes, sounds, emotions, and experiences of Puerto Rican women adjusting to life on the mainland. Winner of the Anisfield Wolf Book Award to honor books "which contribute to . . . our appreciation of the rich diversity of human cultures," *The Latin Deli* is rich in retrospective detail and universal truths. The alternating sections of prose and poetry begin with a portrait of life in El Building in the barrio of Paterson, New Jersey. A sixteen-year-old copes with her excessively protective father's rules by reading. "I felt like an exile in the foreign country of my parents' house. Books kept me from going mad" (16). In another piece, a young woman deals with the racist rejection by her new white boyfriend's mother while the adults around her are mourning the assassination of President Kennedy. In "The Witch's Husband," set in Puerto Rico, Ortiz Cofer's grandmother shares the story of her own flight for freedom while telling her granddaughter an old, old story of a woman who flew away each night to join other women in a ritual of independence. Other pieces explore themes of death and grieving, adultery, self-sacrificing women and patriarchal men, generational conflicts, age, family secrets, and dreams of returning to Puerto Rico after retirement.

A number of the pieces in *The Latin Deli* are autobiographical, and along with *Silent Dancing* provide insight into the life and writing of Judith Ortiz Cofer and her early struggles to consolidate her opposing cultural identities as well as her need and determination to write. She elaborates on the role that literature has played in her life. As a youngster, she discovered fairy tales: "It was the way I absorbed fantasy in those days that gave me the sense of inner freedom, a feeling of power and the ability to fly that is the main reward of the writer" (132). She escaped the turmoils of her nomadic life by turning to books; this insatiable reading, in turn, helped her become more adept with her second language.

Ortiz Cofer also shares her experiences with a dictatorial and straying father, anti–Puerto Rican prejudice, Roman Catholic contradictions regarding the spirit and flesh, and the degradation of African Americans by the educational system. In an especially poignant piece, "The Story of My Body," she describes her physical self; this essay provides a powerful albeit implicit argument for judging people by their character, not their skin color, size, or appearance. The concluding pieces in this moving book provide a glimpse into this gifted author's adult life as a writer, educator, and advocate for communication between and respect for all people.

Grades 12–Adult

• Fiction

The Line of the Sun

New York Library's List of the 25 Most Memorable Books of 1989

Judith Ortiz Cofer's first novel is an eloquent chronicle of the lives of three generations of a Puerto Rican family. It begins in the village of Salud, Puerto Rico, where Mamá Cielo and Papá Pepe are raising their three children, Carmelo, Guzmán, and Ramona. Carmelo, like his father, is a lover of books and solitude. When village gossip reveals that he is gay, he escapes by joining the army, and is killed in Korea a short time later. Ramona is the quiet, obedient daughter who helps take care of the household. She marries Guzmán's best friend, Rafael, who joins the navy soon after the wedding. Guzmán is an exuberant, wild boy whose boundless energy and curiosity constantly propel him into trouble. After a number of escapades, he finally escapes to the United States where the family loses track of him for a number of years.

Years later, the admiration of Ramona's daughter, Marisol, for her adventurous uncle Guzmán and her telling of his life story contrast the world of rural Puerto Rico with that of metropolitan Paterson, New Jersey. The young narrator and secret biographer pieces together the story of her uncle's life through conversations around her mother's kitchen table in their apartment in El Building. Marisol, who has a rebellious streak herself, is elated when the hero of her imagination finally drops in on her family one Christmas Eve. He tells the family how he ended up a prisoner in a labor camp and eventually escaped to become a subway warrior. Marisol, who is feeling alienated from her parents and is frustrated with living in a state of limbo between two cultures, identifies with her uncle and his restless spirit. When he is injured, she becomes his confidante and personal spy, reporting on the imminent labor strike, spiritist meetings, and police surveillance of El Building. The inevitable tragedy results in Guzmán's return to Puerto Rico. Marisol continues to tell his story as she follows her line of the sun, her future as read in the lines in her hand.

Grades 12–Adult

RELATED WORK
The House on the Lagoon by Rosario Ferré. Farrar, Straus & Giroux, 1995.

Silent Dancing:
A Partial Remembrance of a Puerto Rican Childhood

New York Library Best Books for the Teen Age
PEN Martha Albrand Special Citation for Non-Fiction
Pushcart Prize for the Essay "More Room"

These beautifully written memoirs eloquently express the complex experience of growing up in two worlds, of learning to be a "cultural chameleon." Judith Ortiz Cofer relates the story of the first fifteen years of her life through prose and poetry, revealing the ways in which her bicultural/bilingual childhood shaped her identity and contributed to her development as a writer and teacher. Her literary mentor, Virginia Woolf, provided inspiration for her process of reclaiming memories to discover meaning and truth in ordinary events. With insight and sensitivity, Ortiz Cofer addresses the themes of female roles and conditioning, dual existence, and the clash of culture and age.

Ortiz Cofer's parents, as different as fire and ice, symbolize the dichotomies of her childhood. Her father, quiet and serious, joined the navy before Judith was born. He was obsessed with getting out of the barrio and proving that his family was not like other Puerto Ricans. Her mother, earthy and ebullient, reluctantly moved her children back and forth between Puerto Rico and New Jersey, always yearning for her beloved homeland. Ortiz Cofer portrays her maternal grandmother, Mamá, a storyteller and the family matriarch, with admiration and sensitivity. One of Mamá's stories is included in the book; the tale of María Sabida provides a model of the "prevailing woman" who was always alert and never a victim. Grandmother's *cuentos* inspired her young granddaughter and are thus "forever woven into the fabric of my imagination." Ortiz Cofer includes a María Sabida fable that she embroidered to entertain herself when she was quite young.

Grades 10–Adult

Terms of Survival

In these fifty moving poems, Judith Ortiz Cofer explores the process of change, assimilation, and transformation. In "El Olvido," she cautions that it is dangerous to forget the climate of one's birthplace. She writes about her family, both the ones who came to the United States and those who remained on the island of Puerto Rico. Wanting to be released from rituals, she writes about faith, madness, wickedness, always and never, poverty, prostitutes, and dreams, as she confronts customs, rites of passage, and cultural icons. In "So Much for Mañana," her mother urges her to return to the island before her brain splits from all her studying. In "Exile," Ortiz Cofer writes, "I left my home behind me/but my past clings to my fingers/so that every word I write/bears the mark . . . of my birthplace." Writing poetry is her way of recovering the past and creating the future. She wrote most of these poems during a residency at the Virginia Center for the Creative Arts. She elaborates on the themes of some of these poems in her autobiography, *Silent Dancing.* A glossary of Spanish words and terms is provided.

RELATED WORK

See *Poetry* in the Subject Index.

Grades 10–Adult

Lulu Delacre

Puerto Rican American (1957–)

Birthday: December 20
Contact: Publicity
Scholastic Inc.
555 Broadway
New York, NY 10012-3999

"Anything you want, you can achieve, as long as you work hard for it."
(personal communication)

"I believe childhood should be a wonderful stage in a person's life, and if my drawings add a little happiness in a child's day, I consider my life fulfilled." (Something About the Author, *Volume 36, 67*)

Books by Lulu Delacre

WRITTEN AND ILLUSTRATED

Arroz con Leche: Popular Songs and Rhymes from Latin America. Scholastic, 1989.

Golden Tales: Myths, Legends, and Folktales from Latin America. Scholastic, 1996. (Spanish Edition: *De oro y esmeraldas.* Scholastic, 1996.)

Las Navidades: Popular Christmas Songs from Latin America. Scholastic, 1990.

Nathan and Nicholas Alexander. Scholastic, 1986.

Nathan's Balloon Adventure. Scholastic, 1991 (Book Club Edition).

Nathan's Fishing Trip. Scholastic, 1988.

Peter Cottontail's Easter Book. Scholastic, 1991.

Time for School, Nathan. Scholastic, 1989.

Vejigante Masquerader. Scholastic, 1993.

ILLUSTRATED

The Bossy Gallito/El Gallo de Bodas: A Traditional Cuban Folktale retold by Lucía M. Gonzales. Scholastic, 1994.

Lulu Delacre is the accomplished author and illustrator of a number of award-winning books for young readers. A multitalented artist and writer, she speaks three languages fluently: Spanish, English, and French. Her work has been exhibited in the United States, Puerto Rico, and Paris. Sought after as a speaker, she has given presentations at numerous schools, conferences, and institutes.

Born in Rio Piedras, Puerto Rico, Delacre is the middle child in a family of three daughters. Her parents, Marta Orzabal Delacre, a French professor, and Georges Carlos Delacre, a philosophy professor, are from Argentina. Delacre has fond memories of growing up on the sunny, hot island. She often climbed a tamarindo tree with a friend to eat the fruit. On weekends, her father frequently took his three daughters to the beach, where they enjoyed watching the small tropical fish among the rocks along the shore.

Delacre's earliest memory of drawing takes her back to her grandmother's house. Her grandma, who was from Uruguay, took care of the children while their parents taught at the University of Puerto Rico. Delacre spent many happy hours lying on the floor, drawing as they listened to classical music on the record player. Her grandmother saved all her drawings and neatly stacked them in a corner of her closet. The children also loved disguising themselves with their grandmother's scarfs and hats and dancing in front of an old mirror in her room.

When she was ten years old, Delacre's family spent a year in Buenos Aires, Argentina, where her father was on sabbatical leave. It was there that she had her first formal art training. One of her mother's friends, who was a fine artist and who gave lessons to adults, encouraged the talented young artist to join her class. Delacre learned to draw from real life and her joy in being able to create intensified. Her parents encouraged her to pursue her artistic abilities and she enjoyed withdrawing into her own private world of dreams as she drew.

By the time she entered the Department of Fine Arts at the University of Puerto Rico, Delacre knew she wanted to be an artist. At nineteen she was in Paris, where she had been accepted on a full schol-arship at the distinguished art school L'Ecole Supérieure d'Arts Graphiques. She spent three years of intensive study of photography, typography, design, and illustration. During her second year there, she was very impressed with an exhibit of the work of Maurice Sendak. Her honors thesis was an audiovisual project illustrating *Carnival of the Animals* by Saint-Saëns. Her hard work combined with her talent resulted in her graduating first in her class. By then she knew she wanted to become a children's book illustrator.

Delacre has a reputation for high standards in both text and art, often thoughtfully appending fascinating background information such as author's and artist's notes, recipes, pronunciation guides, and bibliographies to her books. She creates books inspired by the folklore from her childhood and the traditions that were a part of her life on the island. One of her favorite mediums is color pencil, and she loves spending hours working on a drawing. She sometimes playfully hides tiny lizards within the pages of a book, adding to the appeal of her already engrossing titles. Her latest book, *Golden Tales: Myths, Legends, and Folktales from Latin America,* is her most extensive work to date. She notes, "If painting the people and places of Latin America true to their own beauty fosters respect, or if sharing some of the golden tales builds bridges among children, I want to keep on doing it. Because for me, that is the true measure of success. ¡*Viva nuestra herencia!*" (Scholastic Brochure).

Delacre enjoys getting to know the people and traditions of different countries and has traveled to Egypt, Turkey, Spain, Mexico, Israel, Greece, Italy, and England. She has lived in Puerto Rico, Argentina, France, and the United States. In addition to writing and illustrating children's books, she has been featured in *Sesame Street Magazine* and other magazines and textbooks. She enjoys walking the cobblestone streets of Old San Juan, Puerto Rico with her children. And as they stroll along the cobblestones, she tells them the legends and tales that were told to her when she was a child.

More Information About Lulu Delacre

Scholastic Brochure.

School Library Journal. February 1993, 71.

Something About the Author. Volume 36, 65–67.

Arroz con Leche:
Popular Songs and Rhymes from Latin America

Horn Book *Fanfare Book*

- Bilingual
- Music
- Nursery Rhymes

This merry bilingual collection of twelve rhymes from Mexico, Puerto Rico, and Argentina features the original Spanish versions and rhyming English translations. Musical notations for nine of the rhymes are appended, and games or fingerplays associated with several of the selections are described at the bottom of the pages. Lovely detailed pastel illustrations accompany each of the rhymes, often portraying actual places such as Old San Juan Cathedral in Puerto Rico. The playful elephants who balance so nimbly on the spider's web in "The Graceful Elephant" are enchanting! And tiny lizards mischievously hide amidst many of the pictures. Lulu Delacre includes an informative Artist's Note, a bibliography, and a tasty recipe for *arroz con leche*, rice and milk. She learned these songs when she was a child and created this book because she wanted to share her favorite childhood poems and music with her two daughters. The cheerful kaleidoscope of songs and rhymes from the oral tradition will be enjoyed by those who know them and provide a pleasurable introduction to those for whom they are new. The positive response to this title inspired Delacre to create a second book of songs with a similar format, *Las Navidades*.

Preschool–Grade 3

RELATED WORKS

Cassette: Available from Scholastic.

Book: *La Navidad: Christmas in Spain and Latin America* by Agnes M. Brady and Margarita Márquez de Moats. National Textbook Company, 1992.

Songs: *Las Navidades: Popular Christmas Songs from Latin America* selected and illustrated by Lulu Delacre. Scholastic, 1990. See page 98.

• Birds
• Roosters
• Folklore
• Cumulative Tales

The Bossy Gallito/El gallo de bodas: A Traditional Cuban Folktale

Notable Trade Book in the Field of Social Studies
Aesop Accolade List
New York Public Library Best Book for Reading and Sharing

An overbearing rooster finds that others do not care for his bossy ways. On his way to his uncle's wedding, he discovers that he needs assistance. Will he make it to the wedding on time? What is the magic word that will summon forth help? This is the Cuban version of a traditional story that came to Cuba and other Latin American countries from Spain long ago. There are many other versions of this popular tale found in various cultures around the world. One is the traditional passover song "Had Gadya," which is believed to have roots in French nursery songs dating back many hundreds of years. Another version is "The Old Woman and the Pig." The author, Lucía M. Gonzales, grew up in Cuba listening to her tía abuela Nena tell stories. *El gallo de bodas* became the author's favorite story, as she listened to her great-aunt tell it many times. She notes that it is known by most Cuban children on the island and she hopes that traditional stories such as this one will continue to be told to Latina/o children in the United States.

Lulu Delacre illustrated this satisfyingly predictable, repetitive story using watercolors with colored pencils and gouache. In preparing to illustrate *The Bossy Gallito*, she took hundreds of photographs of the streets, the people, and the native birds of Little Havana, the Cuban area of Miami. Her research combined with her talent as an artist resulted in a beautifully designed book, filled with amusing and authentic details. Dozens of magnificent birds grace the pages, inviting readers to pore over the enchanting pictures. A glossary of terms and informative notes from both the author and illustrator add to the usefulness of this bilingual title.

Preschool–Grade 3

RELATED WORK

The Rooster Who Went to His Uncle's Wedding: A Latin American Folktale retold by Alma Flor Ada. Illustrated by Kathleen Kuchera. Putnam, 1993. See page 23.

Golden Tales:
Myths, Legends, and Folktales from Latin America

- Legends
- Myths
- Folktales
- History
- Art

Twelve classic tales come together in one volume, bringing thirteen countries and four native cultures from which they emerged into a vivid new perspective. This sparkling treasury combines folklore, history, geography, and art, celebrating the many-faceted cultures of Latin America. Author-artist Lulu Delacre remembers listening to spellbinding tales as she was growing up in Puerto Rico. Years later, she searched for an illustrated collection to share with her own children. Unable to find a volume that conveyed the beauty, complexity, and depth of the stories she knew as a child, she decided to create one herself. This magnificent labor of love is the result. After years of extensive research, writing, and painting, Delacre has succeeded in creating an exquisite volume filled with grace, beauty, drama, and strength.

Each of the sections, featuring the Taino, the Zapotec, the Muisca, and the Inca, is prefaced with an introductory passage that provides historical and cultural information about the group. Fascinating stories explain such phenomena as how the rainbow was born, why the sun is brighter than the moon, how the sea was born, and why you can see a rabbit's picture in the full moon. Here we read about changing cultures, miracles, tragic romance, lightning gods disguised as lizards, a lagoon serpent, the sun who loved all the people and animals who inhabited the earth, messages hidden in a code of colored yarns and knots, and much more. These are the poignant stories of the native peoples of the Americas who found themselves conquered and ruled by Spain. And this is a glimpse of the literature that emerged during this turbulent time of change.

Delacre's vibrant oil paintings convey the mystery and magic of these compelling tales. Her distinctive linocuts enable her to get even closer to the art forms used by some of the indigenous cultures, authentically portraying early design motifs based on realia such as a solar disk from a gold pendant, a funerary vessel, a gold and turquoise earring, the Inca zodiac, a chief's wooden stool, a carved face from a Taino bone vessel, and an early colonial Peruvian tunic. Delicate linocut borders adorn the pages, adding to the beauty of this exquisite book. Delacre's respect for the tales of her childhood, extensive research, loving attention to detail, and imaginative approach to art, design, and storytelling have culminated in her most powerful work to date. She thoughtfully includes detailed notes and sources for each tale, early and modern maps, and an extensive pronunciation guide.

Grades 4–Adult

RELATED WORK

Spanish Edition: *De oro y esmeraldas.* Scholastic, 1996.

- Bilingual
- Christmas
- Epiphany
- Music
- Nursery Rhymes

Las Navidades: Popular Christmas Songs from Latin America

Thirteen holiday songs from Puerto Rico, Santo Domingo, Mexico, and Venezuela are presented in Spanish and English. Following the same format as the earlier collection *Arroz con Leche,* this title features the illustrated rhymes in the first section of the book followed by the musical arrangements for the songs. Arranged chronologically beginning with Christmas Eve to New Year's and Epiphany on the sixth day of January, the order of the songs will help the reader travel through the holidays. Lulu Delacre went to the countryside of Puerto Rico to research the illustrations for this project. She notes, "In the process, something wonderful happened. As nostalgic memories of Christmas on the island came to me, I rediscovered the traditions from my childhood." She adds that because some of these customs are slowly disappearing, she created this book in an attempt to preserve them. As she has done in her other well-researched books, she has added creative touches to this title that make it all the more noteworthy. Many of the rhymes are accompanied by notes depicting traditional activities associated with the holidays. Information about and drawings of the musical instruments traditionally used to accompany the songs are included. A bibliography, artist's note, a mouthwatering picture and recipe for *Rosca de Reyes*—Three Kings Cake—and Delacre's special hidden lizards are all tucked inside this beautifully illustrated book.

Preschool–Grade 3

RELATED WORKS
Cassette: Available from Scholastic.

Book: *La Navidad: Christmas in Spain and Latin America* by Agnes M. Brady and Margarita Márquez de Moats. National Textbook Company, 1992.

Songs: *Arroz con Leche: Popular Songs and Rhymes from Latin America,* selected and illustrated by Lulu Delacre. Scholastic, 1989. See pages 95–96.

- Elephants
- Mice
- Friendship

Nathan and Nicholas Alexander

What happens when a worldly-wise mouse sets up house in the toy chest of a good-natured but territorial elephant? How these two unlikely characters overcome their differences and become friends is the very special story of *Nathan and Nicholas Alexander.* Lulu Delacre's detailed pastels accent this charming story of a friendship that starts out rather violently and ends up with two pals working together to restore order. Somehow we know this is the beginning of something wonderful as the two begin making plans for an outing the following day. Young readers will enjoy viewing the story from both sides, as they listen to or read this gentle lesson about sharing.

Preschool–Grade 2

RELATED WORKS
Nathan's Balloon Adventure. Scholastic, 1991 (Book Club Edition).

Nathan's Fishing Trip. Scholastic, 1988.

Time for School, Nathan. Scholastic, 1989.

Nathan's Balloon Adventure

- Elephants
- Mice
- Hot Air Balloons

Nathan and Nicholas Alexander have traveled long and far to visit Nicholas's cousin Henri. Today's itinerary includes a ride in a hot air balloon. But is Nathan too big, too young, and too clumsy to join the two mice in this exciting adventure? Readers will enjoy this breathtaking flight across field and plain and learn, along with Henri, not to judge someone by their size and age. Lulu Delacre has added another engaging chapter to the escapades of this plucky elephant and his urbane mouse-friend. She delights in the tiniest of detail in her charming watercolors. This book is available only through the book club, but it might already be in your school or public library.

Preschool–Grade 2

RELATED WORKS

Nathan and Nicholas Alexander. Scholastic, 1986.

Nathan's Fishing Trip. Scholastic, 1988.

Time for School, Nathan. Scholastic, 1989.

Nathan's Fishing Trip

- Elephants
- Mice
- Kindness to Animals

When Nathan and his new friend, Nicholas Alexander, set out on their first excursion together, they learn an important lesson about the best laid plans of mice and elephants. What could possibly go wrong on a fishing trip? How did this odd couple end up losing everything including their balance? Lulu Delacre's delightful illustrations and accomplished storytelling add up to a book that young readers will enjoy again and again. And the surprise ending spells relief for those of us who love all creatures great and small. Now what mischief will Nathan and Nicholas Alexander get into next?

Preschool–Grade 2

RELATED WORKS

Nathan and Nicholas Alexander. Scholastic, 1986.

Nathan's Balloon Adventure. Scholastic, 1991 (Book Club Edition).

Time for School, Nathan. Scholastic, 1989.

Peter Cottontail's Easter Book
American Bookseller *Pick of the Lists*

- Easter
- Art
- Music
- Traditions

"Easter was originally an ancient European pagan festival honoring the spring and dawn goddess, Eástre." So begins this sampling of some of the customs associated with Easter. Lulu Delacre skillfully interweaves music, games, recipes, information, and activities into this playful book about Easter. Her engaging illustrations are full of whimsical details, and she is up to her old trick of hiding objects within the pictures. She even takes us to the

White House for an annual event dating from 1878. This lively book begins with an author's note and ends with a bibliography.

RELATED WORK

A Surprise for Mother Rabbit by Alma Flor Ada. Laredo, 1993. See page 24.

- Elephants
- Mice
- Jealousy
- School

Time for School, Nathan

The first day of school is a very momentous occasion, and Nathan wants everything to go just so. But something (or someone) keeps going wrong. Why is poor Nathan sitting so forlornly alone under that tree? And where is his friend, Nicholas? By combining her storytelling and artistic talents, Lulu Delacre has created another engaging tale about the ups and downs of friendship. Nathan and Nicholas fans will applaud this appealing chapter featuring the irresistible duo. And everyone will want a turn to tell about *their* first day of school.

Preschool–Grade 2

RELATED WORKS

Nathan and Nicholas Alexander. Scholastic, 1986.

Nathan's Balloon Adventure. Scholastic, 1991 (Book Club Edition).

Nathan's Fishing Trip. Scholastic, 1988.

- Bilingual
- Carnival
- Fiestas

Vejigante Masquerader

National Council of Teachers of English Notable Children's Book
Américas Book Award
American Bookseller *Pick of the Lists*

A boy fulfills his dream of masquerading with the older boys at Carnival. Each year in February, Carnival brings throngs of masqueraders to celebrate in the streets of cities in Latin America and Spain. The *vejigantes* of Ponce, Puerto Rico, celebrate for the entire month of February, before and after Carnival. This year, Ramón is so determined to take an active role in the festivities that he has secretly made his own costume. He has worked hard to save his earnings from running errands for Doña Ana, who has taken time to teach him how to sew. Now, in disguise, he can join El Gallo's group as they play the traditional, good-natured pranks and no one will recognize him. What problem does Ramón encounter that threatens to ruin his plan? Who steps in to help remedy the situation? Will Ramón have to wait another year to fulfill his dream? These and other questions will be answered as readers enjoy this bilingual story about traditions and persistence.

Lulu Delacre has created a well-researched, fascinating book, made all the more interesting by the creative touches she adds. Early in the book, she challenges her readers to find twenty-eight lizards, one for each day in February, hidden in the pictures. Some are easy to find but others are well hidden and will provide an amusing challenge. This playful strategy encourages readers of all ages to scrutinize the illustrations closely. She also includes background details about *vejigantes,* information about other masqueraders from Latin America and Spain, a glossary, a bibliography, and *vejigantes* chants. Directions for making your own *vejigante* mask are well thought out and easy to follow. The bilingual text and the detailed illustrations pull the reader into the story, capturing the ups and downs of the drama. Readers will enjoy discussing the book, possibly recasting it in the good news–bad news motif. They might even try hiding little lizards or other creatures in their next drawing.   Grades 2–5

RELATED WORK
Tonight Is Carnaval by Arthur Dorros. Dutton, 1991.

Ofelia Dumas Lachtman

Mexican American (1919–)

Birthday: July 9
Contact: Arte Público Press
University of Houston
Houston, Texas 77204-2090

"She was deeply tired but at peace, as if a storm had caught her in its vortex, whirling her around and around and finally tossing her on to a sheltered, tranquil place. . . . Maybe life had to come to a standstill to be grasped at all. Maybe life had to come to a standstill for it to start." (A Shell for Angela, *213*)

Books by Ofelia Dumas Lachtman

Campfire Dreams. Harlequin Books, 1987 (out of print).

The Girl from Playa Blanca. Piñata Books: Arte Público Press, 1995.

Pepita Talks Twice/Pepita habla dos veces. Illustrated by Alex Pardo DeLange. Piñata Books: Arte Público Press, 1995.

A Shell for Angela. Arte Público Press, 1995.

The daughter of Mexican immigrants, Ofelia Dumas Lachtman is a native of Los Angeles. She attended Los Angeles city schools and later Los Angeles City College. After studying at the University of California at Los Angeles for a brief period, she got married and moved to Riverside, California. Dumas Lachtman has a daughter and a son.

During World War II, Dumas Lachtman worked as a medical stenographer. Later, when her children were grown, she became a group worker and eventually assumed a position as the executive director of the West Los Angeles–Beverly Hills YWCA.

Dumas Lachtman's interest in writing started when she was a child. Her first publication came at age twelve, when her work appeared in an anthology of children's poetry. Her writing credits include publication in the *Chicago Tribune, The Christian Science Monitor, The Boston Globe, The Washington Times, Newsday, The St. Petersburg Times, The Dallas Morning News, The Detroit News, Michigan Magazine, Green's Magazine,* and numerous other periodicals.

Recently, three of Dumas Lachtman's books were published by Arte Público Press, one for children, one for young adults, and one for older teenagers and adults. She is also the author of *Campfire Dreams,* a young adult novel which has been translated into French and German. Dumas Lachtman's work explores a variety of important themes including bilingualism, identity, loss, internalized racism, and women's roles. Her books feature Latina protagonists who are resourceful, assertive, and likeable. She has a unique way of writing that leads readers to look forward to her next book. She has written several books that will be published in the near future, including another picture book for children.

Ofelia Dumas Lachtman now makes her home in Los Angeles, where she writes novels and stories. She is a member of the Society for Children's Book Writers, International PEN, and Sisters in Crime, a group for women mystery writers.

The Girl from Playa Blanca

Benjamin Franklin Award for Young Adult Fiction

- Mystery
- Immigration

When Elena and her little brother, Carlos, leave their seaside village in Mexico to search for their immigrant father in Los Angeles, they encounter intrigue, crime, mystery, and friendship. After not hearing from her father for five months, seventeen-year-old María Elena Vargas courageously sets out to find him. But when they arrive in Los Angeles, he has disappeared. Fortunately, Elena has a letter of introduction from her mentor in Playa Blanca to Ana and Salvador Montalvo, a wealthy couple who live in a beautiful Malibu mansion. While she works for them, she conducts her search for her father. The story that unfolds entails stolen letters, an old deed, a mysterious storeroom, a bungled kidnapping, hidden treasure, and a fatal accident. As Elena meets a devious gang member, a taciturn restaurant owner, a mysterious archaeologist, a seemingly kind employer with a puzzling vision impairment, an enigmatic law student, and a household of perplexing servants, she struggles to unravel the tangles of the web. Whom can she trust? "The broken pieces of information that she had gathered were arranging and rearranging themselves in her mind like the fragments of a kaleidoscope" (181).

Elena is a resourceful, likeable protagonist whose sleuthing skills improve as the story progresses. Ofelia Dumas Lachtman, who has an ear for dialogue and a talent for suspense, has written a fascinating book. Perhaps Elena's sleuthing skills will evolve into a new mystery series!

Grades 5–9

Pepita Talks Twice/Pepita habla dos veces

Skipping Stones *Book Award*

- Bilingualism
- Problem Solving
- Canine Companions

Pepita, a little girl who can converse in Spanish and English, decides not to "speak twice" until unanticipated problems cause her to "think twice." Pepita has grown accustomed to using her bilingual skills to help those around her. It seems that everyone calls upon her for assistance. The corner grocer, neighbors, relatives, and teachers are always asking her to translate. Finally, one day she becomes frustrated with her role as translator and decides that she is never going to speak Spanish again. She maintains her position through a number of unanticipated situations. It is her canine companion, Wolf/Lobo, who helps her reconsider her decision.

Ofelia Dumas Lachtman has created an engaging story about the benefits and challenges of bilingualism. Pepita is an assertive, resourceful girl who is gaining skill in solving problems, and young readers will enjoy discussing other options that she might consider in dealing with the constant requests for help. The book might also serve as a reminder to adults to spread the translating tasks around so that one child is not overwhelmed. This charming book is illustrated with detailed, colorful pictures by Alex Pardo DeLange, a Venezuelan-born artist.

Grades K–3

• Identity
• Internalized Racism
• Death
• Grieving
• Passing for Anglo

A Shell for Angela

This poignant novel traces the emotional and cultural journey of a woman whose traumatic childhood experiences lead her to reject her Mexican heritage and family. At the age of nine, living in a barrio in Los Angeles during the Depression era, Angela Martín witnesses the beating and arrest of her father by immigration officials. When her family learns of his death, Angela accompanies her mother on a sad and harrowing trip to Mexico for his funeral. During the service, the young girl is further confused by the words of the priest, who speaks of sin, evil, and the everlasting fires of hell. In fear and bewilderment, she withdraws from the mourners and spends the remainder of the day alone in the cemetery. The wounds inflicted by these experiences are compounded by the racist messages she receives at school and in the community as well as the internalized racism at home. Her mother, cautioning her to wear a hat to shade her from the sun, comments that she is "shamelessly brown" (90). Angela has no one to answer her questions, no one to tell her that her people are beautiful, strong, and good. Instead, she remembers her mother's anguished words after her husband's arrest: "What was his crime, eh? I will tell you. He is a Mexican. And in this country, it is a crime to be a Mexican" (195). And so Angela internalizes the lies that society teaches about Mexican Americans and spends many years denying her heritage. She tries to live the life of a perfect suburban housewife and passes as an Anglo. But a new crisis in her life leads her to revisit her early experiences and decisions. "She became again the little girl with the hand-me-down nationality, caught between two selves, trying to make one fit" (80). As she begins her troubled journey to the past, she struggles to unravel the painful threads of her life.

Ofelia Dumas Lachtman has beautifully captured the complexities, paradoxes, and poignancy of Angela's dilemma. Angela's indecision, vacillation, and ill-defined despair are portrayed with insight and compassion. This fine book explores issues of exploitation of farmworkers, unresolved grief, self-abnegation, the constricting roles open to women, identity confusion, class upward mobility, and life-threatening illnesses.

Note: Regarding the use of the term "Japs" on page 157: When disparaging remarks are made by racist characters, it is clear that they are wrong. But in this case, the word was used by Angela, an otherwise admirable character.

Grades 11–Adult

RELATED WORKS
Internalized Racism: *The Shimmershine Queens* by Camille Yarbrough. Putnam, 1989.

Lyll Becerra de Jenkins

Photo: Natalie Stultz

Colombian (1925–1997)

"I am glad that I write novels for young adults. I feel that, in some small way, I'm endowed with a certain responsibility. Perhaps, through my stories, I can illuminate their lives and stimulate their compassion and understanding, their love for the universal family."
(Lodestar brochure)

Books by Lyll Becerra de Jenkins

Celebrating the Hero. Lodestar Books, 1993; Penguin, 1995.

The Honorable Prison. Lodestar Books, 1988; Penguin, 1989.

So Loud a Silence. Lodestar Books, 1996.

Lyll Becerra de Jenkins was the author of the widely acclaimed *The Honorable Prison* and *Celebrating the Hero,* both written for young adults. Her short stories appeared in periodicals and books around the world, including *The New Yorker, The New York Times,* and *Best American Short Stories.* Dedicated to broadening the scope of literature for young readers, she made a significant contribution to the field.

Born and raised in Colombia, Jenkins's first school was in a convent with Benedictine nuns on the islands of San Andres y Providencia. When her parents moved the family to Colón, Panama, she was enrolled in a bilingual American school inside the Canal Zone. Later, she attended the Convent of Maria Auxiliadora in Soacha, a town to the north of Bogotá. When her family moved to the coastal town of Cartagena, she attended Colegio Biffi, where she was taught by German Franciscan nuns. After graduation, she trained to be a bilingual secretary. Jenkins acted in Teatro Municipal of Bogotá, under the direction of Alejandro Acevedo, a Spanish director from Madrid exiled in Colombia. She also took dancing lessons in Escuela de Danza Jacinto Jaramillo, where she specialized in flamenco.

After she and her husband and their five children were settled in the United States, Jenkins began writing fiction. She remembered her first lesson in fiction when she was a young girl and had no idea she would some day become a writer. It was customary for her family to have discussions after meals in what was called *la sobremesa.* One day, as Jenkins was sharing an incident that had taken place that day at the convent, her sister kept interrupting, saying that she was exaggerating. Their father intervened, encouraging Jenkins to continue expressing her perceptions of what had happened. Years later, when she sat down to write her first stories, she recalled her father's words. She soon learned that facts do not make good fiction. She noted, "It's in the reinvention of the truth that I, as a writer, find the dimensions of my experiences and their full essence and significance."

Jenkins enjoyed writing about family relationships, their joys, pain, and conflicts. Her first short story, a sad tale about one of her brothers, was accepted and published by *The New Yorker*. By fictionalizing the story, Jenkins gained insight into his true character and his motivations. Her next story was about a family living under a military dictatorship. After it too was published in *The New Yorker*, Jenkins received several letters asking what happened to the people in the story. This was the beginning of her first book, the award-winning *The Honorable Prison*, which is a fictionalized account of her personal experiences. Her second book, *Celebrating the Hero*, is also based on family events. Her third book, *So Loud a Silence*, grew out of the experiences of her brother-in-law, who was kidnapped and held for ransom.

Being bilingual, Jenkins found it interesting that she instinctively wrote in English when she is in the United States and in Spanish when she visited her relatives in South America. When one of her editors told her that they wanted to preserve her accent in her stories, she felt a strong incentive to share her experiences and insights. Jenkins's books give a fresh perspective to the traditional coming-of-age novel and bring the country of her birth to life in all its complexity. Reviewers have praised her powerful novels, noting that they will grip the attention of young adults and inject their thinking with new awareness. *The Christian Science Monitor* recommended *The Honorable Prison* highly, and, the Chicago *Sun-Times* proposed that it be required reading for high school students. The response to Jenkins' second novel was equally enthusiastic. The two remarkable books established Lyll Becerra de Jenkins' reputation as a wise and perceptive chronicler of the human condition.

- Family Secrets
- Grandparents
- Colombia
- Gender Roles
- Grieving

Celebrating the Hero

Children's Book of the Year, Bank Street College
Parents' *Choice Story Book Honor Award*
New York Public Library Book for the Teen Age
Consortium of Latin American Studies Award Nominee

After her mother's death, seventeen-year-old Camila Draper travels to San Javier, Colombia, to attend a ceremony honoring her late grandfather and, while trying to learn more about her mother's relatives, uncovers disturbing family secrets. During her early years, Camila had enjoyed listening to her mother reminiscing about her childhood, her homeland, and her father. But as she grew older, she became tired of these stories and told her mother to stop talking about the past. After her mother's unexpected death, she is haunted by the silences she imposed on her mother. She is filled with "questions I want to ask that I cannot formulate to myself, in English or Spanish. I know only that the questions are there, within me, weighty as rocks" (57). As she searches for the truth, she is met with evasions, riddles, hints, and hostility. She wonders if there is a conspiracy to keep her from learning about her grandfather. Was he really the Illustrious Son, the hero he is purported to have been? As she unravels the tangled threads of the past, she learns some painful but important truths about the subjugation of women, the lengths relatives and community members will go to to protect prominent men, and the abuses of power, loyalty, and trust within a family and a community. This is a perceptive novel about grieving, denial, contradictions, silences, misogyny, fabricated truths, remorse, and illusions.

Lyll Becerra de Jenkins notes that *Celebrating the Hero*, her second novel, like her first, is based on family history. Even though her grandmother had a beautiful voice and studied singing and piano in an exclusive music school in Bogotá, Colombia, her husband had prohibited her from singing. Jenkins didn't know all the details because she, like Camila, had been bored with stories about her relatives and had not listened attentively. When she began writing the book, she struggled to remember everything she had heard about her grandmother. Then she realized that the facts did not matter—that the creative process involves sorting out and choosing the ideas that fit the work. The book has been praised by critics as a beautifully crafted novel that makes an eloquent contribution to the growing body of immigrant literature.

Grades 7–12

The Honorable Prison

Scott O'Dell Award for Historical Fiction
Booklist *Best Book of the Decade*
Booklist *Children's Editors' Choice*
Parents' *Choice "Shoe-in Winner"*
New York Public Library 100 Titles for Giving and Sharing
ABA-CBC Children's Books Mean Business
National Conference of Christians and Jews Recommended Book
Zilveren Griffel *for the Best Book Published in the Netherlands*

- Historical Fiction
- South America
- Political Prisoners
- Freedom of Speech

Because of the political stand taken by her father, a newspaper editor who persistently opposes the military dictatorship of their unnamed country, Marta Maldonado and her family are imprisoned by the government. Seventeen-year-old Marta, her thirteen-year-old brother, and their parents are preparing to flee the country when they are taken from their home and jailed in an isolated pueblo near a military outpost in the Andes. Marta's first-person narrative provides an unflinching portrayal of the traumatic year they spend in the "honorable prison," as well as of her own personal growth and political awakening. As the family struggles with the cold, damp climate, the shortage of food and medicine, the fear of impending violence, and the isolation and monotony of their imprisonment, Marta gradually realizes that she has lived a privileged, self-absorbed life. She reexamines her resentment of the position Papa has taken against the atrocities committed by their government, and she tries to hold on to her dream of freedom as her father's chronic lung condition deteriorates and they all face starvation.

The Honorable Prison is a gripping story that reveals the devastating impact of political repression on one family. It is an eloquent tribute to all those courageous individuals who have taken a stand against social injustice and human rights abuses. As Papa taught Marta to understand and respect the *campesinos,* so will this poignant book inspire readers to educate themselves about the injustices of class oppression. Jenkins wrote the book as a "fusion of personal experiences and invention." She notes that while she was writing the novel, she "was full of doubts. Was I properly conveying to American readers the meaning of living in house imprisonment under a dictator general? I never expected my novel to be so well received or so fully understood" (Lodestar brochure). Indeed, the critical response to her book has been overwhelmingly positive. *Horn Book* stated, "Like *The Diary of Anne Frank,* it is a stern reminder of the dangers inherent in government gone mad and a celebration of the best in our common humanity—the spiritual triumph of those refusing to be subjugated."

Grades 7–12

RELATED WORK
Spanish Edition: *La prision de honor.* Editorial Norma, 1989.

Carmen Lomas Garza

Photo: Helleah Tsinhnahjinnie

Chicana (1948–)

Birthday: September 12, 1948
Contact: Children's Book Press
246 1st Street, #101
San Francisco, CA 94105

"From the time I was a young girl, I always dreamed of being an artist. I practiced drawing every day." (Family Pictures)

"If you see my heart and humanity through my art then hopefully you will not exclude me from rightfully participating in this society."
(A Piece of My Heart, *13*)

Books by Carmen Lomas Garza

Family Pictures/Cuadros de familia. Children's Book Press, 1990.

In My Family/En mi familia. Children's Book Press, 1996.

Papel Picado: Paper Cutout Techniques. Xicanindio Arts Coalition, 1984.

A Piece of My Heart/Pedacito de mi Corazón: The Art of Carmen Lomas Garza. Laguna Gloria Art Museum, 1991; The New Press, 1994.

Carmen Lomas Garza was born in Kingsville, Texas, near the border with Mexico. From the time she was a young girl she dreamed of becoming an artist. Her mother inspired her to be an artist and both her mother and her father helped her plan her future. Lomas Garza studied art in school and she practiced drawing every day. She earned her bachelor of science at the Texas Arts and Industry University in Kingsville, her master's in education at Juarez-Lincoln/Antioch Graduate School in Austin, Texas, and her master's of art at San Francisco State University in California.

Lomas Garza has won many awards, grants, and fellowships for her art. She has had numerous solo exhibitions as well as group exhibitions. Her work is displayed in museums, libraries, and schools including the Hirshhorn Museum and Sculpture Garden, and the Smithsonian Institution in Washington, D.C. She works in a wide variety of media including oil on canvas, acrylic on canvas, gouache on arches paper, lithographs, *papel picado* (paper cutouts), and metal cutouts.

Lomas Garza presently lives in California. She is considered one of the major Mexican American painters in the United States. She is also an art instructor, curator, and writer.

Lomas Garza's first book, the award-winning *Family Pictures/ Cuadros de familia,* recounts her childhood experiences growing up in Texas. It is an excellent book for studying traditions as well as for inspiring young artists and writers to follow their dreams. Her second book for children, *In My Family/En mi familia,* is a companion volume to the first and features a continuation of her memories and family themes, lovingly depicted through text and art.

More Information About Carmen Lomas Garza

NEWSPAPERS AND JOURNALS

Brown, Betty Ann. "A Community's Self-Portrait." *New Art Examiner.* December 1990, 20–24.

Crohn, Jennifer. "What's the Alternative?" *The East Bay Guardian.* March 1991, 41.

Kutner, Janet. "Art with Roots." *The Dallas Morning News.* February 17, 1990, pp 1C–2C.

Lewis, Valerie. "A Celebration of Family." *San Francisco Chronicle.* July 29, 1990, 9.

Matthews, Lydia. "Stories History Didn't Tell Us." *Artweek.* February 14, 1991, 1, 15–17.

Santiago, Chiori. "Mano a Mano: We Have Come to Excel." *The Museum of California Magazine.* March/April 1989, 8–13, back cover.

Santiago, Chiori. "The Mexican Museum." *Latin American Art.* Fall 1990, 95–98.

Van Proyen, Mark. "To Touch Both Body and Soul." *Artweek.* April 11, 1991, 11–12.

Wasserman, Abby. "The Art of Narrative." *The Museum of California Magazine.* Winter 1991, 24–28, front cover.

Woodard, Josef. "Not So Naive After All." *Artweek.* April 14, 1991, 9–10.

BOOKS

¡Latinas! Women of Achievement edited by Diane Telgen and Jim Kamp. Visible Ink, 1996.

A Piece of My Heart/Pedacito de mi Corazón by Carmen Lomas Garza. The New Press, 1994.

VIDEOTAPES

Maldonado, Betty. *Hispanic Artists in the United States: The Texas Connection.* De Colores Productions, 1988.

Rodríguez, Laura. *Aqui y Ahora/Female Creators: A Profile of Carmen Lomas Garza.* KTVU, Channel 2, Oakland, CA, 1982.

Family Pictures/Cuadros de familia

American Library Association Notable Book
Texas Bluebonnet Award

- Art
- Artists
- Bilingual
- Autobiography
- Traditions

Carmen Lomas Garza's memories of her childhood in a rural Mexican American community in Kingsville, Texas, near the Mexico border inspired her to create *Family Pictures/Cuadros de familia.* Through story pictures she shares fond memories of her life from ages five to twelve years. In Spanish and English, she recounts her great dream of becoming an artist and how her mother inspired and supported this aspiration. Carmen Lomas Garza used a variety of materials in her paintings: oil on canvas, acrylic on canvas, and gouache on arches paper. The paper cutouts (*papel picado*) images on the text pages were cut from black paper with X-Acto knives. *Papel picado* is a traditional Mexican folk art technique which Carmen often uses to portray intricate images. Her engaging, detailed pictures and accompanying bilingual text portray day-to-day experiences such as making tamales, going to a fair in Mexico, picking cactus, a cakewalk, picking oranges, and birthday celebrations. The appeal of this book has been far-reaching in intergenerational literacy and writing programs. It is an excellent resource for stimulating discussion of and writing about cultural customs and family activities.

All Ages

RELATED WORK
In My Family/En mi familia by Carmen Lomas Garza. Children's Book Press, 1996 (companion volume, see below).

In My Family/En mi familia

- Art   • Artists   • Bilingual
- Autobiography   • Traditions

In this companion volume to *Family Pictures/Cuadros de familia,* Carmen Lomas Garza shares more memories of her childhood through story pictures and text.

All Ages

A Piece of My Heart/Pedacito de mi Corazón: The Art of Carmen Lomas Garza

This beautiful book gathers thirty-seven vivid full-color and black-and-white reproductions of Carmen Lomas Garza's work. It includes a poignant autobiographical piece by the artist; an interpretive essay by Amalia Mesa-Bains, a nationally known artist, curator, critic, and scholar of Latino art; a biographical listing of Lomas Garza's grants, fellowships, awards, and exhibition history; and an extensive bibliography.

In her autobiographical essay, Lomas Garza describes the pain and discrimination she and her brother suffered at school. She has vivid memories of an incident that happened when she was five years old. Her older brother came home crying because his teacher had hit him with a ruler for speaking Spanish. Later, Lomas Garza, too, suffered many emotional and physical punishments. "Each time I spoke English I was ridiculed for my accent and made to feel ashamed" (12). Her Anglo classmates made fun of the food she took for lunch. "By the time I graduated from high school I was confused, depressed, introverted and quite angry" (12). The university art classes offered to her excluded information about the rich art history of her people, and her own work was criticized as being too political, too primitive, and not universal.

Lomas Garza turned to her art to heal the wounds inflicted by years of exclusion and humiliation. She writes, "If you see my heart and humanity through my art then hopefully you will not exclude me from rightfully participating in this society" (13).

The works of art presented in *A Piece of My Heart/Pedacito de mi Corazón* take us into the heart of one of the most distinguished chroniclers of Chicano/a life. Her canvases preserve the traditions and practices of daily life among families, friends, and neighbors in southern Texas. As we enter the world of Lomas Garza's paintings, we are struck by the intricate details and the empowerment of the familiar. Each piece invites the viewer to study the central figures, the paintings on the walls, the furniture, dishes, and curtains. The pieces depicting outdoor scenes pay special attention to the flora and fauna of the area, with cats and dogs abounding. The centralized positioning of women in her work is noteworthy. They are actively engaged in healing, preparing food, storytelling, and nurturing. Lomas Garza's pictures often show the whole family involved in projects such as making tamales, preparing *empanadas*, painting Easter eggs, and eating watermelon. For readers interested in interpretations of the paintings, Mesa-Bains's analysis of each is placed on the same page. This beautifully designed book makes Lomas Garza's art available to a wider audience. Art enthusiasts of all ages, interests, and backgrounds will be enriched by the heartfelt work of this gifted artist.

All Ages

RELATED WORKS
Family Pictures/Cuadros de familia by Carmen Lomas Garza. Children's Book Press, 1990.

In My Family/En mi familia by Carmen Lomas Garza. Children's Book Press, 1996.

Nicholasa Mohr

Puerto Rican American (1938–)

Birthday: November 1
Address: c/o Arté Público Press, University of Houston, 4800 Calhoun, Houston, TX 77204-70900.

"Because of who I am, I feel blessed by the work I do, for it permits me to use my talents and continue to 'make magic.' I can recreate those deepest of personal memories as well as validate and celebrate my heritage and my future."   (Bantam brochure)

Books by Nicholasa Mohr

All for the Better: A Story of El Barrio (Stories of America Series). Illustrated by Rudy Gutierrez. Steck-Vaughn, 1993.

El Bronx Remembered. HarperCollins, 1993.

Felita. Illustrated by Ray Cruz. Dial, 1979; Bantam Skylark, 1990.

Going Home. Dial, 1986; Bantam Skylark, 1989.

In My Own Words: Growing Up Inside the Sanctuary of My Imagination. Messner, 1994.

In Nueva York. Arte Público Press, 1988.

The Magic Shell. Illustrated by Rudy Gutierrez. Scholastic, 1995. Spanish Edition: *El Regalo Magico.* Spring 1996.

Nilda. Harper & Row, 1973.

Old Letivia and the Mountain of Sorrows. Viking, 1996.

Rituals of Survival: A Woman's Portfolio. Arte Público, 1985.

The Song of El Coqui and Other Tales of Puerto Rico/La Cancion del Coqui. Written with Antonio Martorell. Viking, 1995.

Nicholasa Mohr was born in New York City's oldest Spanish-speaking community, known as El Barrio (the neighborhood) or Spanish Harlem. When she started school, she moved with her family—mother, father, and six older brothers—to the Bronx, where she spent most of her growing-up years. "Growing up in a household of six older brothers, and being part of a family who still held old-fashioned Puerto Rican concepts about the male and female roles, was often a struggle for me" (Bantam brochure). Mohr elaborates on some aspects of this struggle in her books.

From the beginning, she found magic in creating pictures and writing letters. Her art provided adventure, freedom, and space in the small crowded apartment where she lived with her extended family. Her mother lovingly provided support and encouragement for Mohr's achievements. (Mohr's father died when she was eight years old.)

Drawing and painting sustained Mohr through otherwise depressing conditions in both her home and school life. By using her imagination, she was able to create something pleasing and interesting. She used her skills and imagination to further develop her creativity, first in visual arts and later in her writing.

Mohr wanted to attend a college preparatory high school, but due to the intervention of a bigoted guidance counselor, she attended a trade school instead. She writes about the racism of the counselor and other teachers in her memoir, *Growing Up Inside the Sanctuary of My Imagination*. At the trade school, she majored in fashion illustration. After she graduated, she attended the Art Students' League in New York City where she studied drawing and painting. Her love for books led her to discover the work of Mexican artists; she later studied art and printmaking in Mexico. Subsequently, she has taught art in colleges in New York and New Jersey.

As Mohr's art developed, her feelings and experiences as a Puerto Rican woman born in the United States came through. This led to a publisher asking her to write about her life. She was aware of the lack of Puerto Rican literature, so she eventually agreed to the suggestion. "I was well aware that there were no books published about Puerto Rican girls or boys. . . . I was also reminded that when I was growing up, I'd enjoyed reading about the adventures of many boys and girls, but I had never really seen myself, my brothers or my family in those books. We just were not there "(Bantam brochure). In her memoir, she elaborates on her love for books and libraries. She writes, "One of the most thrilling events I can recall was when I got my first library card" (61). The library became a home away from home for Mohr, providing a quiet place where she could study, read, and write.

Years later, writing her first books was difficult, but with her characteristic determination and by applying some of the techniques she had developed as a visual artist to her new challenge as a writer, she has become a successful author. Mohr writes about the ongoing struggles of the Puerto Rican people on the mainland to gain their basic human rights. Her work, often incorporating a strong social statement, reflects the perspectives of the Puerto Rican people in all their complexity and variety. She has written numerous books for children, young adults, and adults in addition to plays, screenplays, articles, and essays. She has won many awards and honors and in 1989 she was awarded an honorary doctorate from the State University of New York. The National Hispanic Academy of Media Arts and Sciences honored her with the Annual Achievement in Literature Award in 1996.

More Information About Nicholasa Mohr

Authors and Artists for Young Adults. Volume 8, 161–167.

Dictionary of Literary Biography. Volume 145, 170–177.

Hispanic, Female and Young: An Anthology. Phyllis Tashlik, editor. Arte Público Press, 1994. See page 185.

Growing Up Inside the Sanctuary of My Imagination by Nicholasa Mohr. Julian Messner, 1994. See pages 116–117.

¡Latinas! Women of Achievement edited by Diane Telgen and Jim Kamp. Visible Ink, 1996.

"Puerto Rican Writers in the United States, Puerto Rican Writers in Puerto Rico: A Separation Beyond Language," by Nicolasa Mohr. In *Barrios and Borderlands: Cultures of Latinos and Latinas in the United States,* edited by Denis Lynn Daly Heyck. Routledge, 1994.

Something About the Author, Volume 8, 138.

• Biography
• Boycotts
• Depression Era
• Moving
• Puerto Rico

All for the Better: A Story of El Barrio

This is the touching biography of Evalina Lopez (Antonetty) (1922–1984). The book focuses on her early years, but the epilogue and afterword provide information about her later years. In 1933, when Evalina was eleven years old, her mother was forced by economic hardship to send her daughter to live with her aunt in New York City. The Great Depression had brought hard times to everyone, but things were even worse in Puerto Rico. With many tears, Evalina reluctantly bid her family good-bye and bravely traveled by ship to live in Spanish Harlem's El Barrio. There she gradually adjusted to a new city, new home, and new school as well as a new language. She pitched in and helped her relatives and neighbors whenever she could. When she realized that many of her neighbors were too ashamed to apply for the government food packages that were available, she was determined to find a solution. Meanwhile, she saved her money and with the help of her aunt, her mother and sisters were eventually able to join her in New York.

Evalina Lopez Antonetty became an activist on behalf of her community; she founded the United Bronx Parents Group. Through her leadership, determination, and ingenuity, she made a difference; her life serves as an inspiration to those who hope one person can improve things.

Nicholasa Mohr has written an easy-to-read, inspiring biography of a truly special person. The black-and-white detailed drawings add to the warmth of the story. *All for the Better* is one of twenty-eight books in the Stories of America Series, edited by Alex Haley.

Grades 2–5

El Bronx Remembered

National Book Award Finalist
New York Times *Outstanding Book*
School Library Journal *Best Book for Fall*

- Short Stories
- Bronx

Nicholasa Mohr's second book, a memorable collection of eleven short stories and a novella, "Herman and Alice," eloquently captures the joy, tragedy, humor, and irony of life. Depicting Puerto Rican life in the Bronx in New York City, she describes the struggle to find meaning in spite of the cultural contradictions faced by her characters. Taking place during the postwar years from 1946 to 1956, the focus is on rural Puerto Ricans adjusting to the big city. The introduction states: "These migrants and their children, strangers in their own country, brought with them a different language, culture and racial mixture. Like so many before them, they hoped for a better life, a new future for their children, and a piece of that good life known as the 'American dream.' " Mohr explores a number of significant themes, including cultures in transition, dreams and disillusionments, cross-cultural interactions, family fortunes and hard times, class structure and social mores, and intergenerational conflicts. Her novella, "Herman and Alice," is one of the earliest U.S. Latino works to deal with the topic of homosexuality. When gay thirty-eight-year-old Herman Aviles and pregnant fifteen-year-old Alice get married, they agree that they are not interested in a physical relationship. After the baby is born, Alice's feelings change and she starts going out with her old friends. Eventually Herman decides to return to Puerto Rico and to try to contact his former lover, David. In another piece, Uncle Claudio decides to return to Puerto Rico because "there he is Don Claudio and in New York, he is Don Nobody." In "A Lesson in Fortune-Telling," a new student in school tells her classmates' fortunes. (For a positive portrayal of Gypsies—or Rom, which is their proper name, the name they use to refer to themselves—read the books listed below under Related Works.) Other *El Bronx Remembered* stories deal with a mother who is accused of dealing drugs; a valedictorian who suffers the embarrassment of wearing his uncle's "roach killer" shoes to graduation; three girls who find a dead man in an abandoned building; a lonely elderly Jewish man who is welcomed into the home of his generous Puerto Rican neighbors; a Catholic girl who wants to eat lunch with her Jewish friend during Passover; and a young girl who experiences the death of a beloved dog because of the stinginess of adults. *El Bronx Remembered* is a significant work, exploring the circumstances and values of a changing culture.

Grades 7–12

RELATED WORKS

Puerto Ricans in the Bronx: *The Boy Without a Flag: Tales of the South Bronx* by Abraham Rodriguez, Jr. Milkweed Editions, 1992 (for mature readers).

Gypsies (Rom): *Uncertain Roads: Searching for the Gypsies* by Yale Strom. Four Winds Press, 1993 (for young readers).

Gypsies (Rom): *Bury Me Standing: The Gypsies and Their Journey* by Isabel Fonseca. Knopf, 1995 (for adults).

- Moving
- Grandmothers
- Death
- Nonviolence
- Newcomers
- Gender Roles

Felita

Notable Children's Book in the Field of Social Studies

Eight-year-old Felita Maldonado loves her neighborhood in New York City. To her disappointment, her parents decide to move. "We're off to a better future," her father announces. Only her wise and loving grandmother, Abuelita, who moved to New York from Puerto Rico, understands how much Felita will miss her old neighborhood and Gigi, her best friend. The people in the new neighborhood taunt and tease Felita, yelling "Go on back to your own country" (37). Faced with unrelenting prejudice in their new location, Papi, Mami, Felita, and her two brothers finally decide to return to their old neighborhood. Felita finds that many things have changed while she was gone, and some of the most significant changes are within herself. She has learned much about her heritage and about how to deal with the prejudice the family has faced. When her beloved grandmother dies, Felita vows to visit Puerto Rico—a trip she had long hoped to take with her grandmother.

In her first book for this age group, Mohr not only provides information about the pain of discrimination as experienced by a young girl, but offers insight into how one might cope with such bigotry. In Abuelita's words, "Felita, it is important for you to know that no one is better than anyone else because they have a lighter skin or a different kind of hair. Inside, you must know this and feel strong" (61).

In her memoir, *Growing Up Inside the Sanctuary of My Imagination*, Nicholasa Mohr reveals that *Felita* was based on her own family's experiences. She writes, "That experience—when in my young life I witnessed hatred, abuse, brutality, and xenophobia based solely on the fact that we were Puerto Ricans—will remain with me for the rest of my life" (52).

RELATED WORK

Sequel: *Going Home.* Dial, 1986; Bantam Skylark, 1989. See below.

Grades 4–7

Going Home

Parents' *Choice Remarkable Book for Literature*
Notable Trade Book in the Field of Social Studies

- Puerto Rico
- Travel
- Identity
- Gender Roles

Before reading this book, read the prequel, *Felita.* At the end of *Felita*, when her beloved Abuelita dies, Felita Maldonado vows to visit Puerto Rico. In *Going Home*, twelve-year-old Felita takes this important journey, the one she had long hoped to take with her grandmother. The first half of the book is devoted to the period before the trip to Puerto Rico and describes Felita's family, friendships, neighborhood, and school. Since her eleventh birthday, her parents have become increasingly protective and her brother, Tito, has picked on her and become even more bossy than ever. Supervised and chaperoned, Felita says, "Sometimes I feel like I am in jail" (66). Frustrated with her parents' double standard for their sons and daughter, she longs for Abuelita and their heart-to-heart talks. When school is out, the family leaves for the long-anticipated trip to Puerto Rico. But the experience is not quite what Felita expected. She is surprised that she is considered an outsider and called a Gringita. "All my life I've been Puerto Rican, and now I'm told I'm not. . . . At home I get called a spick and here I'm a Nuyorican" (122). Even her aunts and uncles are a disappointment. As Felita becomes involved with a community play, she is met with both admiration and jealousy. However, by summer's end, she has made a close friend, used her creativity and talent, developed more insight into human interactions, and learned about her heritage. She goes home with a richer understanding of herself and an increased appreciation of life on the island.

Felita's first-person narrative is lively and straightforward; her colloquial, spirited language brings an exuberance and veracity to her experiences in New York City and Puerto Rico. Mohr skillfully continues her character development of the maturing protagonist, sensitively depicting her emotions, reactions, and increasing awareness. The author has a keen sense of the strict rules imposed on young Puerto Rican women and a sharp eye for the ups and downs of friendships among adolescents. Readers of all backgrounds will relate to the need to develop independence and to shape one's own identity. In addition, they will meet an admirable Latina character, learn more about Puerto Rico, and perhaps begin to perceive their relatives and friends with new insight.

Grades 4–7

RELATED WORK

Prequel: *Felita.* Illustrated by Ray Cruz. Dial, 1979; Bantam Skylark, 1990. See previous page.

Growing Up Inside the Sanctuary of My Imagination

In this compelling memoir, Nicholasa Mohr shares the poignant story of her first fourteen and a half years growing up Puerto Rican, poor, and female in the 1940s in Spanish Harlem in New York City. The youngest of seven children and the only girl, she learned early to create her own space in the crowded, noisy environment. She describes slipping consciously into the world of her imagination, erasing the dissonance from her mind. This is an inspiring portrayal of a creative mind and the blossoming of a young girl's imaginative powers.

Mohr introduces us to her brothers, her wonderfully eccentric aunt, her father, and most important, her beloved mother, who provided the emotional support for her hopes and dreams. She remembers her mother's generosity, always making room for relatives and friends who needed a place to stay. She credits her mother with teaching her to love and respect animals, noting that "It is one of the many precious things she gave me from her treasure chest of human values" (83). Her father and mother were very different in their beliefs and behavior; Mohr feels that their opposing points of view helped her to look at all sides of an issue and to seek out her own truth.

The chapters that deal with Mohr's experiences at school should be required reading for all educators. Starting in kindergarten with a rigid, cruel teacher, her years in school were, for the most part, demoralizing and stifling. During her thirteen years in elementary and high school, she found only two teachers who were caring and supportive. She and her classmates were routinely chastised and punished for speaking Spanish, even informally at recess. Mohr notes that the school system seemed to have no place for children like her. Her experiences with the heartless guidance counselor who ignored her request to attend the High School of Music and Art are appalling. This is a chilling example of how institutional racism works to ignore and stifle the talents and dreams of young people of color.

Mohr was dealt another crushing blow when her mother died of cancer at the young age of forty-nine. The passages that describe her last pain-filled weeks and especially their last loving talk are beautifully written. Mohr writes, "There are two major components that have helped me survive and thrive. The first was my imagination and the powers of my inner life. The second was my mother's faith in me and her determination that I succeed" (111). A list of published works by the author and black-and-white photographs of Nicholasa Mohr and her relatives are included. *Growing Up Inside the Sanctuary of My Imagination* is part of the In My Own Words Series, which features memoirs by authors of books for young readers.

Grades 4–Adult

RELATED WORKS
Television adaptation: *The Dignity of the Children*. ABC documentary, winter/spring 1996.

Silent Dancing: A Partial Remembrance of a Puerto Rican Childhood by Judith Ortiz Cofer. Arte Público Press, 1990. See page 93.

The Invisible Thread by Yoshiko Uchida (In My Own Words Series). Julian Messner, 1991.

In Nueva York

Notable Trade Book in the Field of Social Studies
American Library Association Best Books
New York Times *Outstanding Book of the Year*
School Library Journal *Best Book*

- Lower East Side: New York
- Short Stories

This is a moving collection of eight interrelated short stories that depict life in Losaida, one of New York City's Puerto Rican communities. Writing candidly, sympathetically, and with wry humor, Nicholasa Mohr portrays her characters with warmth and sophistication. Some of the same characters appear in several stories, sometimes as major characters and in other stories in a minor role.

In Nueva York is Mohr's third book; it is a significant contribution of humor and pathos to the usual bleak depiction of life on the Lower East Side. She portrays authentically the pull of the two cultures that are present in the lives of her characters: the culture of the big-city neighborhood with its deterioration and danger contrasted with the generous, caring people who remember their lives on the island of Puerto Rico where the way of life was much different.

In "The Perfect Little Flower Girl," Mohr writes about Johnny and Sebastian, two gay men. Johnny is concerned about providing for Sebastian, who is disabled with asthma and migraine headaches. Finally they find a way around the homophobic system by arranging a marriage to a lesbian friend with the agreement that benefits will go to Sebastian. Mohr also shows insight into size discrimination in her portrayal of Chiquitín, a very small person who appears throughout the book. She writes, "Chiquitín had learned early that because he was physically different from the average person, life for him would have limits. From the simple tasks of buying clothing that fit, . . . being able to speak face to face with people without being ignored, to the more serious task of getting a job, commanding respect as an adult, and speaking another language, life for Chiquitín was a series of obstacles to be overcome" (141). Mohr's portrayal of these characters as complex, honorable people is a step forward in shattering the stereotypes that surround them.

Mohr uses Spanish liberally throughout the text. Instead of setting these words off in italics and repeating with English, the translation is embedded in the context of the stories. Perhaps Mohr intended her readers to feel the connection between the two cultures through the languages. Indeed, she succeeds admirably in drawing her readers into her stories and the lives of her characters.

Grades 9–12

RELATED WORK
Play: *I Never Even Seen My Father.*

The Magic Shell

When Jaime reluctantly moves with his parents from the Dominican Republic to New York City, he has a difficult time adjusting. The problems in his new environment seem endless: the noise, the cold weather, the heavy winter clothing, being cooped up in an apartment, a new language, and most of all, he misses his old friends. Just when he thinks things can't get any worse, he remembers the conch shell his great-uncle gave him as a going-away present. The magic of the shell transports him back to his beloved homeland where he was free to play in the warm out-of-doors with his friends. These magic times with the shell provide enough comfort and time for him to start learning the new language, make new friends, and gradually adjust to his new home. By the time his family is ready for a visit to the Dominican Republic, Jaime would rather attend the Discovery Summer Day Camp with his new friends. But once he gets back to his old home and reunites with his old friends, he remembers the joys of life on the island. When he visit his great-uncle and discusses the magic of the shell with him, Jaime realizes that the magic was really within himself.

Nicholasa Mohr has created a touching story of a child learning to live within two cultures; she eloquently captures the pain and frustration felt by the newcomer, the outsider. She portrays the new children Jaime meets as welcoming and friendly; unfortunately, this is quite often not the case. Readers may be interested in the books listed under Related Works in which the role of the newcomer is also explored.

Grades 2–5

RELATED WORKS

For Educators
The Inner World of the Immigrant Child by Cristina Igoa. St. Martin's Press, 1995. See page 209.

For Older Students
How the García Girls Lost Their Accents by Julia Alvarez. Algonquin Books, 1991; Dutton, 1992. See pages 40–41.

For Children

Newcomer from Dominican Republic
Over Here It's Different: Carolina's Story by Mildred Leinweber Dawson. Photographs by George Ancona. Macmillan, 1993.

My Two Worlds by Ginger Gordon. Clarion, 1993.

Newcomers
Aekyung's Dream by Min Paek. Children's Book Press, 1978.

Angel Child, Dragon Child by Michele Maria Surat. Scholastic, 1983.

Molly's Pilgrim by Barbara Cohen. Lothrop, Lee and Shepard, 1983.

Making a New Home in America by Maxine Rosenberg. Illustrated with photographs by George Ancona. Lothrop, Lee and Shepard, 1986.

Nilda

School Library Journal *Best Book*

New York Times *Outstanding Book of the Year*

American Library Association Best Book of 1973

Jane Addams Children's Book Award of U.S. Women's International League for Peace and Freedom

Society of Illustrators Citation of Merit for Art

- Mother-Daughter Relationship
- Death
- Barrio
- Art

Nicholasa Mohr dedicated *Nilda,* her first novel, with love to the children of El Barrio—and of all the many barrios all over the world. As is often the case with first books, this novel includes autobiographical elements. It is the story of three years in Nilda's life—from age ten to thirteen—and takes place in the barrio in New York City from 1941 to 1945. It chronicles the day-to-day experiences of a poor Puerto Rican family. When her father's heart attacks and eventual death force the family into the welfare system, Nilda finds that this social service organization is indeed a fearsome institution. She tells about going to the welfare office with her mother and then later having their apartment inspected by the social worker. Her humiliation is further compounded when officials at the health office inspect her head for lice.

School provides no sanctuary. Students have their hands rapped with a ruler for speaking Spanish. One teacher makes no attempt to understand Hispanic mourning customs; another who teaches Spanish demands Castilian accents from Puerto Rican students.

Nilda suffers many losses during these three years. The most devastating is the death of her mother. Subsequently, the family is separated and Nilda goes to live with her aunt in the Bronx. The young woman copes with all these problems by escaping into her art: "she lost herself in a world of magic achieved with some forms, lines and color."

This is an exceptional story of hardship, family ties, and neighborhood interactions. It is rich in detail, full of a child's thoughts and feelings. Fascinating and frank, humorous and sad—a classic coming-of-age story.

Note: Contains strong language.

Grades 7–12

Rituals of Survival: A Woman's Portfolio

- Short Stories

This fine collection of five short stories and a novella provides inspiration to women everywhere who are trying to break out of the restrictive roles in which society has placed them. Nicholasa Mohr offers powerful portraits of six New York Puerto Rican women who are, each in her own way, issuing declarations of independence and pursuing domestic and social revolutions. Facing isolation, poverty, illness, depression, demanding relatives, death of loved ones, and lack of support for their dreams, they somehow persevere. Zoraida, resilient and shy, finds a way to deal with her controlling husband and interfering family. When they take away her beloved rocking chair, "the one place where she felt she could be herself, where she could really be free" (29), she retreats further within herself. After her husband dies, sixty-six-year-old Carmela asserts her independence and finds a way to make her own life at last. After a brief return home, Virginia, a bisexual textile designer, leaves to continue her wanderlust ways. Amy, isolated and poverty stricken after the accidental death of her husband, finds a way to bring a little joy into the lives of her four children on Thanksgiving Day. A former prostitute, Lucia celebrates her twentieth birthday in the hospital on Welfare Island where she is dying of tuberculosis.

In the novella, Inez struggles to follow her dream of going to art school. When her parents die, she goes to live with her pernicious aunt. She cherishes and keeps alive the memories of her mother who told her, "Someday you must study so that you can become an important artist . . . make an important contribution to the world and really be somebody" (106). After six years of neglect and emotional abuse in her aunt's home, Inez enters into a marriage as a passport to freedom. However, she soon realizes that she has jumped from the frying pan into the fire; her new husband is insanely jealous and violent. She finds a creative albeit unusual way to disentangle herself from this abusive relationship and with great determination follows her dream of attending art school. In all of these stories, the women struggle to remain true to themselves. Their rituals of survival serve as guides for those who follow in their footsteps.

Grades 10–Adult

RELATED WORK

Intaglio: A Novel in Six Stories by Roberta Fernández. Arte Público Press, 1990. See pages 208–209.

- Folklore
- Frogs
- Guinea Hens
- Mules
- Slavery

The Song of el Coquí and Other Tales of Puerto Rico

Dedicated "to the children of the barrios who live far away from the Caribbean magic that weaves the stories of this book," this engaging collection of three folktales was written with respect and affection for the rich and complex ancestral traditions that make up Puerto Rican culture. In the first tale, the god Huracán enjoys his mountain home on the beautiful island of Borinquén. However, he soon becomes sad because there is no music, so he creates a storm that lasts for a million years. Soon after the cataclysm subsides, the air is filled with the sweet song of the tiny coquí. The second tale, "La Guinea, the Stowaway Hen," begins in West Africa where slave traders are kidnapping people. La Guinea, seeking refuge, ends up on the slave ship en route to Puerto Rico. She finally finds a new home where she provides inspiration for Don Elias, a maskmaker. In the final folktale, "La Mula, the Cimarron Mule," Mula is worked to near exhaustion by Spanish bandits until she escapes and joins a community of *cimarrones* (escaped slaves) in the hills. Each of the animals represents a group of people in Puerto Rico. El coquí represents the indigenous Tainos, La Guinea symbolizes the African people who were brought to the island as captive slaves, and the story of La Mula is a parable about the Spaniards who conquered the island. Together, the three folktales form a composite of a culture comprised of three very different and very special strands.

The paintings in this book are extraordinarily exquisite! The resplendent art combined with the fascinating stories make this a book that will jump off the bookshelves and into the hands of readers of all ages and backgrounds.   All Ages

RELATED WORKS

Spanish Edition

La canción del coquí: y otros cuentos de Puerto Rico. Viking, 1995.

Folktales from Puerto Rico

Juan Bobo and the Pig, a Puerto Rican folktale retold by Felix Pitre. Lodestar Books, 1993.

Juan Bobo: Four Folktales from Puerto Rico, retold by Carmen T. Bernier-Grand. HarperCollins, 1994.

Pat Mora

Mexican American (1942–)

Birthday: January 19
Contact: Arte Público Press
University of Houston
Houston, Texas 77204-2090

"Cultures can be bridges. They're not walls. When we learn about other cultures, we realize how much alike people are."
(Experience Exchange, *1*)

"We have a whole generation growing up without ever seeing themselves in print. What does it mean if you don't see yourself in books? There is a strong connection between images and identity."
(Albuquerque Journal)

"I began writing picture books because I am drawn to the form, but also because I believe there was and is a great need for such books written by Latinas and Latinos describing our values, customs, realities. Not only Latino youngsters need and deserve such books—all young people do in our multicultural society."
(The Horn Book Magazine, *299*)

Books by Pat Mora

Agua Agua Agua (Let Me Read Series). Illustrated by José Ortega. Good Year Books, 1994.

Agua Santa/Holy Water. Beacon Books, 1995.

Ana Meets the Wind. Clarion Books, forthcoming.

A Birthday Basket for Tía. Illustrated by Cecily Lang. Macmillan, 1992.

Borders. Arte Público Press, 1986.

Chants. Arte Público Press, 1994.

Communion. Arte Público Press, 1991.

Confetti. Lee and Low, 1996.

The Desert Is My Mother/El desierto es mi madre. Illustrated by Daniel Lechon. Arte Público Press, 1994.

The Gift of the Poinsettia/El regalo de la flor de Nochebuena. Written with Charles Ramirez Berg. Illustrated by Daniel Lechon. Arte Público Press, 1995.

The House of Houses. Beacon Press, 1997.

Listen to the Desert/Oye al desierto. Illustrated by Francisco X. Mora. Clarion, 1994.

Nepantla. Essays from the Land in the Middle. University of New Mexico Press, 1993.

Pablo's Tree. Illustrated by Cecily Lang. Macmillan, 1994.

The Race of Toad and Deer. Illustrated by Maya Itzna. Orchard, 1995.

Tomas and the Library Lady. Knopf, 1997.

Uno, Dos, Tres: One, Two, Three. Illustrated by Barbara Lavallee. Clarion Books, 1996.

Water Rolls, Water Rises. Clarion, forthcoming.

Pat(ricia) Mora has earned distinction as both a writer and an educator. In each of these fields, she has gained a reputation as a strong advocate for cultural conservation. A former teacher, university administrator, museum director, and consultant on United States–Mexico youth exchanges, Mora now spends her time writing and speaking to audiences of all ages. Best known for her award-winning poetry, she also writes children's books and essays.

Mora was born in El Paso, Texas; she grew up in this border city to which her grandparents came during the Mexican Revolution. Her parents, Raul Antonio Mora, an optician, and Estella Delgado Mora, a homemaker, were very supportive parents. At considerable personal sacrifice, they sent their children to Catholic schools, where her mother was a president of the PTA. Books were an important part of Mora's childhood; her mother took the children to the library regularly and encouraged them to read and write. Mora credits her mother with being her first and best editor. In "My Fierce Mother," printed in *Nepantla,* Mora affectionately describes her as a woman who is determined to be treated fairly. No one, no matter how powerful, can intimidate her. "She read every paper I wrote," and "saves every piece I write and any piece written about me."

Mora grew up in a society that did not value her cultural heritage, and so, like most young people in a similar situation, she tried to fit in. She writes that her personal experience with internalized racism helps her understand how young people may be feeling today. As a child, she couldn't have known that assimilation means a loss of cultural identity. She spoke Spanish at home with her parents, grandmother, and aunt, but at school the pressure to conform led her to ignore her ethnicity.

Until she was seventeen, she never considered being anything but a nun. Then she became interested in being a physician, but at that time women were not encouraged to enter that male-dominated field. So, like many women before her and since, she went into teaching. She was an English major and a speech minor in both her bachelor's and master's programs. She notes that the university virtually ignored her cultural heritage while she was a student there. Even though she grew up in a middle-class family and neighborhood, she was the first in her family to graduate from college. She soon married and began teaching at a high school in the El Paso Independent School District.

During the ensuing years, Mora earned her master's degree, had three children, and worked as a teacher, lecturer, university administrator, and museum director. She hosted a radio show, "Voices: The Mexican American in Perspective" on KTEP, a National Public Radio affiliate. She began making time for writing in 1980 and in 1983 she received the first of many awards when she was recognized by the National Association for Chicano Studies. Her career as a writer and an advocate for cultural conservation blossomed during the eighties; the recipient of a Kellogg National Fellowship as well as many other honors and awards, Mora continued her work as an educator and museum director until 1989.

For the first thirty-seven years of her life, Mora lived in El Paso. In September 1989 she moved with her new husband, an archaeologist, to Cincinnati, where she spends her time writing, speaking, facilitating workshops, and traveling. She continues to create poetry but also writes picture books and prose. She has become increasingly aware of the absence of the U.S. Latina voice in American literature. She longs for a world free of the pollution of bias and bigotry. She believes in the power of words to awaken, to heal, and to create change.

More Information About Pat Mora

Albuquerque Journal. February 24, 1995, page numbers unavailable.

Contemporary Authors. Volume 129, 306.

Experience Exchange. Houghton Mifflin Newspaper, 4–5.

"A Latina in Kentucky." *Horn Book Magazine.* May/June 1994, 298–300.

¡Latinas! Women of Achievement edited by Diane Telgen and Jim Kamp. Visible Ink, 1996.

Nepantla: Essays from the Land in the Middle by Pat Mora. See pages 128–129.

Notable Hispanic American Women edited by Diane Telsen and Jim Kamp. Gale Research, 1993, 280–282.

- Aesop's Fable
- Crows
- Water

Preschool–K

Agua Agua Agua

In this charming little book, Crow finds a way to relieve her thirst by using her head. Pat Mora's lyrical text is accompanied by whimsical illustrations by José Ortega. Let Me Read books use playful language, such as repetition and rhyme, to build interest and success. They are designed to develop positive attitudes toward reading, build on successful reading experiences, and create a positive, supportive role for parents. Suggestions are included for activities to help children relate to the written word, such as "Find and learn the Spanish words." Three levels are available to provide gradual challenges to help young readers gain confidence and become lifelong learners.

- Poetry

Grades 11–Adult

Agua Santa/Holy Water

Poet Pat Mora draws readers into the bountiful rivers of her poems, paying tribute to women who resist, create, nurture, and heal. The interior design of this collection of poetry flows beautifully with the waves of words and images, rich in history, mythology, and experience. As in her other collections, Mora draws inspiration from her Mexican American roots; here she contrasts cascading waters with the desert images of earlier works. In "Coatlicue's Rules: Advice from an Aztec Goddess," the rules include "Beware of offers to make you famous," "Retain control of your own publicity," "Protect your uterus," "Avoid housework," and "Verify that the inside voice is yours." Malinche's tips include "In an unfriendly country, wear a mask," "Monolinguals know about linguistics like atheists know about theology," and "Beware historians citing only themselves." Other themes center around birth, death, adoption, racism, guilt, Frida Kahlo, Sor Juana, La Llorona, the Day of the Dead, Honduras, and more. One of the most powerful poems is "Let Us Hold Hands," calling on women of all backgrounds, past and present, to support each other, forming a ring around the world. One poem, "Corazón del corrido," is entirely in Spanish, while the others have Spanish words and phrases interspersed with English. The notes in the back of the book give historical and cultural information about some of the poems. A fellowship from the National Endowment for the Arts enabled Pat Mora to do the final editing on this magical and affirming collection.

RELATED WORKS

Borders by Pat Mora. Arte Público Press, 1986. See pages 125–126.

Chants by Pat Mora. Arte Público Press, 1994. See page 126.

Communion by Pat Mora. Arte Público Press, 1991. See pages 126–127.

A Birthday Basket for Tía

With the help of her feline friend Chica, Cecilia selects a surprise gift for her great-aunt's ninetieth birthday. On the birthday morning, as her mother is preparing food for the surprise party, Cecilia, always accompanied by Chica, searches through the house for the perfect gift for her beloved Tía. She chooses objects that invoke special memories—a favorite book her aunt reads to her; a bowl in which they mix cookie dough; a flowerpot in which they grow flowers for the kitchen window; a teacup in which Tía serves *hierbabuena*, hot mint tea, when Cecilia is sick; and a red ball they throw back and forth—and lovingly places them in a basket. Later, Cecilia and Mamá fill a piñata with candy and decorate the living room with balloons, flowers, and tiny cakes. Soon the musicians, family, and friends arrive and everybody shouts "SURPRISE! *¡Feliz cumpleaños!* Happy birthday!" as Tía walks through the door. After Tía carefully inspects each object in the basket, the music begins. Now Tía has a surprise for Cecilia: she sets down her cane and invites her beloved niece to dance with her.

The pleasing cumulative text is accompanied by bright cut-paper collages which echo the excitement of the celebration and the closeness of the intergenerational bond. This book, along with *Pablo's Tree,* offers a refreshing approach to birthday celebrations, in which gifts are much-loved items that have meaning for the characters; there is no need for expensive presents. *A Birthday Basket for Tía* is an excellent read-aloud and read-alone book.

Preschool–Grade 3

RELATED WORKS

Hello, Amigos! by Tricia Brown. Holt, 1986.

Pablo's Tree by Pat Mora. Macmillan, 1994. See pages 129–130.

Serafina's Birthday by Alma Flor Ada. Translated from the Spanish by Ana M. Cerro. Illustrated by Louise Bates Satterfield. Atheneum, 1992.

Borders

Southwest Book Award

- Poetry

In a richly lyrical style, Pat Mora explores the complex borders that divide us. With a piercing look at the political, social, cultural, and emotional divisions that create painful chasms among people, she speaks with a spirited, inspiring voice. Her words about gender, prejudice, indifference, language, class, education, isolation, health, and anger are powerful and mesmerizing. As a poet and educator who lives between two cultures, two traditions, two languages, and two nations, Mora's poems call for validation and healing. Her fascination with the pleasure and power of words is evident here: "Perhaps my desert land waits to hear me roar, waits to hear me flash: NO. NO" (24); "Risk my differences, my surprises. Grant me a little life, America" (33). Her poems about immigration, Tomás Rivera, being among the first of a people to go to college, bilingualism, cleaning women, maids, hysterectomies, addiction to approval, archaeology,

Grades 11–Adult

healing, ancestors, thoughts of suicide, intimacy, love, disillusionment, and cancer demonstrate the wide range of themes she explores.

RELATED WORKS

Agua Santa by Pat Mora. Beacon Books, 1995. See page 124.

Chants by Pat Mora. Arte Público Press, 1994. See below.

Communion by Pat Mora. Arte Público Press, 1991. See below.

Chants

Southwest Book Award
El Paso Times *Best Book of Poetry*

• Poetry

In her first book of desert incantations, Pat Mora speaks with muted, yet spirited tones as she explores the themes of womanhood, political, gender, class, and age borders; of loss, and of healing. She celebrates the beauty and power of the desert, praising the magical presence of the telluric force.

Two of Mora's poems have recently been adapted into books for children. "Mi Madre" grew into *The Desert Is My Mother,* and "Poinsettia" has been expanded into *The Gift of the Poinsettia/ El regalo de la flor de Nochebuena.* Several poems feature old women: a grandmother who treasures her solitude; a beloved elderly aunt with whom Mora has switched roles; and a small gray-haired woman who makes and sells crepe paper flowers to sell to bargain-hunting tourists. In "Bailando" we catch a glimpse of the dear aunt who might have provided the inspiration for another children's book, *A Birthday Basket for Tía.*

Grades 11–Adult

Mora cries out against violence against women in several poems, and speaks unflinchingly of fear, resentment, loneliness, and despair. Hers is a healing voice, one of promise and hope.

RELATED WORKS

Agua Santa by Pat Mora. Beacon Books, 1995. See page 124.

Borders by Pat Mora. Arte Público Press, 1986. See pages 125–126.

Communion by Pat Mora. Arte Público Press, 1991. See below.

• Poetry

Communion

Communion is Pat Mora's third collection of poetry. In this sensitive collection she adds a global perspective while building on her previous themes of political, gender, class, and age borders, loss, healing, and womanhood. Nostalgia, literacy, tenacity, poverty, assimilation, violence, loneliness, language, aging, friendship, parenthood, and sisterhood are all here in this moving volume of poignant poems. Mora's experiences when she traveled to Pakistan, Peru, and Cuba are integrated into her poetry. Women carry water on their heads, cook beans and rice, sell vegetables, clean houses, weave rugs, gather herbs, and wear veils. In "Señora X No More" a determined woman struggles to learn English. Love of the earth is expressed beautifully in "Divisadero Street, San Francisco": while living in the cement heart of the city, a woman finds a way to plant flowers. "Lost without dirt," she says as she greens her little corner of the world (17). Butterflies, snow geese, sandhill cranes, Canadian geese, sand, trees, dandelions, and wild grapes anchor these poems to Mother Earth. Mora explores the role the past plays in our lives, and in two poems, she again exposes domestic violence against women: in "Perfume," a woman is stabbed and killed by her partner (43–44) and in "Emergency Room" a woman is covered from neck to knee in bruises (45). Spanish words and phrases are translated into English at the bottom of each page.

Grades 11–Adult

RELATED WORKS

Agua Santa by Pat Mora. Beacon Books, 1995. See page 124.

Borders by Pat Mora. Arte Público Press, 1986. See pages 125–126.

Chants by Pat Mora. Arte Público Press, 1994. See above.

The Desert Is My Mother/El desierto es mi madre

Skipping Stone Honor Award

- Deserts
- Bilingual
- Environment
- Poetry

Here the desert is lovingly portrayed as a place of great beauty and power rather than the barren, boring setting featured in many stories. Mora, an award-winning poet, and Daniel Lechon, a prize-winning painter, collaborated to present the desert as a provider of food, healing, comfort, music, spirit, and life. On each double-page spread, a young girl makes a request and the desert responds. "I say heal me. She gives me chamomile, oregano, peppermint." The book ends with "The desert is my strong mother." The design of the cover and interior of the book is also very appealing. This beautiful celebration of the relationship between nature and humans is a significant contribution to literature for young readers. Books such as this one and those listed below under Related Works provide hope that young readers will develop a conservation ethic and learn to love and respect the earth. Superb for reading aloud, discussion, and art activities.

Preschool–Grade 3

RELATED WORKS

Listen to the Desert /Oye al desierto by Pat Mora. Clarion, 1994. See page 128.

Keepers of the Earth by Joseph Bruchac and Michael Caduto. Fulcrum, 1988.

The Gift of the Poinsettia/El regalo de la flor de Nochebuena

- Bilingual
- Christmas
- Mexico
- Posadas

This beautifully illustrated bilingual picture book is based on the Mexican tradition of *las posadas,* in which villagers reenact Mary and Joseph's search for shelter for the nine nights before Christmas. The book begins, "Long ago, a boy named Carlos lived in the small Mexican town of San Bernardo." Carlos lives with his Aunt Nina and his canine companion, Chico; they are poor but their house is full of love. Night after night, traveling from house to house, Carlos enjoys the festivities of *las posadas* but worries about finding a special gift for the baby Jesus. On Christmas Eve the children each will place a gift before the manger. Finally his aunt, sensing his concern, makes a suggestion; she reassures him that "Love makes small gifts special." On Christmas Eve, when Carlos presents his humble present, he realizes that love is the best gift of all. The authors not only tell the story of *las posadas,* but lovingly weave in information about other Mexican traditions such as *papel picado, piñatas,* and *cascarones.* This exquisitely designed and illustrated book concludes with the music and text for the songs of *las posadas.*

RELATED WORKS

Las Posadas: *Fiesta U.S.A.* by George Ancona. Lodestar, 1995.

Search for a Special Gift: *The Gift* by Helen Coutant. Knopf, 1983.

Grades 2–5

- Animals
- Bilingual
- Deserts
- Environment
- Poetry
- Sounds

Listen to the Desert/Oye al desierto

Pat Mora and Francisco X. Mora have teamed up to create an enchanting book that will help the reader and listener perceive the desert anew. This bilingual portrayal of animal sounds heard in the southwestern desert is an excellent choice for reading aloud and for dramatization. Listeners of all ages will love the predictable, repetitive text and enjoy joining in to repeat the sounds. The lines on each page, two in English and two in Spanish, provide an opportunity to compare and contrast the sounds of the two languages—they are different and yet alike. "Listen to the dove say coo, coo, coo. La paloma arrulla, currucú, currucú, currucú." We hear the owl, toad, snake, dove, coyote, fish, and mice as well as the rain and the wind. The watercolor illustrations feature a vast expanse of light blue sky with geometric shapes at the bottom of each page. The cheery animals face the text and seem to be reciting the poetry along with the reader. The desert will never quite be the same again after one enjoys this book.

Preschool–Grade 2

RELATED WORK

The Desert is My Mother/El desierto es mi madre by Pat Mora. Arte Público Press, 1994. See page 127.

- Autobiographical Essays
- Authorship

Nepantla: Essays from the Land in the Middle

These twenty inspiring essays are so significant and powerful, they should be required reading for all educators and prospective educators. In her first collection of prose, Pat Mora writes with remarkable sensitivity and insight about many significant issues including race, class, age, and gender. Using an analytical and yet accessible style, she examines issues related to bilingualism, cultural awareness, ethnic loyalty, assimilation/acculturation, internalized oppression, shackling stereotypes, education, class privilege, children's literature, authorship, and much more. *Nepantla* means "place in the middle" in Nahuatl, one of Mexico's indigenous languages. Mora finds herself in the middle in a number of ways: she is in the middle of her life, she is between her daughter and her mother, and she is presently living in the middle of the United States. For years she worked in the middle land between the university and the community. From these unique perspectives, she is able to offer opinions, insights, concerns, and visions, all strengthened by her voice of poetic experience.

What Mora has to say is so important and expressed with such care and in such readable language, I found myself marking every other sentence to use for quotes. She explores issues of cultural conservation, beginning with the preservation of her own Mexican American culture. In her travel essays, she confirms the necessity of preserving the heritage of diverse ethnic groups. She chronicles her trips to Puerto Vallarta, Pakistan, the Dominican Republic, Guatemala, and Cuba and the ways in which they have given her a unique perspective on the United States from which she can better perceive its weaknesses and strengths.

This collection of essays, which includes speeches, reminiscences, poetry, and lectures, provides validation and encouragement to others who are committed to social change. Mora affirms the need for and the right of Latinas and Latinos to be heard and to participate in the shaping of our country. She asks difficult and sometimes unwelcome questions, questions that must be addressed. *Nepantla* is a significant contribution to the growing body of Chicano nonfiction as well as to American literature.

Grades 12–Adult

Pablo's Tree

- Adoption
- Birthdays
- Grandfathers
- Trees
- Single Motherhood
- Traditions

Each year on his birthday, Pablo eagerly looks forward to seeing how his grandfather, Lito, has decorated the tree he planted on the day the boy was adopted. When Mamá first told her father that she planned to adopt a child, he lovingly selected a special tree for his new grandchild. And on the day that Mamá brought the baby home, Lito planted the tree in the sun in his backyard. Each year since then, Pablo has spent the night after his birthday at his grandfather's house. And each year, Abuelito has decorated the tree in a different way as a surprise for Pablo. The two have established a loving tradition of sitting under the tree while they take turns telling the story of Pablo's arrival and the story of the tree.

Pat Mora has created a unique birthday story, special in many ways. Planting a tree is such a wonderful way to honor a loved one; this book is a step forward in nurturing a love of nature. Also refreshing is the lack of materialism—here is a child who looks forward to seeing a tree, not to how many toys he receives for his birthday! Both this birthday story and the earlier *A Birthday Basket for Tía* by the same author and illustrator are a welcome contrast to the usual birthday stories.

Lang's exuberant collages using bright cut paper with dyes combined with the lively story, make this a great read-aloud as well as read-alone book.

Preschool–Grade 3

RELATED WORKS

Adoption

Abby by Jeannette Caines. Harper and Row, 1973; Harper Collins, 1996.

Birthdays

Hello, Amigos! by Tricia Brown. Holt, 1986.

A Birthday Basket for Tía by Pat Mora. Macmillan, 1992. See page 125.

- Folklore
- Guatemala

The Race of Toad and Deer

Pat Mora based this folktale on one she heard from Don Fernando Tesucún, a mason of restoration at a Guatemalan archaeological site in Tikál. Similar to the tortoise and the hare fable, this sly tale is about a race between Venado, an overconfident deer, and Sapo, a resourceful toad. Venado is swift but Sapo is clever. Which one will win the race? A cast of enthusiastic animals turn out to watch the big event.

The author has written a satisfying book about the small and courageous triumphing over the large and tyrannical. She has woven Spanish words and phrases such as *silencio, buenos días, adelante,* and *amigos* into the text. She has also created an authentic setting with animals and plants indigenous to the area. Readers will meet bush dogs, spider monkeys, javelinas, tapirs, iguanas, armadillos, and anteaters. First-time illustrator Maya Itzna Brooks provides playful paintings to accompany the text. She was born in Germany but returned to her parents' native country, Guatemala, when she was fourteen. There she followed in her parents' footsteps by becoming an artist. She now lives in New Mexico, where her work is exhibited at a local gallery.

This folktale lends itself nicely to dramatization. While the teacher or a student reads the story, a few children pantomime the main parts. The remainder of the class repeat lines such as "Race time! *¡Carrera!*", and "*¡Adelante, Tío Venado!*" This happily involves the whole group in a spontaneous activity without rehearsals or memorizing lines.

Preschool–Grade 2

RELATED WORKS

Guatemala: See the works by Omar Castañeda on pages 76–81.

Folklore: See the Subject Index.

- Bilingual
- Birthdays
- Counting Book

Uno, Dos, Tres: One, Two, Three

Two girls go to a Mexican market to select presents for their mother's birthday. As they shop, the marketplace comes alive with music, dancing, singing, waterfalls, birds, and people. They carefully choose among the gorgeous items, counting as they go. They pick out ten presents, including a gaily decorated piñata horse, a dancing marionette, and a delicately painted wooden animal. This charming books ends when the girls surprise their mother by presenting the assortment of wrapped presents. "*¡Feliz cumpleaños, Mamá!*"

"Uno one/We'll buy Mamá a sun." So begins this exquisite counting book. One of the many things that make this book so special is the refreshing images of the round characters. Fat-oppressive sentiments have permeated every aspect of our lives, including children's literature. What a nice surprise to find full figures in this charming little picture book! Add to that the vibrant, colorful watercolors that provide just the right touch of whimsy and humor to a special day of shopping for a loved one. The trip through the market is filled with unique, inventive folk art, which is breathtaking. The textures of the rhythmic text correspond with the illustrations to inspire readers of all ages to learn to count in Spanish and English and to enjoy the pleasure of being bilingual. The resplendent book ends with a note from the author and a pronunciation guide.   All Ages

RELATED WORKS

Bilingual Counting Books

Fifty on the Zebra, Counting with the Animals by Nancy María Grande Tabor. Mariuccia Iaconi, no date available.

Three Friends/Tres Amigos by Maria Cristina Brusca and Tona Wilson. Holt, 1995. See page 74.

Birthdays

A Birthday Basket for Tía by Pat Mora. Macmillan, 1992. See page 125.

Pablo's Tree by Pat Mora. Macmillan, 1994. See pages 129–130.

Michael Nava

Photo: C. F. Berkstresser

Mexican American (1954–)

Birthday: September 16
Contact: Charlotte Sheedy Literary Agency
65 Bleecker Street, 12th Floor
New York, NY 10012

". . . if you are a member of an oppressed group in this country, then you have to really, really believe in principles like equal protection under the law. They're not intellectual abstractions to which you feel some sort of vague intellectual allegiance. They really have to exist, they really have to mean something, because they're your only protection in this society." (Bloomsbury Review, 2)

"The aberration in my life is not that I'm a lawyer who writes, but that I'm a writer who practices law." (Bloomsbury Review, 1)

"I'm an outsider. . . . I'm no one's stereotype . . . I think that the great mass of the American public still thinks that all homosexuals are white hairdressers, are promiscuous, are . . . well, fill in the blank. I'm here to say, Look at me: I'm Latino, I'm a lawyer . . . you can't make generalizations about my people, Latino or gay."
(Bloomsbury Review, 1)

Published Works by Michael Nava

FOR YOUNG ADULTS

"Abuelo: My Grandfather, Raymond Acuña," in *A Member of the Family: Gay Men Write About Their Closest Relations,* edited by John Preston. Dutton, 1992.

"The Marriage of Michael and Bill," in *Friends and Lovers: Gay Men Write About the Families They Create,* edited by John Preston. Dutton, 1995.

Created Equal: Why Gay Rights Matter to America, written with Robert Dawidoff. St. Martin's Press, 1994.

FOR MATURE TEENAGERS AND ADULTS

"Boys Like Us," in *Boys Like Us,* edited by Patrick Merla. Avon, forthcoming.

The Death of Friends. Putnam, 1996.

Finale: Short Stories of Mystery and Suspense (editor). Alyson Publications, 1989.

Goldenboy. Alyson Publications, 1988.

The Hidden Law. HarperCollins, 1992.

How Town. Harper and Row, 1990.

The Little Death. Alyson Publications, 1986.

Michael Nava is the highly acclaimed writer of an award-winning mystery series featuring a gay Latino lawyer. He is recognized as a first-rate novelist whose work is set apart by its insight, compassion, and sense of social justice. Nava attended Stanford Law School before becoming a Los Angeles city prosecutor in 1981. After several years, he opened a private law practice and later moved to a position in the California Appellate Court, where he helped a judge write opinions that were codified into law. Currently he lives in San Francisco, where he is a full-time writer.

Nava was born and raised in Sacramento, California, in a semi-rural barrio called Gardenland. Isolated from Sacramento proper, the poor neighborhood was "across the bridge instead of across the tracks." There were no sidewalks and no streetlights. Nava's great-grandparents came to the United States from Mexico during the Mexican Revolution, starting as migrant workers and working their way to the Sacramento Valley, where they stayed. The second oldest of six children, Nava was an unhappy, moody child, "precocious at one moment and withdrawn the next" ("Abuelo," 16), turning to books for solace. "I knew that I was gay when I was 12, which was not a good thing to be in my family situation. I knew I had to leave Sacramento . . ." (*Gay Community News [GCN]*, 1). He was fourteen when he started writing poetry; since he couldn't talk to anyone about his feelings, he wrote about them. "I was a frenetic over-achiever . . . I focused in at an early age that education was going to be

my way out of my family and the poverty-stricken community where I grew up" (*Bloomsbury Review*, 1). When he graduated from high school, he was the class valedictorian, captain of the debating team, and student body president. He earned a full academic scholarship to Colorado College and graduated cum laude with a major in history in 1976. Nava was awarded a Thomas J. Watson Fellowship and spent the following year in Buenos Aires, where he studied and translated the poetry of Ruben Dario.

After graduating from Stanford Law School in 1981, Nava embarked on a career as a prosecutor for the City of Los Angeles. He was intoxicated with the romance of being a trial lawyer and the feeling that he was doing something that had social utility. But after three years of toiling in grimy courtrooms and run-down prisons, he burned out. "The criminal justice system is a depressing place. It is a system of victims, no matter what side they're on. Terrible things happen to decent people, and there's nothing you can do about it" (*Los Angeles Times*, E1). He opened a private law practice in Los Angeles and later became a research attorney for the California Court of Appeals. There he researched legal issues and wrote opinions that were published and became a part of the body of California common law.

"When I was in college, I set out to be the great American poet" (*Bloomsbury Review*, 1). Some of his poetry was published in the early eighties, but Nava decided to turn his attention to fiction. He started writing his first mystery, *A Little Death*, during his last year of law school.

Rejected by mainstream publishers, it was published in 1986 by Alyson Publications, a small gay-owned press in Boston. Publisher Sasha Alyson says, "It is rare for an unsolicited first book to be outstanding. . . . In a lot of mysteries, the mystery is good but the writing is so-so. Michael's work is different. He is a poet, and it shows" (*LA Times*, 2). Alyson also published his second mystery, the award-winning *Goldenboy*, and *Finale*, a collection of mysteries edited by Nava. Then in 1990, Nava made the leap from the small press to one of the largest commercial publishers in the United States, a move that has brought his work to the attention of a wider audience. The success of *How Town* firmly establishes Nava as one of the gay community's leading literary figures. He recently completed another mystery titled *The Death of Friends*.

Because of his day job, Nava wrote at night and on weekends, generally writing three hours each evening and all day Saturday or Sunday. His work as a lawyer involves writing and his fiction involves the law. His mystery series feature Henry Rios, a gay Latino lawyer who has much in common with his creator. But in a number of interviews, Nava makes it clear that Rios is not Nava: "if you've spent much time with me you know we're not the same character" (*GCN*, 2). Nevertheless, they are similar in a number of ways: both are attorneys, gay, Latino, workaholics, recovering alcoholics, and they both grew up poor in central California. And they both live and work in Los Angeles and the San Francisco Bay Area. Unlike earlier generations of lesbian and gay writers, Nava never agonized over the sexual orientation of his protagonist. He knew that the best writers write from their own experience, and his experience is that of a gay Latino lawyer. He longs for the day when sexual orientation will be viewed as one of the many features of our nature. Given society's unrelenting hostility toward lesbians and gays, Nava is making an important contribution toward that awareness by creating a positive and affirming figure like Henry Rios.

Nava notes, "I try to depict the reality in which I live, which in California is multi-ethnic, multi-cultural, and certainly multi–sexual orientation. I live in a very rich world here, and I try to depict it with some veracity. This is one of my goals as a writer, to accurately paint a picture of my world" (*GCN*, 1). Nava has a worldview that stems from his experience of having grown up as an outsider. "I have spent my life being uncomfortable. As assimilated as I am, I have never for one day forgotten who I am and what I am: a homosexual Latino. Being uncomfortable makes you think, and mindless prejudice sparks anger. My fury has fueled all my accomplishments" (*LA Times,* E13). In accepting his gayness, he remembers saying to himself, "I am a homosexual, and I am still a good human being, notwithstanding what the Catholic

Church, or my classmates, or my family members say. That act of compassion toward myself compels me to be compassionate toward others" (*LA Times,* E13).

In addition to his mystery series, Nava has cowritten a book calling for Americans to stand up for the Bill of Rights and the Constitution of the United States and give lesbian and gay people what should already be theirs: first-class citizenship. In *Created Equal: Why Gay Rights Matter to America,* the authors explain why anything less denies the guarantee of equality for all American citizens and widens the chasm between what our country promises and what it delivers.

Nava's gay-affirming voice addresses crucial social problems and issues. He unflinchingly tackles tough subjects such as child molestation and abuse, the psychology of addiction, political corruption, and the inequities in the criminal justice system. He has been praised for his insight into character and relationships, his skill with language, and his ability to create a suspenseful book. Although his mysteries are written for adults and mature teenagers, some of his other work is appropriate for use with high school students. Given his interest in social and political issues and the paucity of good books for young readers about gay Latinos, perhaps Nava will choose

the field of adolescent literature for some of his future writing projects. He is currently writing a memoir titled *Unlived Lives: The Memoirs of a Misfit.*

More Information About Michael Nava

JOURNALS AND NEWSPAPERS

"Brains and Rage." *The Bloomsbury Review.* June 1991, 1–2.

"Gay Latino Lawyer Mystery Writer." *Gay Community News,* July 15–20, 1990, 1–4.

"Poetic Justice." *Los Angeles Times.* May 6, 1990, E1, E13.

"The Mysteries of Writer Michael Nava." *San Francisco Sentinel,* June 1990, no page available.

"Tough, Smart and Gay." *Los Angeles Times,* April 19, 1990, J1, J13.

BOOKS

"Abuelo: My Grandfather, Raymond Acuña," in *A Member of the Family: Gay Men Write About Their Closest Relations,* edited by John Preston. Dutton, 1992. See below.

Contemporary Authors. Volume 124, 323.

Contemporary Gay American Novelists, edited by Emmanuel S. Nelson. Greenwood, 1993.

Gay and Lesbian Characters and Themes in Mystery Novels by Anthony Slide. McFarland, 1993.

The Gay and Lesbian Literary Heritage, edited by Claude J. Summers. Henry Holt, 1995.

• Autobiographical Short Story

"Abuelo: My Grandfather, Raymond Acuña," in *A Member of the Family*

Michael Nava's poignant piece in *A Member of the Family* not only will give readers insight into his childhood but will lend support to isolated gay teenagers and speak to the desperation of anyone who feels confined in a family and society that does not value who they are. "Childhood had been a form of imprisonment for me," he writes (19). Neither paraphrase nor quote can convey the complexity of what Nava says in this revealing statement about a very painful time in his life. Nava writes about his grandfather, who was a Yaqui Indian, intelligent and solitary, and the only person in Nava's family, besides Michael, who read for pleasure. "He represented a kind of masculinity from which I was not excluded by reason of my intelligence, or, later, my homosexuality. . . . Fat, myopic, and brainy, I escaped sissyhood only because of the aggressive gloominess I shared with my grandfather" (17). Nava's mother and grandmother loved the young boy and worried about his moodiness, but they did not know how to help him. And he didn't know how to ask for support, because he didn't understand his own pain. He spent his childhood waiting for his life to begin, and when he left for college, he vowed never to return home again. When he did return later, his grandmother had died and his grandfather had remarried. Nava observed the changes in his abuelo and later regretted that he hadn't talked with him about those years of estrangement. But Nava learned some important lessons from his grandfather. One of the most significant was that masculinity and self-denial are not the same thing. Nava writes with unflinching honesty about the isolation and unhappiness of his youth. His eloquent words will stimulate discussion and writing about family, culture, and society.

The twenty-four essays commissioned specifically for *A Member of the Family* feature some of the most talented gay male writers of our time. They turn their hearts and psyches inside out to show us the families who gave birth to them, raised them, rejected them, exiled them, and loved them. They write about the hurts they received and sometimes gave, the letters they left or sent, and of unresolved conflicts and reconciliations. This is a powerful collection that exposes the pain and isolation gay people often experience even within their own families. It is an excellent resource for educators and for high school students.

Grades 8–12

RELATED WORKS

Fiction

Tommy Stands Alone by Gloria Velásquez. Arte Público Press, 1995. See pages 174–175.

Who Framed Lorenzo Garcia? by R. J. Hamilton. Alyson Publications, 1995. See page 202.

Nonfiction

Chicana Lesbians: The Girls Our Mothers Warned Us About by Carla Trujillo. Third Woman Press, 1991. See page 212.

Compañeras: Latina Lesbians: An Anthology by Juanita Ramos. Routledge, 1994. See page 211.

Different Drummer: Homosexuality in America by Elaine Landau. Messner, 1986.

Growing Up Gay, Growing Up Lesbian: A Literary Anthology edited by Bennett L. Singer. New Press, 1994.

Young, Gay, and Proud! edited by Sasha Alyson. Alyson Publications, 1991.

"The Marriage of Michael and Bill," in *Friends and Lovers: Gay Men Write About the Families They Create*

Michael Nava's eloquent piece in this anthology not only will lend insight into his childhood and young adulthood but will provide hope to isolated gay teenagers whose relatives often deny their existence, disown and disinherit them, and throw them out of the house. Nava unflinchingly describes the despair of his early years when he blamed himself for his family's poverty and his stepfather's irresponsibility. When he realized he was gay, it was "the final, crushing blow" (112). He shares the ways in which he tried to compensate by being a model child: smart, well behaved, and respectful of elders. After a suicide attempt when he was fourteen, he cut himself off from his feelings and became "driven to make up in outside achievement the inner deficiency I felt . . ." (114). Years later at Stanford Law School, he met Bill, a fellow student, who would become his lover. After years of tortured boyhoods, the two set out to build a life together. Nava writes, "Bill was not the first family I had, but he was the first family I chose" (124).

Nava beautifully describes the ways in which love "softened the harshness with which I viewed myself and . . . opened up to me a possibility of happiness that I had never even considered" (112). His story will help educators and parents comprehend the wounds inflicted on young gays and lesbians by a homophobic society. Growing up in a world that teaches them to hide their sexual orientation and to hate themselves has resulted in a national tragedy: lesbian and gay youth who take their own lives account for 30 percent of all teen suicides in the United States. Information such as that provided in Nava's writing and the materials listed under Related Works (below) is desperately needed to counteract the oppression experienced by lesbian and gay youth. In places where books such as those listed in this chapter might be considered controversial, teachers should familiarize themselves with their school district's policy on controversial materials. They should always protect themselves by informing their supervisors in advance before using these materials.

RELATED WORKS

Bridges of Respect: Creating Support for Lesbian and Gay Youth: A Resource Guide by Katherine Whitlick. American Friends Service Committee, 1989.

Death by Denial: Studies of Suicide in Gay and Lesbian Teenagers, edited by Gary Remafedi. Alyson Publications, 1994.

Helping Gay and Lesbian Youth: New Policies, New Programs, New Practice, edited by Teresa DeCrescenzio. Haworth, 1994.

The Last Closet: The Real Lives of Lesbian and Gay Teachers, by Rita Kissen. Heinemann, 1996.

One Teacher in Ten, edited by Kevin Jennings. Alyson Publications, 1995.

Two Teenagers in Twenty: Writings by Gay and Lesbian Youth, edited by Ann Heron. Alyson Publications, 1993.

Created Equal: Why Gay Rights Matter to America

- Civil Rights
- Lesbians and Gay Men

Michael Nava and Robert Dawidoff have written a compelling and galvanizing book calling for Americans to stand up for the Bill of Rights and the Constitution of the United States and give lesbian and gay people what should already be theirs: first-class citizenship. Anything less denies the guarantee of equality for all American citizens and widens the chasm between what our country promises and what it delivers. Everyone interested in justice, liberty, and the future of civil rights for all people in the United States will want to read this powerful book. Nava and Dawidoff answer crucial questions, debunk debilitating myths, define prejudice, and analyze the current campaign against lesbian and gay equality. Of necessity, their book is about what gays and lesbians do *not* want. The authors provide accurate information about the real lesbian and gay agenda, which is *not* to have special privileges but to have the ordinary rights that all Americans enjoy.

Why should heterosexual Americans care about the rights of lesbians and gay men? Because the movement for equality for gay and lesbian people is central to the continuing defense of individual liberty in America. What is at stake is the future of constitutional principle and the rights of free individuals in American society. The struggle is about privacy, civil equality, individuality, and the right of all citizens to be free. "The traditional American doctrine that governments are instituted for the purpose of protecting the fundamental rights of individuals, and the historical process by which these rights have been extended to groups who were enslaved, oppressed, and otherwise unacknowledged at the time of the founding, are the twin pillars of the gay rights movement—as they have been of every struggle to extend the promise of individual liberty to Americans" (8).

Grades 11–Adult

RELATED WORKS

Gay and Lesbian Rights: A Reference Handbook. ABC-CLIO, 1994.

Hearing Us Out: Voices from the Gay and Lesbian Community by Roger Sutton. Little, Brown, 1995.

Lives of Notable Gay Men and Lesbians, edited by Martin Duberman. Chelsea House Series. Dates vary.

A More Perfect Union: Why Straight America Must Stand Up for Gay Rights by Richard D. Mohr. Beacon Press, 1994.

The Henry Rios Mystery Series: The Little Death, Goldenboy, How Town, The Hidden Law

- Mystery
- Gay Males
- AIDS
- Homophobia
- Child Abuse

Note: Michael Nava's mystery series is included as a resource for adults. His books are faithful to the conventions of the mystery genre, but they are set apart by their sensitivity, insight, and sense of social justice. Featuring Henry Rios, an ethical, compassionate gay Chicano lawyer, the award-winning books in the series are well written, perceptive, and entertaining. However, they deal with issues such as sexual violence, child pornography, and pedophilia, which are considered controversial in many parts of the country. Educators in areas where consciousness is more advanced might choose to use the series with very mature high school seniors. The series also provides important reading for adults who want to educate themselves about crucial issues facing their gay male students, colleagues, and community.

Please note the books listed in the Related Works section below for information about lesbian mysteries. The issues lesbians face are different from those faced by gay men. It is extremely important that educators note this difference; lumping the issues faced by lesbians and gay men together leads to distortion, erasure, and marginalization and can be extremely harmful to both groups. For readers interested in additional information concerning lesbian issues, please see Gloria Anzaldúa's chapter beginning on page 54.

The Little Death is the first novel in the Henry Rios mystery series for adults by Michael Nava. Henry Rios is a gay Chicano lawyer who practices law in a fictional college town near San Francisco. He graduated from law school ten years earlier, determined to be a good lawyer and an ethical person. At thirty-three, Henry is still a dedicated, but burned-out, public defender who has recently been demoted to handling arraignments after losing a major case. Increasingly disillusioned with the criminal justice system, he decides to quit his job and set up his own private practice. He meets and enters into a relationship with Hugh Paris, heir to a railroad fortune and a recovering heroin addict. Paris expresses fear for his own life, having recently become suspicious that his grandfather killed his grandmother and uncle. When his body is found in three feet of water in a creek near campus, the police call it an accident. Rios thinks it is murder, and with a heavy heart sets out to prove his theory. As he takes on some of the most powerful people in the country, he finds himself in a tangled web of greed, corruption, and legal trickery. With unexpected twists and turns, Nava keeps the reader guessing up until the last pages of this engaging book.

Goldenboy is the second book in the Henry Rios mystery series. Rios, who was a hard drinker in *The Little Death,* has fortunately three years later identified himself as an alcoholic, undergone treatment, and is now drinking tea and mineral water. The book opens with Rios reluctantly agreeing to join his friend Larry Ross in Los Angeles to work on a murder case. Ross and Rios had worked together several years earlier to knock a sodomy initiative off the California ballot with a lawsuit. Nava explains that sodomy is "a generic term for every sexual practice but the missionary position" (12). When Rios arrives in Los Angeles, he is saddened to discover that Ross has AIDS. As the book progresses and his friend's health deteriorates, he tries to provide emotional support, but communication between the two is somewhat limited by years of socialization, resulting in difficulty expressing feelings.

The case involves Jim Pears, a gay teenager who was arrested for the murder of a coworker who threatened to reveal his sexual orientation to his conservative parents. Ross asks Rios to help "balance the accounts" by representing Pears, who is a victim of the same disease he is—bigotry. Nava does an excellent job of exposing the ways in which the media distorts and sensationalizes the case. He also portrays the abhorrent ways that homophobia has taught Pears to hate himself. Even the compassionate Rios finds himself having difficulty dealing with Pears' self-loathing. Everyone, even Rios, thinks that Pears is guilty, and the district attorney seeks the death penalty. But as mystery lovers have learned to expect, there is much more to this case than is apparent at first.

This book is definitely for the mature reader, with its sexual violence and somewhat explicit lovemaking scenes, but it provides information about the complexities of a number of important issues. *Goldenboy* won the Lambda Award for the Best Small Press Publication in 1988.

How Town is the third book in the Henry Rios mystery series. The plot revolves around the subjects of pedophilia and child abuse. Rios is adamant that he doesn't defend child molesters, so readers will be surprised to find him representing Paul Windsor, a wealthy, abominable pedophile accused of murdering a dealer in child pornography. Rios takes the case only after his estranged sister (a lesbian) appeals to him on behalf of her friend Sara Windsor, Paul's wife. As Rios unravels the tangled threads of the intricate crime, the reader is invited to examine a number of important issues including racism, homophobia, poverty, family secrets, alcoholism, and sexual violence against children. While entertaining the reader with a tale of suspense, Nava stretches the psychological and emotional boundaries of the genre, as a number of lesbian mystery writers have been doing for some time.

The Hidden Law is the fourth book in the Henry Rios mystery series. Rios defends Michael Ruiz, a bitter, confused teenager who is accused of murdering State Senator Agustin Peña, a suavely corrupt politician. Peña has just returned to public life after killing an elderly man while driving drunk and doing a stint in an alcohol rehabilitation center. As Rios investigates the case, he uncovers information about family violence, turf conflicts in a halfway house, political turpitude, and the losses incurred by upward mobility. The resolution of the case strikes a painful chord for Rios and helps him make an important decision about his career.

Nava has recently completed two Rios books titled *The Death of Friends* and *The Burning Plain.*

RELATED WORKS

Gay Male Mysteries for Adults
Dave Brandstetter Mystery Series by Joseph Hansen. Viking Press, P.O. Box 120, Bergenfield, NJ 07621, 1-800-331-4624.

Lesbian Mysteries for Adults
Kate Delafield Mystery Series by Katherine V. Forrest. Naiad Press, P.O. Box 10543, Tallahassee, FL 32302.

Lauren Laurano Mystery Series by Sandra Scoppettone. Ballantine Books, 400 Hahn Road, Westminster, MD 21157, 1-800-733-3000.

Stoner McTavish Mystery Series by Sarah Dreher. New Victoria Publishers, P.O. Box 27, Norwich, VT 05055.

Chicana/o Mysteries

Gloria Damasco Mystery Series by Lucha Corpi. Arte Público Press, University of Houston, Houston, TX 77204-2090, 1-800-633-ARTE.

Sonny Baca Mystery Series by Rudolfo Anaya. See page 53.

Latina Mystery for Young Adults

The Girl of Playa Blanca by Ofelia Dumas Lachtman. Arte Público Press, University of Houston, Houston, TX 77204-2090, 1-800-633-ARTE. See page 103.

Luis J. Rodríguez

Chicano (1954–)

Birthday: July 9
Address: P.O. Box 476969
Chicago, IL 60647

"I began a new season of life. Intellect and body fused, I now yearned to contribute fully, embodied with conscious energy, to live a deliberate existence dedicated to a future humanity which might in complete freedom achieve the realization of its creative impulses, the totality of its potential faculties, without injustice, coercion, hunger and exploitation." (Always Running, 243–244)

Books by Luis J. Rodríguez

Always Running: La Vida Loca: Gang Days in L.A. Curbstone Press, 1993; Touchtone Books/Simon & Schuster, 1994; Libros en Español, Simon & Schuster, 1996.

America Is Her Name. Curbstone Press, 1997.

The Concrete River. Curbstone Press, 1991.

Poems Across the Pavement. Tía Chuchu Press, 1989; 1991.

Luis J. Rodríguez is an award-winning writer, journalist, and critic. His poetry and prose have been widely published in anthologies, magazines, textbooks, and newspapers. He is the director/founder of the Tía Chucha Press, the publishing wing of the Guild Complex, a nonprofit, cross-cultural, multiarts center in Chicago. He has conducted writing workshops in homeless shelters, prisons, and migrant camps as well as for gang members and Spanish-speaking children and their parents. He travels throughout the United States, Europe, and parts of Latin America, where he lectures, reads, and performs.

When Rodríguez was born, his family lived in the border town of Juárez, Mexico. But his mother made sure that he and his siblings were born on the El Paso side of the border. His father, Alfonso, was the principal of a local high school and his mother, María Estela, was a secretary at the school. His parents were opposites: his father was a stoic intellectual and his mother was full of fire, pain, and love. "This dichotomous couple, . . . this *curandera* and biologist, dreamer and realist . . . molded me; these two sides created a life-long conflict in my breast" (*Always Running,* 16). After his father was driven out of his position by trumped-up criminal charges, of which he was later found innocent, the family moved to the Mexican section of Watts in Los Angeles. Although Rodríguez's father was convinced that they would find a better life in the United States, he struggled to find employment, working at construction or factory jobs and finally settling for a position as a glorified custodian at a college. Rodríguez's mother found work cleaning houses and in the garment industry.

Describing himself as a quiet, withdrawn child, Rodríguez writes about the countless barriers set in their path. The Río Grande became a metaphor for their lives. "Our first exposure in America stays with me like a foul odor. It seemed a strange world, most of it spiteful to us, spitting and stepping on us, coughing us up, us immigrants, as if we were phlegm caught in the collective throats of this country" (*Always Running*, 19). The name-calling, the job hurdles, the geographical boundaries that kept Mexicans on the east side of the city, the language restrictions, the school environment that failed to validate their culture, and the poverty all led Rodríguez to feel invisible, to feel that he didn't belong. He notes, "I . . . would learn to hide in imaginative worlds—in books; in TV shows, where I picked up much of my English . . ." (*Always Running*, 14). He describes the humiliations at school, where speaking Spanish was considered a crime. He spent his first year building with blocks in the back of the classroom because his teachers didn't know what to do with a child who spoke only Spanish. There he suffered the indignity of not knowing how to ask to go to the bathroom and the danger of not understanding what to do during a fire drill. His older brother physically abused him, and they both suffered violence from other boys in the neighborhood. His anger and frustration festered, and when he was eleven he joined his first club, which gradually became a gang. There were no sports groups, Boy

Scouts, or camping groups available to him and other clubs were popping up all around him, challenging any young male who wasn't part of a clique. His memoir, *Always Running*, is his chilling account of his seven years as an active gang member. By the time he was fifteen, his parents had kicked him out of the house and he was living in the garage.

Somehow, amidst the violence and drugs, Rodríguez became involved in a number of constructive projects. He joined a group that studied politics, philosophy, economics, and the dynamics of social revolution. At thirteen, he participated in his first conscious political act when he led a school walkout to demand quality and accountable education. He painted murals and wrote and acted in plays. Later, he became a mural project supervisor, and painted several murals that are currently documented at the Social Public Research Center as part of the Smithsonian Institution's Chicano Mural Documentation Project. He was also a columnist for his school newspaper, a student council Speaker of the House, and president of the Chicano/a student group. He discovered the magic in books and read works such as *Down These Mean Streets* by Piri Thomas, which became his bible. At eighteen, he was an honorary winner in a literary contest and signed a book contract with a publisher in Berkeley.

When he was twenty, Rodríguez moved to South-Central Los Angeles to distance himself from his gang. He worked as a blast furnace operator, carpenter, truck driver, steel worker, and chemical refinery mechanic and took night classes in creative writing and journalism. From 1980 to 1985,

he worked as a journalist and organized Latino literary workshops. Then in 1985, he moved to Chicago to edit the *People's Tribune*. He became involved with the burgeoning poetry scene, joining performance poets in theaters, clubs, and bars. His poetry books were published, winning awards for their literary excellence. Rodríguez founded his own press, Tía Chucha Press, named for his beloved aunt, "the most creative influence of my childhood" (*Always Running*, 59).

The recipient of numerous awards and honors, Rodríguez received a 1992 Lannan Fellowship for Poetry; 1992 and 1994 Illinois Arts Council Fellowships; a City of Chicago Neighborhood Arts Program grant to do workshops in homeless shelters; and a 1990 Chicago Artists Abroad Grant to lecture and read in Paris. In 1993 he participated in a reading tour of Germany, Holland, and Austria with five other American poets.

The publication of Rodríguez's autobiographical account of his days as a gang member in Los Angeles, *Always Running*, has led to the next step in his career. As an expert on gangs, he travels the world on the lecture circuit, reading poetry and lecturing on the issues of youth, empowerment, and social justice. He has written a number of articles on this topic such as "Throwaway Kids: Turning Youth Gangs Around," printed in *The Nation*, in which he writes, "It's time the voices for viable and lasting solutions be heard. . . . First, that we realign societal resources in accordance with the following premises: that every child has value and every child can succeed. That schools teach by engaging the intelligence and creativity of all students. . . . And, that we root out the basis for the injustice and inequities that engender most of the violence we see today."

More Information About Luis J. Rodríguez

BOOKS AND ARTICLES

Always Running: La Vida Loca: Gang Days in L.A. by Luis J. Rodríguez. Curbstone Press, 1993; Touchstone Books/Simon & Schuster, 1994; Libros en Español, Simon & Schuster, 1996. See below.

Speaking of Poets II: More Interviews with Poets Who Write for Children and Young Adults, edited by Jeffrey S. Copeland and Vicky L. Copeland. National Council of Teachers of English. 1996.

"Gangs: The New Political Force in Los Angeles," by Luis J. Rodríguez. *Los Angeles Times,* September 13, 1992, no page available.

"Like Father, Like Son," by Rosalind Cummings. *Reader: Chicago's Free Weekly,* June 30, 1995, 1, 13–18, 23.

"Throwaway Kids: Turning Youth Gangs Around," by Luis J. Rodríguez. *The Nation,* November 21, 1994, 605–609.

"Who We Are," by Luis J. Rodríguez. *Hungry Mind Review,* Fall 1994, 7–8.

VIDEOTAPE

Luis J. Rodríguez. Lannan Literary Video #31. 1-800-869-7553.

Always Running: La Vida Loca: Gang Days in L.A.

Carl Sandburg Literary Arts Award for Nonfiction
Chicago Sun-Times *Book Award*
New York Times Book Review *Notable Book Award*
New York Public Library *Book for the Teen Age*

- Memoir
- Gangs

Always Running is Luis J. Rodríguez's riveting account of his years growing up in poverty in East Los Angeles, his turning to gang life as a means of preservation, and his ultimate triumph against the odds. He started writing the book when he was sixteen, but didn't complete it until his own son, Ramiro, joined a gang. He wrote it as a gift to his son, to provide support for him to find his way out of gang life. Hopefully, its message will reach other young people and help them understand the futility of gang warfare. Combining straightforward retrospection, philosophical commentary, and poetic insights, Rodríguez has created an unflinching book that will help readers understand why young people get involved in gangs. It provides insight into the roots of the problems while it describes the symptoms in raw detail. The author chronicles his experiences with racism in the schools, on the streets, in the police departments, and in the criminal justice system.

Rodríguez describes the uprootings, evictions, humiliations, and violence of his early years. He was a withdrawn, quiet child. "I was a broken boy, shy and fearful." His first encounter with gang members made a powerful impression on him. He realized that "All my school life until then had been poised against me: telling me what to be, what to say, how to say it" (42). He explains how the groups started as clubs and metamorphosed into gangs. Rodríguez was involved with gangs from age eleven to age eighteen. During this time, twenty-five of his friends died. Those years were filled with alcohol, drugs, sex, stealing, fighting, hijacking, shooting, and firebombing, as well as police harassment and brutality, jail cells, juvenile courts, and alternative schools. However, Rodríguez also became involved in painting murals, playing the saxophone, writing a book, student organizing, study groups, boxing, and writing plays, and he worked at various jobs including mowing lawns, delivering papers, and washing cars. He would take one step forward just to end up taking one step back.

Always Running has some important messages for educators. Rodríguez's brother was put in a class for mentally disabled children because he couldn't speak English. Luis spent his first year of school building with blocks because the teachers didn't know what to do with him. The students weren't allowed to speak Spanish; if a Spanish word slipped out, even on the playground, they were sent to the office for detention or corporal punishment. Later, Rodríguez's high school "had two principal languages. Two skin tones and two cultures. It revolved around class differences. . . . The school separated these two groups by levels of education: The professional-class kids were provided with college-preparatory classes; the blue-collar students were pushed into industrial arts" (84).

How did Rodríguez find his way out of the world of gangs? How did he overcome all the problems that threatened to pull him into a bottomless chasm? How did he find the courage to stop running? These questions and more are answered in this anguished, lyrical memoir. Reviewers have praised the book as an absolutely unique work, richly literary and poetic, a work of enormous beauty, a forceful story of triumph, as fierce and fearless, and an instant classic.

Grades 9–Adult

RELATED WORKS

Crews: Gang Members Talk to Maria Hinojosa by Maria Hinojosa. Photographs by German Perez. Harcourt Brace, 1995.

Don't Spit on My Corner by Miguel Durán. Arte Público Press, 1992.

New York Times Book Review. February 14, 1993, 26. (Review by Gary Soto.)

Voices from the Streets: Young Former Gang Members Tell Their Stories by Beth S. Atkin. Little, Brown, 1996.

America Is Her Name

Grades K–5

Luis J. Rodríguez has written a story for young children about a Latina girl who wants to be a writer. Followers of his work anxiously await the release of this important picture book.

• Poetry

The Concrete River
PEN Oakland/Josephine Miles Award for Literary Excellence

The Concrete River presents forty-three poems written by Luis Rodríguez. Dedicated to Nelson Peery, "who taught me the poetry of the fight, and the fight of the poetry," the book provides a tour of East Los Angeles with Rodríguez as the guide. With raw honesty and lyrical beauty, he describes the living conditions, the social realities, and the people who shaped his life. He paints vivid pictures of shattered glass, burned-out buildings, crumbling factory walls, and rusting cars. In "Watts Bleeds," he writes about the teachers who "threw me from classroom to classroom, not knowing where I could fit in" (13). The title poem of the collection tells about his near-death experience sniffing glue, the "plastic death in a can" (39). One of the most powerful poems in the collection is "The Best of Us," which is based on the trial of a police officer charged with the willful and unlawful murder of a seventeen-year-old Latino. Rodríguez captures the voice of Delia Torres, the young woman who was engaged to the victim and who witnessed the murder. Skillfully weaving actual courtroom proceedings into his verse, Rodríguez contrasts the officer's pattern of brutality with his official record of exceptional conduct. "The lies come dressed in suits and ties; they lurk behind badges and smothered grins" (43). Rodríguez writes about his experiences working in a steel factory. These poems are filled with the sounds and images of overhead cranes with huge iron jaws, the jackhammer's staccato song, the fiery blast furnace, and the reddened pots of molten metal. Inspired by writers like Piri Thomas, Rodríguez traded his wrenches, hammers, and screwdrivers for the tools of his new trade, words and ideas.

Rodríguez's poetry has been praised by reviewers for its poetic power, perceptive gaze, passion and compassion. In an interview on National Public Radio, Gary Soto said, "He's one of the most honest poets I've read in a long time, and that includes all other contemporary American writers. And his sense of tragedy in this area is . . . not overdone. I think it's accurate, and that's what makes him so compelling as a writer is . . . his accuracy and his willingness to get involved in the surroundings of his life."

Grades 12–Adult

RELATED WORKS

Poetry: *Poems Across the Pavement* by Luis Rodríguez. Tía Chucha Press, 1989; 1991. See below.

Interview: National Public Radio's "Morning Edition," May 14, 1992.

Poems Across the Pavement

• Poetry

San Francisco State University Poetry Center Book Award

This collection of nineteen poems by Luis J. Rodríguez embodies twenty years of revolutionary and literary endeavors. A former gang member and industrial worker, Rodríguez draws from his Los Angeles and Chicago experiences to weave an urban tapestry of voices, violations, and visions. His poetry speaks of class and race battles, industrial displacement, street turmoil, and police brutality. From a homeless shelter in Chicago, to a coastal town in Oaxaca, to an immigrant's trek across the border, to empowerment elections in Alabama, Rodríguez creates an alchemy of words, interlaced with anguish and hope. Throughout this collection, we hear the sounds of sweet music from a saxophone, the whisperings of people hungering for dignity, the humming of a soul lost to heroin, the blue chords of a guitar. What makes Rodríguez's poetry so powerful is its mixture of raw honesty and lyrical beauty, its passion about people, experiences, and conditions that are often distorted, ignored, and erased.

Grades 12–Adult

RELATED WORK

The Concrete River by Luis Rodríguez. Curbstone Press, 1991. See above.

Jan Romero Stevens

Hispanic/Latina (1953–)

Birthday: September 8
Contact: Northland Publishing
P.O. Box 1389
Flagstaff, AZ 86002

"Writing within a particular cultural setting validates the importance of that culture, its customs and language for those children who are a part of it. Just as importantly it brings understanding and appreciation to those children who are not familiar with it. Through my writing, my goal is to foster pride in our cultures, recognizing the differences between us but celebrating the equality of us all in God's world."   (personal communication)

Books by Jan Romero Stevens

Carlos and the Cornfield/Carlos y la milpa de maíz. Illustrated by Jeanne Arnold. Northland Publishing, 1995.

Carlos and the Skunk. Illustrated by Jeanne Arnold. Northland Publishing, 1997.

Carlos and the Squash Plant/Carlos y la planta de calabaza. Illustrated by Jeanne Arnold. Northland Publishing, 1993.

Jan Romero Stevens is a journalist and writer from Flagstaff, Arizona. She often speaks to students about her writing and conducts workshops for adults. Her engaging bilingual books for children have identified her as an important emerging writer in the field of children's literature.

Romero Stevens, whose birth mother is Latina, was adopted by an Anglo family as an infant. Years later, she started the search for her birth mother. Unlike many people in her situation, she found her rather quickly through a newspaper story she was researching. The subject of the story, a woman who makes sopaipillas, led her to her birth mother, Tommie Trujillo. Romero Stevens's adoptive mother, Charlotte Farmer, supported the search and went with her to meet Trujillo. The reunion was a very positive, joyful one for everyone. "It's about as wonderful as you can imagine" (*Arizona Daily Star [ADS]*, 5C), Romero

Stevens notes, still astonished by her good fortune.

Born in Las Vegas, New Mexico, Romero Stevens has lived in New Mexico and Arizona all her life. She has been a writer and columnist for Flagstaff's *Arizona Daily Star* for fifteen years, where she is currently the community news editor. "I like to write about the good news. I like to tell people what's good about this community" (*ADS,* 1C). She chooses to work part-time, to be able to spend more time with her family. She is married to Fred Stevens, the alumni director of Northern Arizona University. They have two sons, Jacob and Paul.

Romero Stevens's life as a writer is very much tied to her role as a mother. Carlos, the hero of three of her books, is a composite of her two sons. "I didn't want him to be a real modern-day boy. I wanted him from a time when family was important and things were safe, because that's the way I think things should be" (*ADS*, 5C). The plots for her books were taken from her personal experiences. She based her first book on her childhood memories of her mother warning her that if she didn't wash her ears, a potato plant would sprout in them. She repeated the warning to her own children, and later used it as the basis for *Carlos and the Squash Plant*. This bilingual book was met with such enthusiasm that she was inspired to continue writing about Carlos and his adventures. The second book, *Carlos and the Cornfield,* was based on her younger son's penchant for planting too many seeds in each hole in the family garden. The forthcoming third book features Carlos's encounter with a skunk.

Schools and libraries frequently invite Romero Stevens to speak with young readers. After she reads from her books, she talks with the students about the writing process. She shows them revised copies of her own writing, pointing out all the words that have been crossed out and all the revisions that have been made. Encouraging them to relax and enjoy writing, she reassures them that everyone makes mistakes on the first draft and that numerous revisions are common even for the most accomplished writers. She also talks about the differences between newspaper writing and fiction writing.

In her workshops for adults, Romero Stevens explores writing and publishing literature for children. She encourages participants to submit a work in progress to be critiqued in class. She also consults with individuals, sharing her experiences and insights into the world of writing for youngsters. She believes that the most important requirement for becoming a successful writer for young readers is that we love children and love writing for them, in addition to being familiar with the body of children's literature.

Romero Stevens has always been entranced by the culture, history, food, and people of the Southwest. She is exploring her Latina heritage by studying Spanish with her children and by writing bilingual books. She writes her books to help her children develop connections with their Latino culture. "We live in such a diverse society, I wanted them to appreciate their own heritage and also learn to appreciate other cultures" (*Mountain Campus News,* 2, 6).

More Information About Jan Romero Stevens

The Arizona Daily Star. October 26, 1995, 1C, 5C.

The Mountain Campus News. Northern Arizona University, October 15, 1993, 2, 6.

Sierra Vista Herald. March 15, 1994, 1A, 3A.

Carlos and the Cornfield/Carlos y la milpa de maíz

- Bilingual
- New Mexico
- Gardening

In this engaging story, Carlos finds out what his father means when he says, "You reap what you sow." The book begins with Carlos admiring a beautiful red pocket knife in Señor Lopez's store. In order to earn the money to buy it, he agrees to plant the sweet corn in the family garden. Papá explains that the seeds must be planted in a very special way, exactly three kernels in each hole. As Carlos works and works, he decides that it won't hurt to take a few shortcuts. All goes well at first and he rushes off to buy the knife. But when the corn sprouts, he has an uneasy feeling. Instead of confessing to his parents, he sets out to correct his mistakes, with humorous results. In the prequel, *Carlos and the Squash Plant,* Carlos learned a lesson about the importance of listening. Now in the sequel, he learns about the rewards of hard work, and another lesson about listening. Romero Stevens has created another funny book that young readers will enjoy. They will sympathize with Carlos's plight and, no doubt, have stories of their own about a time when they tried to take shortcuts in completing their chores. As in her first book, the details for this one came from Romero Stevens's own experience. When her family planted its own garden, her younger son always wanted to dump more seeds into the holes than were needed. The bilingual text is accompanied by colorful illustrations by Jeanne Arnold. The book ends with a mouthwatering recipe for cornmeal pancakes/*panqués de maíz.*

RELATED WORKS

Carlos and the Squash Plant/Carlos y la planta de calabaza by Jan Romero Stevens. Illustrated by Jeanne Arnold. Northland Publishing, 1993. See below.

Green Corn Tamales/Tamales de elote by Gina Macaluso Rodríguez. Illustrated by Gary Shepard. Hispanic Book Distributors, 1994. 1-520-882-9484. See page 183.

The Harvest Birds/Los pájaros de la cosecha by Blanca López de Mariscal. Children's Book Press, 1995.

Grades K–3

- Bilingual
- New Mexico
- Gardening

Carlos and the Squash Plant/Carlos y la planta de calabaza
Western Books Exhibition Award of Merit

This humorous tale features Carlos, a boy with a yen for gardening. He lives on a farm in the fertile Española Valley in northern New Mexico where he helps his parents tend a large garden plot. As he works, the rich brown soil ends up between his toes, under his fingernails, and inside his ears. His mother warns him that if he doesn't wash his ears, a squash will grow in them. But Carlos doesn't believe her and besides, he hates washing his ears. As the story sprouts, Carlos finds himself with a problem he didn't anticipate. What is that itchy feeling in his ear? Why is he wearing that wide-brimmed hat? And why does he go right to bed after dinner each evening?

Jan Romero Stevens has created an original story based on her own childhood experiences. Her mother told her that if she didn't wash her ears, a potato plant would grow out of them. Years later, she repeated the warning to her children and eventually she elaborated on it for her first book. Romero Stevens wrote the book for her two sons, to show them where she grew up and to teach them Spanish.

The consistent page layout features the English passage at the top of the page with the Spanish translation below, separated by miniature pictures. On the opposite page are Jeanne Arnold's large oil paintings. She studied the works of Latin American folk artists, painters from Mexico such as Diego Rivera, and Taos painters before embarking on the work for the book. Young readers and listeners of all backgrounds will enjoy this inventive tale and look forward to further adventures with Carlos. The book ends with a recipe for *calabacitas,* a spicy dish which features the tasty vegetables from Carlos's garden.

Grades K–3

RELATED WORK

Carlos and the Cornfield/Carlos y la milpa de maíz. Illustrated by Jeanne Arnold. Northland Publishing, 1995. See above.

Gary Soto

Chicano (1952–)

Birthday: April 12
Address: 43 The Crescent
Berkeley, CA 94708

"I'm a fan of Old Yeller, but wouldn't it be wonderful to discover in books the names of our dogs—Humo, Pecas, Tigre, Macho, and Princesa." (personal communication)

Books by Gary Soto

Baseball in April: And Other Stories. Harcourt Brace, 1990.

Boys at Work. Illustrated by Robert Casilla. Delacorte, 1995.

California Childhood: Recollections and Stories of the Golden State (editor). Creative Arts Books, 1988.

Canto Familiar. Illustrated by Annika Nelson. Harcourt Brace Children's Books, 1995.

The Cat's Meow. Illustrated by Joe Cepeda. Scholastic, 1995.

Chato's Kitchen. Illustrated by Susan Guevara. Putnam, 1995.

Crazy Weekend. Scholastic, 1994.

Everyday Seductions (editor). Ploughshares, 1995.

Father Is a Pillow Tied to a Broom. Slow Loris, 1980.

A Fire in My Hands: A Book of Poems. Scholastic, 1990.

I Thought I'd Take My Rat to School: Poems for September to June. Written with Karla Kuskin. Little, Brown, 1993.

Jesse. Harcourt Brace, 1994.

Lesser Evils: Ten Quartets. Arte Público Press, 1988.

Living up the Street: Narrative Recollections. Dell, 1992.

Local News. Harcourt Brace, 1993.

The Mustache. Putnam, 1995.

Neighborhood Odes. Illustrated by David Diaz. Harcourt Brace, 1992.

New and Selected Poems. Chronicle, 1995.

The Old Man and His Door. Illustrated by Joe Cepeda. Putnam, 1996.

Pacific Crossing. Harcourt Brace, 1992.

Pieces of the Heart: New Chicano Fiction (editor). Chronicle, 1993.

The Pool Party. Illustrated by Robert Casilla. Delacorte, 1993.

The Skirt. Illustrated by Eric Velasquez. Delacorte, 1992.

Small Faces. Dell, 1993.

Snapshots of the Wedding. Putnam, 1996.

A Summer Life. University Press of New England, 1990.

Summer on Wheels. Scholastic, 1995.

Taking Sides. Harcourt Brace, 1991.

Too Many Tamales. Illustrated by Ed Martinez. Putnam, 1993.

Films by Gary Soto

These films are available directly from Gary Soto. Call (510) 845-4718 to order or for more information.

The Bike. Rudy's odyssey around the neighborhood on his new bicycle. VHS, 11 minutes.

Novio Boy. Rudy's first date. VHS, 30 minutes.

The Pool Party 1993 Andrew Carnegie Medal winner. VHS, 28 minutes. For more information, see the review for the book on pages 160–161.

Gary Soto, recognized as one of America's best Chicano writers, was a senior lecturer at the University of California at Berkeley for many years. A celebrated poet, he also creates short stories, picture books, novels, and films. He is one of the few Mexican American authors who writes for adults, young adults, and children. He celebrates and remains true to his heritage in his writing; the universality of his vision and his skill with the use of words have established him as a major contemporary writer. His writing springs from his Chicano heritage and working-class background; his probing-yet-lyrical poetry and prose provide inspiration for all his readers, especially those who seldom read about themselves in books.

A third-generation Mexican American, Soto was born and raised in the San Joaquin Valley, in Fresno, California. Like many Latinos in the area, his parents and grandparents worked in the fields hoeing cotton and picking grapes, or worked in the packing houses, factories, or warehouses. In addition, his mother candled eggs for a major supermarket. When Gary was only five years old, tragedy struck his family: his father, aged twenty-seven, was killed in a factory accident. Soto has written about this trauma repeatedly; almost every collection of poetry or prose refers to it in some way. In *Lesser Evils,* he writes that his mother never talked about his father's death; his name was never mentioned in their house. They saw his grave only in photographs: "a quiet settled on us like dust . . . We lived poor years because he died. We suffered quietly and hurt even today" (83).

Soto's mother remarried two years later; his stepfather was an alcoholic white man who worked loading boxes onto a conveyor belt at a warehouse. Soto describes him as "a tired man when he came into my life . . . He hurt from the house payments, the asking wife, the five hungry kids to clothe . . ." (*Small Faces,* 17–18). Soto and his siblings were home alone much of the time while their parents were at work. In "Being Mean," he writes, "We were terrible kids, I think. My brother, sister, and I felt a general meanness begin to surface from our tiny souls . . ." (*Living up the Street,* 1). Living in the middle of industrial Fresno, once rated the worst city in the United States by the *Rand-McNally Report,* surrounded by factories, warehouses, and junkyards, Soto remembers the summers he was four and five. He writes that there was much to do: "Wrestle, eat raw bacon, jump from the couch, sword fight with rolled-up newspapers, steal from neighbors, kick chickens, throw rocks at passing cars . . ." (*Living up the Street,* 2). They also drank Kool-Aid, fought, set fires, swiped apricots and peaches from the trees in neighbors' yards, and watched television, where Soto learned about "the comfortable lives of white kids. There were no beatings, no rifts in the family. They wore bright clothes . . . They hopped into bed with kisses and woke to glasses of fresh orange juice . . ." (*Living up the Street,* 30). Soto attended parochial school until he was in the fifth grade; at St. John's Catholic School, nine-year-old Gary, nicknamed Blackie, was seated among the "stupids" (*Living up the Street,* 28). When asked what he wanted to do when he grew up, Soto's responses ranged from priest to hobo, and later in sixth grade, paleontologist. He decided to attend summer school one year; there he took a special interest in history and earned his first A. He became a school cadet in junior high; when he was sixteen and couldn't find a summer job, he worked as a volunteer recreational assistant for the city parks department. In high school, he joined the wrestling team. During his younger years, he tried various schemes to earn money, doing yardwork and running errands. When he was old enough, he started working in the fields, hoeing cotton and picking grapes, to earn money to buy his school clothes. Peer pressure from his classmates, whom he describes as "clothes conscious and small time social climbers" (*Living up the Street,* 107), pushed him to endure the backbreaking, mindnumbing work in the fields. In one strikingly poignant piece, Soto described a jacket, the color of day-old guacamole, that he was forced to wear for several years; this hated jacket symbolized all the hurts and embarrassments that he suffered during his childhood (*Small Faces,* 37–41).

Soto was often told by those around him that he "would never do anything, be anyone. They said I would work like a donkey . . ." (*Living up the Street,* 110). When he was seventeen, he ran away from home for the summer to work in a tire factory in Glendale, California. He had a 1.6 average at Roosevelt High School. But he was afraid he would have to spend his life working in the fields, so he decided to go to a community college and later to Fresno State University. It was there that he discovered poetry. At first he majored in geography, but when he stumbled across an anthology of contemporary poetry in the library, his life changed forever. "I was really little more than a boy when I first scribbled out a few sad lines of poetry. . . . Having come from a family with no books . . . I began writing my first poems in 1973 . . ." (*New and Selected Poems,* 1–2). Suffering through college poverty, he worked at all kinds of odd jobs, including washing cars, picking grapes, digging weeds, mowing lawns, and chopping beets and cotton. He believed in César Chavez and the United Farm Workers and was "given over to the destiny of poverty, unmanageable and angry in my ragged Levis, . . . given . . . over to the alchemy of poetry" (*New and Selected Poems,* 1–2). "When I first studied poetry, I was single-minded. I woke to poetry and went to bed with poetry" (*A Fire in My Hands,* 5). From the poetry that he was reading,

he saw that he was not alone in his alienation; he discovered the power of the written word to capture his experience and share it with others.

With strict discipline, he developed his gift for writing. He graduated from Fresno State University magna cum laude in 1974 and married Carolyn Sadako Oda in 1975. In 1976 he earned an M.F.A. in creative writing from the University of California at Irvine, spending that year as a visiting writer at San Diego State University. In 1977 he started teaching at the University of California at Berkeley, where he was until recently a senior lecturer in the English Department. His poetry appears frequently in literary magazines and he has received fellowships from the Guggenheim Foundation, the National Endowment for the Arts, and the California Arts Council. The recipient of many honors and awards, Gary Soto has written numerous books; over twenty of these books of poetry, prose, and children's stories are currently in print.

When asked about his writing process, Soto reveals that he works on one book at a time because he is afraid of getting scattered if he tackles too many projects. He writes in the mornings because his mind is clear and he can concentrate then. He works in his garage, which he has turned into a study. If he gets stuck on a line, he stops and works out with a bench press until his imagination kicks in again. He feels that "It is a brave act to keep the rush of words going. It . . . is utter loneliness and uncertainty" (*Pieces of the Heart,* vii–x).

Although Gary Soto is best known for his poetry, he also writes in a

number of other genres. Most of his work is unflinchingly personal; the majority of it springs from his memories of a childhood spent in the barrio. When asked how he remembers the details of his childhood so precisely, Soto answered, "For a long time I never left my childhood. I was always thinking about it . . . my father was killed in an industrial accident . . . I kept going over those events in my mind until I was into my 30s—thinking that if we'd done this instead of that, everything would have been different" (*NEA Today,* 9). Looking back on his early years, he does not think that he came from a culturally rich family in the educational or academic sense of the word. "We had our own culture which was more like the culture of poverty, as I like to describe it" (*Dictionary of Literary Biography,* 246). He notes that "I don't think I had any literary aspirations when I was a kid. In fact we were pretty much an illiterate family. We didn't have books and no one encouraged us to read" (*Something About the Author,* 211). This was before the belief in ethnic pride gained momentum; Soto remembers feeling "that being poor and Mexican was wrong" (*Lesser Evils,* 84). Assimilation was the rule of the time, and as a result, Soto did not become fluent in Spanish. In all his writing, he never mentions a teacher who took a special interest in him when he was a child or encouraged him to pursue his dreams.

But Soto believes that "Literature can make a difference to the marginal kid" (*NEA Today,* 9). He read *To Sir with Love* in high school and felt it was written for him, although now he thinks it is poorly written. This sensitivity to young people's concerns and the ability to portray the world as it is perceived by youngsters enables Soto to write books that appeal to young readers of all backgrounds. As could be expected, his books for children and young adults are more playful and humorous than his writing for high school students and adults. Though entertaining and often tinged with humor, these works often have an angst at their core, reflecting his concern with social issues such as poverty, violence, and racism. Soto asserts, "I write because there is pain in my life, our family, and those living in the San Joaquin Valley. . . . I write because those I live and work with can't write" (*Contemporary Literary Criticism*, 275). He speaks for those who have been relegated to the fringes of society, who do not have a voice to express the pain, humiliation, and disillusionment of their lives. He is able to incorporate information about significant issues into his stories and poems in such as way as to leave the reader with hope and renewed determination to continue the important work that needs to be done.

The critical reception to Gary Soto's writing has been overwhelmingly positive. Time and again, reviewers praise his ability to tell a story, to transcend the boundaries of ethnicity and age, and to transport his readers beyond the present time, place, and perspective. His work has filled a gap in literature for children and young adults; hopefully, his books are reaching young people who may feel doomed, as Soto once did, to a future in the fields or factory. Eloquently speaking to the aspirations and dilemmas in young people's lives, his voice helps to encourage them to strive to fulfill their dreams. Hopefully, his work will inspire young Chicanos and Chicanas to become writers themselves.

More Information About Gary Soto

Authors and Artists for Young Adults. Volume 10, 176–182.

Contemporary Authors. Volume 119, 352.

Contemporary Authors. Volume 125, 424–427.

Contemporary Literary Criticism. Volume 32, 401–405.

Contemporary Literary Criticism. Volume 80, 275–303.

Dictionary of Literary Biography. Volume 82, 246–252.

NEA Today. November 1992, 9.

Something About the Author. Volume 80, 209–215.

• Short Stories

Baseball in April: And Other Stories

American Library Association Best Book for Young Adults
Booklist *Editor's Choice*
Horn Book *Fanfare Selection*
California Library Association's John and Patricie Beatty Award
Parenting Magazine *Reading Magic Award*

This award-winning collection of eleven short stories depicts the everyday experiences of young Latino/a people growing up in Fresno, California. The main characters ride bicycles, try out for Little League, study karate, play with Barbie dolls, participate in the school talent show, compete in a marbles tournament, and try to earn money to buy a guitar. Soto writes the stories of the kids we usually don't read about: the ones who do not make it into Little League, who do not excel at karate, and who ride old bicycles that break down. These refreshing stories show what young people do when they are not chosen to play on Little League teams: they find a way to play baseball anyway. In "Broken Chain," Alphonso's family cannot afford braces for his teeth, so he decides to fix them by pushing on them. "After breakfast that Saturday he went to his room, closed the door quietly, turned the radio on, and pushed for three hours straight" (3). In "The No-Guitar Blues," Fausto earns a twenty-dollar reward for finding a lost dog, but ends up putting the money in the collection plate at church instead of buying a long yearned-for guitar. In "Mother and Daughter," Yollie and her mother dye an old dress for her to wear to the eighth-grade fall dance. In "The Karate Kid," Gilbert's experiences with karate classes are nothing like the movies. Soto's stories, moving, yet humorous, present themes of friendship, family relationships, independence, success, and learning to cope with failure. The glossary defines the Spanish words, phrases, and expressions used in the book.

Grades 5–9

RELATED WORK
Local News by Gary Soto. See pages 157–158.

Canto Familiar

• Poetry

Hungry Mind Review *Children's Book of Distinction*

This companion volume to *Neighborhood Odes* includes twenty-five poems about the pleasures and woes that Mexican American children experience growing up. The *cantos* (songs) sing the praises of familiar activities such as picnics, soccer, gathering *nopales,* dancing *folklórico,* and eating watermelon. Children wear their shoes on the wrong feet and put their coats on backwards just for fun. They gaily toss *bebé* into the air on an old hand-me-down sarape. They create drums out of oatmeal boxes and guitars out of shoe boxes. They savor *menudo, chicharrones,* sunflower seeds, and snow cones. They roll out tortillas into the shapes of faraway lands. They do the dishes, iron, take math tests, lose eyeglasses, and accidently lock handcuffs on their wrists. Teachers will especially enjoy "My Teacher in the Market." As in all of Soto's books, feline companions have a featured place in this volume: we meet Hambre, who loves tortillas; Pleitos, who wrestles socks and bullies yarn; Slinky, who tips over garbage cans; and the good-luck kitten, who gets stranded on the roof. These poems sing about an ironing board that squeaks with pain, a face as shiny as a moon over a hill, the animals of hunger inside a growling stomach, and the big hand on a clock washing its face over and over. Soto has done it again—found an exuberant way to celebrate the ordinary events of life. No glossary is provided for the Spanish terms, which can be understood through the context of the poetry. This is illustrator Annika Nelson's first children's book; eleven of her prints grace the pages of this jaunty volume, one of Soto's most lighthearted works.

Grades 3–6

RELATED WORKS
Companion volume: *Neighborhood Odes* by Gary Soto. See page 158.

The Cat's Meow

• Cats
• Language
• Humor

Eight-year-old Graciela can't believe her ears when her feline friend, Pip, looking at her empty food bowl, says, *"Quiero más,* Graciela." ("I want more.") But when Graciela tries to get her to say something else, she clams up and runs across the street. Graciela tries to discuss this strange development with her good-natured and absentminded parents, but they are too distracted with their daily events and, both having hearing losses, misunderstand her.

This pattern continues until Graciela finally convinces Pip to explain how she learned to talk. It seems that once when the humans were out of town on vacation, Pip made friends with a kindly neighbor, Sr. Medina, who taught her to speak Spanish. After hearing this story, Graciela is anxious to meet Sr. Medina. As the story unfolds, she also meets a tarantula, a snake, some mice, a nosy neighbor, several news reporters, and a police officer. She even receives a Spanish dictionary in the mail. But why did Pip and Sr. Medina disappear? And who is this new cat who knows how to speak French?

This is one of Gary Soto's most humorous books. Revised from an earlier version published by Strawberry Hill Press in 1987, this story is illustrated with whimsical black-and-white drawings. Spanish words are translated at the bottom of each page; non-Spanish-speaking students may pick up a few words or develop an interest in learning a second language. Animal lovers will be relieved with the way the story ends.

Grades 2–5

• Cats
• Mice
• Food
• Humor

Chato's Kitchen

Parents' *Choice Honor Award*
Parenting Magazine *Reading Magic Award*

Chato, the coolest low-riding cat in East Los Angeles, can't believe his luck. The new neighbors busily moving in next door are none other than the plumpest, juiciest little *ratoncitos* (mice) that he has ever seen. Ever the quick thinker, he extends a neighborly invitation to the tasty, er, lovely family for a surprise dinner at his house. The *ratoncitos* RSVP in the affirmative, if they can bring a friend. The roguish cat gleefully agrees, figuring six mice are better than five. Whistling "La Bamba," he starts to prepare the feast; his best friend, Novio Boy, a cat with the loveliest growl in the barrio, drops by. Soon the feline duo is whisker deep in food-fixing: fajitas, carne asada, chiles rellenos, salsa, enchiladas, and a sweet, smooth *flan*. Meanwhile the mice family, although busy settling into their new home, remember to prepare a special dish—*quesadillas*—to take to their evening engagement. Soon their friend, Chorizo (sausage), arrives and they all descend upon Chato's door at the appointed hour. Chato and Novio Boy are all set for the main course to walk through the door but they haven't prepared themselves for Chorizo, who turns out to be a cool, road-scraping dachshund. Foiled, the two would-be villains resign themselves to a meal sans mouse. With this minor change in the menu, the dinner party assembles at the table and proceeds to enjoy the meal.

This tale is rendered hilarious by Soto's scintillating wit and Guevara's bold, innovative illustrations. Each page, with the savory seasoning of Spanish words and the feast of salty paintings, captures the flavor of life in *el barrio*.

RELATED WORK

"Chato's Kitchen," by Gary Soto. *Book Links,* January 1996, 54–55.

All Ages

Crazy Weekend

- Robbers
- Photography
- Humor

Seventh graders Hector Beltran and Mando Tafolla spend a zany weekend in Fresno visiting Hector's uncle, Julio Silva. When Hector's mother first suggested that he needed to get out of East Los Angeles and see some of the world, he had visions of Paris or Madrid. But now here they are in Uncle Julio's messy apartment sleeping on a lumpy couch and eating cold cereal. When Julio, a photographer, takes them on an aerial photo shoot of a local farm, the boys find themselves in the back of a rickety, rusted-out old airplane. While flying, they spot a broken-down armored truck and two suspicious men; Uncle Julio quickly snaps some pictures of the robbers. The next morning they read about a robbery in the newspaper and Uncle Julio takes his photographs to the paper. Hector and Mando are interviewed for the Today's Youth section and the article is mistakenly printed in the next paper. The two robbers, Freddie Bork and Huey "Crybaby" Walker, see the article and decide they have to teach the boys a lesson. But the bumbling villains are not prepared for the scared but quick-witted boys. The resulting comedy of errors is hilarious.

This is an action-packed, humorous adventure story. The lively sprinkling of Spanish words and phrases are translated in a glossary at the end of the book; Soto throws in some interesting information about photography and journalism as well. His characters are likeable and welldrawn; even minor characters such as Mrs. Inouye, whose farm is photographed, are portrayed with complexity. After reading this crime-doesn't-pay thriller/comedy, readers will want to check out the further adventures of Hector and Mando in the sequel, *Summer on Wheels*.

Grades 5–9

RELATED WORK
Sequel: *Summer on Wheels*. See page 163.

A Fire in My Hands: A Book of Poems

- Poetry

This collection of twenty-three poems originally intended for adults celebrates small, significant moments in the poet's life. In the foreword, Gary Soto notes that he thinks of his poems as a "working life, by which I mean that my poems are about common, everyday things. . . ." His unusual poems celebrate ordinary topics such as baseball, earning money, music, dancing, hitchhiking, oranges, and feeding birds. Each poem is prefaced by a short introduction in which the poet explains its origin. Arranged in roughly chronological order beginning in childhood, and moving through adolescence and young adulthood, the poems provide a glimpse into the way the poet's mind works. The informal free verse utilizes consciously plain language; the skilled use of words and images will stay with readers of all ages.

In the foreword, Soto shares that at first he was scared to write poetry, in part because his poetry teacher, to whom the book is dedicated, was a stern man who could see the errors in his poems. There is a message here for teachers and for young writers who are seeking to express themselves through language. The friendly four-page "Questions and Answers about Poetry" section at the end of the book provides gentle encouragement for poetry enthusiasts and struggling writers of all ages.

Grades 7–12

• Art
• College
• Farm Labor
• United Farm Workers
• Vietnam War

Jesse

Loosely autobiographical, this tenderly written, contemplative novel is one of Gary Soto's most poignant books. Set in Fresno, California, in the late 1960s and using a first-person narrative, the book chronicles seventeen-year-old Jesse's painful search for a way out of a lifetime of poverty and backbreaking labor in the fields. He and his older brother, Abel, know that the way to get ahead is to work hard and get an education. Jesse leaves home and quits high school during his senior year to join Abel in community college. Sharing a rundown apartment, they supplement their meager Social Security payments by spending the weekends working in the fields and scrounging junk to sell. (Their father was killed in an factory accident when they were "small, twigs of flesh.") Introspective Jesse, plagued by self-doubts, searches for meaning in his dubious classes, often succumbing to pressure from his politicized friends to join the protests led by César Chávez and Dolores Huerta. His art classes provide the most comfort; he enters his drawing, titled ¡Huelga!, of the United Farm Workers strike in an art exhibit at the college after working and reworking it "until I thought I had finally got their sadness right . . ." (122). After months of work and study, the brothers attempt to hitchhike to the beach during spring break; however, they spend two forlorn days camping beside the highway waiting for a ride. When passing teenagers throw eggs at them, they trudge off in different directions to cry; eventually they get back home and spend the remainder of their vacation chopping cotton.

Jesse finds pleasure in the small things in life: a field trip to the country with his biology class, inner-tubing on the Piedra River, eating huevos con weenie burritos with his brother, memories of elementary school, and riding in the back of a truck with the wind in his face. All the while, the Vietnam War and the threat of being drafted cast a cloud over their lives. The story ends when Abel is drafted and leaves for Vietnam and Jesse is left alone to ponder his future. He fears that he will never escape the "fields running for miles with cantaloupes like heads, all faceless in the merciless sun" (166). And yet, the reader is left with the feeling that somehow, Jesse will find a way to follow his dreams.

Grades 9–Adult

RELATED WORKS

Calling the Doves By Juan Felipe Herrera. Children's Book Press, 1995. See page 182.

Voices from the Fields: Children of Migrant Farmworkers Tell Their Stories by Beth Atken. Little, Brown, 1993. See page 201.

. . . y no se lo tragó la tierra/ . . . And the Earth Did Not Devour Him by Tomás Rivera.
Translated by Evangelina Vigil-Piñon. Arte Público Press, Third Edition, 1995. See
page 183.

Living up the Street: Narrative Recollections

American Book Award from the Before Columbus Foundation

• Autobiographical Short Stories

Gary Soto offers twenty-one narrative recollections of his life growing up in
Fresno, California; he dedicates this book to the people who lived these stories: his brother, Rick, his sister, Debra, and Little John and Scott. These
autobiographical short stories cover over twenty years of Soto's life, beginning when he was five years old and proceeding roughly chronologically until
shortly after his first book was published in 1977. The book opens with a
description of the street where Soto's family lived in 1957; Braly Street was in
the middle of industrial Fresno, surrounded by factories and a junkyard. In
the second vignette, Soto shares more details about his father's accidental
death and his reactions than he does in any other work; he refers to this
tragedy in a number of other poems and stories. He writes about summers
spent drinking Kool-Aid, fighting with his siblings and neighbor kids, participating in the local city park's recreational activities, and watching television,
where he learned about the "comfortable lives of white kids" (30).

Soto writes with amazing detail about the traumas and triumphs of his
early years. He generously shares information about his mistakes and embarrassments as well as his successes. This collection will help readers gain
insight into his other works. His prose often reads like poetry: "We walked
without saying too much because talking ruined the joy of noiseless minds"
(77). This book includes three school photographs of Soto and his classmates
in first grade, fifth grade, and sixth grade.

Grades 10–Adult

RELATED WORK

A Summer Life by Gary Soto. See page 162.

Local News

• Short Stories

In this companion book to *Baseball in April,* Gary Soto again touches a universal chord. In his second volume of short stories, as in his poems, the
author uses his ability to perceive and share the common events that make
life interesting. Readers are introduced to Araceli, whose adventurous spirit
leads her to take a long-awaited but disappointing nickel-a-pound airplane
ride to benefit Children's Hospital. We meet Blanca Mendoza, whose determination to stay up until midnight on New Year's Eve results in her being
accidentally locked out of the house in the cold. Elizabeth and Leonard
Aguirre's experiences going door-to-door selling candy and coloring books
of superheroes no one has ever heard of bring back memories of selling
greeting cards in the 1950s. Other stories feature a school play, radio program
requests for "Oldies but Goodies," racquetball games, and a mean older

brother who plays dirty tricks on his little brother. After enjoying thirteen-year-old Alma's trick-or treat escapades, readers might want to read *Willie Bea and the Time the Martians Landed* by Virginia Hamilton for another fascinating Halloween story. And those wanting more information after reading about Ignacio "Nacho" Carrilla's frustrating attempts to become a vegetarian can turn to *Much Ado About Aldo* by Johanna Hurwitz. The lost raider's jacket is reminiscent of another book by Soto, *The Skirt*.

The small touches make these stories even more special: the hot coffee over soggy cornflakes; the dark paneled walls hung with pictures of happy and sad clowns and the Kennedys; the Sears catalogue game, in which the children take turns choosing the toys they like; and the tennis shoes lined with plastic sandwich bags to keep one's feet dry. Readers searching for positive portrayals of fat people will be disappointed in "Nickel-a-Pound Plane Ride" but may find "El Radio" somewhat more encouraging. The peppering of Spanish words and phrases adds to the vitality of the vignettes. A glossary is included.

RELATED WORKS

Baseball in April by Gary Soto. See pages 152–153.

The Skirt by Gary Soto. See page 161.

Grades 4–7

• Poetry

Neighborhood Odes

Twenty-one poems full of laughter, love, joy, regret, and humor celebrate everyday things such as lawn sprinklers on a hot day, a day in the country, feline and canine friends, and eating warm tortillas with butter. Soto shows us that there is poetry in the common, ordinary events of our lives. The Spanish words in the text can be understood by non-Spanish readers through the context of the poems; a glossary is available so one can confirm the meanings. These poems are written with such humor and perceptivity that they will even appeal to youngsters who are reluctant poets. Soto's sensitivity is apparent in poems such as "Ode to Mi Gato," in which he expresses his love for the white cat he had found abandoned as a kitten: "We lap up his love and/He laps up his welcome." Librarians will enjoy "Ode to My Library," in which the poet confides that he devoured thirty books in a summer read-a-thon, researched the Incas, and helped paint a mural about the Aztecs. This is Caldecott Award–winning illustrator David Diaz's first children's book; his playful black-and white cut paper illustrations accompany ten of the poems.

Grades 4–7

RELATED WORK

Companion volume: *Canto Familiar* by Gary Soto. See page 153.

• Poetry

New and Selected Poems

Selected poems from six of Soto's previous books, some of which are out of print, and twenty-three new poems comprise this brilliant collection. The poems are organized into chapters, titled from the previous books: "The

Elements of San Joaquin," "The Tale of Sunlight," "Where Sparrows Work Hard," "Black Hair," "Who Will Know Us?", and "Home Course in Religion." In the preface, "Sizing Up the Sparrows," Soto chronicles his early development as a poet, beginning when he "was really little more than a boy when I first scribbled out a few sad lines of poetry . . ." (1).

Soto draws upon his experiences growing up in Fresno, California, to present a multifaceted collage of vividly drawn characters living amid urban violence, racism, backbreaking labor, and disillusionment; with a vision that transcends the ordinary, he chronicles the small joys and large angers of their lives. The opening poem, dedicated to César Chávez, focuses on the elements of field, wind, stars, and sun. "Already I am becoming the valley,/A soil that sprouts nothing/For any of us" (6). The harvest will not go to the ones who have worked the fields. Soto's poems are about alienation, struggle, and the universal themes of birth and death, but they also confirm the power of the human spirit to survive and soar. He has a special gift for speaking eloquently and unflinchingly of the struggles of his life: the accidental death of his father when he was five years old, the poverty and economic hardships he grew up with in California's central valley, and the racial prejudice against his people. His poetry calls into question the social and political order of America, asking profound questions that need to be addressed. Soto has the rare ability to write about the harsh realities of life and at the same time evoke feelings of hope.

Grades 10–Adult

Pacific Crossing

- Exchange Programs
- Japan
- Martial Arts
- Travel

In this sequel to *Taking Sides*, fourteen-year-old Lincoln Mendoza and his *carnal*, Tony Contreras, participate in a six-week summer exchange program in Japan. From their Noe Valley school in San Francisco, the two almost–eighth graders are selected for the cross-cultural experience because of their interest in the Japanese martial art of *shorinji kempo*. After the nine-hour flight to Tokyo, they travel to Atami, a town of twenty thousand people, where they meet their host families. They encounter new experiences, meet interesting people, and discover a Japan much different from the one they expected. When they prepare a feast of frijoles, salsa, and tortillas for their host families, they realize that cooking Mexican food is not as easy as they had assumed. They learn to enjoy the public baths, attend a sumo wrestling match, Lincoln tolerates an ear cleaning, and they spend interminable hot hours tending the eggplants in the family gardens. On a camping trip, Lincoln, unlicensed and nervous, drives his host family's father to a hospital after a deadly spider bite. And Lincoln spends many arduous, satisfying hours practicing *shorinji kempo*; in his final test, he passes to *nikkyu* rank, two steps from black belt. He establishes a special friendship with fourteen-year-old Mitsuo Ono, his new Japanese brother; the two look forward to the day Mitsuo can visit Lincoln in San Francisco; this reunion has interesting potential as a sequel.

With humor and sensitivity, this book challenges numerous misconceptions each boy has about the other's culture and language, and brings to life the truism that people are more the same than different. The reader, along with the characters, learns much about both cultures and about the potential people have to grow and change as a result of multicultural experiences. Soto includes numerous terms in Spanish and Japanese which non-Spanish and non-Japanese speakers will enjoy trying to translate from the context; glossaries are available for confirming the meanings. Followers of Lincoln's problems adjusting to his move to suburbia in *Taking Sides* will be interested in the fact that the family decided to move back to San Francisco, this time settling in the Noe Valley near the Mission District where Linc had spent his first twelve years.

Grades 6–10

Mature students might be interested in reading *El Yanqui* by Douglas Unger, a book about a student exchange program in Argentina.

RELATED WORKS

Prequel: *Taking Sides* by Gary Soto. See pages 163–164.

For mature teenagers: *El Yanqui* by Douglas Unger. Ballantine, 1988.

• Parties
• Socioeconomic Class

The Pool Party

Ten-year-old Rudy Herrera is surprised and excited when he receives an invitation to a pool party from Tiffany Perez, the richest and most popular girl in school. He has spent most of the summer helping his father with his gardening jobs. Now his thoughts turn to finding just the right inner tube to take to the party. His family has plenty of advice: his older sister tries to improve his manners and his father teaches him how to make small talk. Gently reassuring his son that Tiffany will like him because he is real, Father adds, "Listen, they may be rich folks, but don't worry. Just go and have fun . . ." (80). After a narrow escape involving a stolen car and a trial ride down the river on the inner tube, Rudy is ready to make a big splash at the party. The party-goers snicker at first ("Tiffany invited *him* to the party?"), but their snobbishness soon turns to curiosity as they compare their fancy pool toys with Rudy's huge, decorated inner tube. By the time Rudy leaves the party, his eyes are red from the chlorine and the tube is nearly flat because everyone has used it.

Gary Soto gives young readers a light, funny story with likeable characters. The contrasts between Rudy's and Tiffany's lives are evident. While Rudy's family eats frijoles, *papas*, and Kool-Aid and snacks on corn nuts and root beer, Tiffany serves brie, carrot sticks, ambrosia, and miniature cobs of corn at her party. When Rudy tells Tiffany about his adventures on Francher's Creek, she responds that her parents usually take her to Hawaii. When the harpist who is providing music for the party finishes playing, Rudy is puzzled that she cannot play his requests for "'96 Tears" or "Woolly Bully." But Rudy, undaunted, follows his father's advice and has fun.

Within this story are the stories told by Rudy's grandfather, "El Shorty," who lives with the family and helps with the gardening jobs. These are the stories about the poor days in California, just after he arrived from Mexico with the dream of a home with an orange tree in the backyard. He tells of hitchhiking to California and after his shoes were stolen, using cardboard to jump from place to place. Rudy and his family usually ignore these stories. Rudy sometimes "wondered if his Grandfather was right in the head" (7). Grandfather spends his spare time "taping a splintered shovel back to life" (7) and digging a swimming pool in their backyard. Perhaps when Rudy is older, he will want to know more about those difficult years and listen more patiently to what his grandfather is trying to say.

Grades 3–5

RELATED WORKS
Film: *The Pool Party* by Gary Soto. See pages 205–206.
Sequel: *Boys at Work* by Gary Soto.

The Skirt

- Dance
- *Folklórico*
- Lost and Found

Fourth grader Miata Ramirez has lost something again—this time she left her treasured *folklórico* skirt on the schoolbus. This is the skirt that belonged to her mother when she was a child in Hermosillo, Mexico. Now Miata needs all her wits to retrieve the precious skirt before her upcoming dance group performance, for which she has practiced three long months. Rallying all her courage and enlisting the help of her best friend, Ana, she slips into the bus yard and rescues the skirt. However, an unexpected twist near the end of the book finds Mama giving her daughter a new skirt. With characteristic ingenuity, Miata, feeling sorry for the old skirt, finds the perfect solution—she wears the old skirt under the new one.

Set in the San Joaquin Valley in California where the Ramirez family moved to escape the pollution and long commute in Los Angeles (and where Gary Soto grew up), this lightly suspenseful story weaves information about Hispanic culture and Spanish words into the text. Taking a situation many young readers can identify with—losing something and trying to explain it to parents—the author brings us an engaging female protagonist and a good read-aloud story that invites discussion and writing extensions. Gary Soto used the lost-and-found theme again later in his picture book *Too Many Tamales*.

Grades 3–5

RELATED WORKS
Too Many Tamales by Gary Soto. See page 164.

Small Faces

- Autobiographical Short Stories

The thirty-one prose reminiscences that make up this moving collection were written in 1983 and 1984. Gary Soto is always observing and thinking about the world and weighing his place in it. Describing himself as mercurial, fickle, and capricious, he confides that he and his wife are constantly moving. In the first ten years of marriage, they "lived in twenty different places, two states, two countries, eight cities and five counties" (27). He muses that maybe this moving around is due to his migrant genes; perhaps he is destined to continually break camp and hit the road for another field. Some days he wants money and nice things and other days he thinks about the richness a poor life can bring (16). He finds himself looking forward to the future and yet mourning for the past—"the same past that won't lie down and die for good" (48). The book ends with Soto wondering if we can really make a difference. "We can say things but solve nothing. Today I've listened to a line in my head over and over: 'the past seems horrible to me, the present gray and desolate, and the future utterly appalling'" (137). This book of highly poetic prose has much to think about and discuss.

RELATED WORKS

Living up the Street by Gary Soto. See page 157.

A Summer Life by Gary Soto. See below.

Grades 10–Adult

• Autobiographical Short Stories

A Summer Life

A Summer Life consists of three parts, each made up of thirteen short stories and essays about growing up in the industrial section of Fresno, California. Soto reminisces about the years when he was around four or five years old in Part 1; Part 2 is about his life between the ages of six through twelve; and Part 3 covers his years from thirteen through seventeen. Writing in the first person with vivid language and rich imagery, he captures the innocence, humor, loneliness, and energy of a Latino childhood spent in a working-class neighborhood surrounded by factories, diesel trucks, and junkyards during the fifties and sixties. The first story, "The Buddha," features a ceramic statue of Buddha that Soto's Uncle Shorty brought back from the Korean War. Five-year-old Soto carries the statue with him as he plays in the neighborhood. The Buddha, half hidden in the weeds, watches as the young boy runs under a slow moving diesel truck and skids in the dust on the other side. In "The Hand Brake," Soto writes about fashioning a brake for a child's running legs from an old bicycle hand brake. Running in the hot sun, he races a train, a taxi, and a tumbleweed. As Soto grows older, he starts developing a sensitivity toward animals, which is evident in many of his books. In "The Chicks," he tries unsuccessfully to protect three baby chicks from the neighbor's cat. Later, his loneliness is temporarily eased by the company of a stray dog in "The Stray."

The stories in *A Summer Life* are excellent models for young writers. Soto's example of writing about everyday events and experiences will inspire others who may at first think they have nothing about which to write. Most of the stories have a happy, carefree tone in spite of the dangers the unsupervised children face playing on busy streets while their parents try to eke out a living working in the factories.

Grades 10–Adult

RELATED WORKS

Soto has adapted two of the stories, "The Bike" and "The Inner Tube," into films. See page 205.

"The Inner Tube" was rewritten for another book, *The Pool Party*. See pages 160–161.

Living Up the Street by Gary Soto. See page 157.

Small Faces by Gary Soto. See pages 161–162.

Summer on Wheels

In this sequel to *Crazy Weekend,* thirteen-year-old Hector Beltran Molina and his amigo, Mando Tafolla, end the summer by hitting the road on an exciting bicycle trip from East Los Angeles to the Santa Monica beach. They have barely left home when Hector finds himself in the starring role in a television commercial. Before long, they are singing backup for a recording Uncle Ricardo is making. Next, when they attend a baseball game, Hector is the one-millionth fan to enter the stadium. Staying with relatives in East Los Angeles, Maywood, Culver City, Beverly Hills, West Los Angeles, and Santa Monica, the two happy-go-lucky boys find new adventures at each stop—painting a "Reading Is Power" mural on a library, pretending to be wax figures at the Hollywood Wax Museum, teaching a cousin how to ride a bicycle, and finally surfing the waves at the beach. They also renew connections with relatives and meet new friends along the way. When they return home, Hector's enthusiasm influences his parents to put old disagreements aside and invite everyone to a family reunion. Hector and Mando even paint a mural of their trip on the family garage.

- Bicycling
- Travel
- Vacations

Grades 5–9

RELATED WORK
Prequel: *Crazy Weekend* by Gary Soto. See page 155.

Taking Sides

Fourteen-year-old Lincoln Mendoza faces some tough questions when he and his mother move from the Mission District of San Francisco, an urban barrio, to Sycamore, a suburban town with tree-lined streets. He often wonders if their new location is really an improvement. At first he liked the peacefulness of the new neighborhood but he soon starts missing his old school and its mural of brown, yellow, and black kids. "There are no brown people here," he muses as he compares the pluses and minuses of each location. He notices that he and his mother have started using English, even at home, and that his Spanish is getting worse and worse. On the other hand, he and his new friend Monica bemoan the fact that their parents often reminisce about their hard work in the fields, saying the kids are spoiled. And Linc is tired of "nine years of hauling bologna sandwiches to school" as well as the pollution, graffiti, and noise of the old neighborhood.

One of Linc's biggest challenges is coming to terms with his divided loyalties to the two basketball teams. A racist coach, an injured knee, a disagreement with his old friend Tony, his mother's Anglo boyfriend, and a burglary attempt on the Mendozas' new house add to the confusion. Near the end of the book during the big game between his two schools, Linc realizes that "he was a Franklin boy beneath a Columbus uniform. He was brown, not white; poor, not rich; city, not suburbia" (127).

- Basketball
- Single-Parent Family
- Socioeconomic Class
- Moving

Besides providing an interesting look at class and race issues, the book also lightly addresses gender issues. Linc is surprised and then pleased to learn that Monica is also a basketball player and interested in math. His father, who left the family when Linc was seven, sends Linc birthday cards with one-dollar bills while his mother provides daily support, continuity, and love. And Linc notices that it is his new basketball buddy's mother and not his father who brings in the big bucks.

One of the many noteworthy nice touches in the story is the relationship between Linc and his canine companion, Flaco, who also has an injured leg. Another is the integration of Spanish terms and phrases into the text (a glossary is available). Readers will want to read the sequel, *Pacific Crossing*, to find out what new adventures await Lincoln and his family and friends.

Other multicultural books about basketball include *Hoops* and *The Mouse Rap*, both by Walter Dean Myers. For another book about the problems of moving to a "nicer" neighborhood, read *Felita* by Nicholasa Mohr.

Grades 6–10

RELATED WORK

Felita by Nicholasa Mohr. Bantam Skylark, 1990. See pages 114–115.

- Christmas
- Food
- Keepsakes
- Lost and Found

Too Many Tamales

Maria happily helps her parents make tamales for a Christmas family gathering. When her mother leaves her diamond ring on the kitchen counter while she leaves the room to answer the telephone, Maria cannot resist trying it on. Hours later, while playing with her cousins, Maria remembers the ring. Assuming it fell into the *masa*, cornmeal dough, while she was kneading it, she desperately enlists the help of her cousins. Together they eat every one of the twenty-four tamales, all the while waiting to bite down on something hard. Corn husks littering the floor, stomachs stretched till they hurt, the only clue they discover is cousin Danny's confession that he thinks he swallowed something hard. Finally, a guilt-ridden Maria decides she must confess to her mother. Just as the words start to form, she spies the ring sitting safely on her mother's finger. The story ends on a happy note with the family good-naturedly gathering in the kitchen to cook up another batch of tamales.

Everyone who has ever lost something, especially if it belonged to someone else, will identify with this story. During the course of producing the rich oil paintings with their delightful facial expressions, illustrator Ed Martinez and his wife cooked and ate more tamales than they ever dreamed possible. This book, a refreshing change from the usual Anglo holiday story, is an excellent choice for creative dramatics.

Grades K–3

RELATED WORKS

The Farolitos of Christmas by Rudolfo Anaya. Hyperion, 1995. See page 50.

Green Corn Tamales by Gina Macaluso Rodríguez. Hispanic Book Distributors, Inc., 1994. (520) 882-9484. (Includes a recipe.) See page 183.

Who Will Know Us?

In the poem from which the title of the book was taken, dedicated to Jaroslav Seifert, Gary Soto asks, "Who will know us when we breathe through the grass?" (19). A number of the poems in this volume are about death: the untimely death of his father; the death of Moses, his friend's gallant collie dog; and the death of Sadao Oda, who had thinned grapes and hoed beets, for whom Soto writes an elegy. He writes about his seventy-year-old grandfather, who wants to die. Soto's poems are about the emotions we all experience—shame, grief, worry, loneliness, melancholia, guilt, boredom, and uncertainty—but he has a way of writing about these feelings that gives us hope that we can move on to happiness, joy, and tranquillity. His use of language is always fresh, often surprising: "The sun is a red blister/Coming up in your palm" (2). Soto writes about being "bored with the holes/In our souls . . ." (46). The fear of returning to the poverty of his childhood still haunts him: in "Worry at the End of the Month" (52–53), he sees his perfect life overturning and he prepares to say good-bye to his fancy clothes and weekend trips. Other poems are about trying to fly when he was a child, worrying about disease, a stray dog eating in an alley, playing chess with his daughter, visiting a sugar plant, masturbation, the joys of swimming, and traveling by train. In poem after poem, Soto remains faithful to the common things in life.

Grades 10–Adult

RELATED WORK

New and Selected Poems by Gary Soto. See pages 158–159.

Leyla Torres

Colombian (1960–)

Birthday: October 28
Contact: Publicity Department
Farrar, Straus & Giroux, Inc.
19 Union Square West
New York, NY 10003

"Do not be afraid of taking a risk, even if you fail. Without failing you won't get the chance to succeed. Failure is something you can only avoid by saying nothing, doing nothing, and being nothing."
(*personal communication*)

Books Written and Illustrated by Leyla Torres

Saturday Sancocho. Spanish version: *El sancocho del sábado.* Farrar Straus Giroux, 1995.

Subway Sparrow. Spanish version: *Gorrión del metro.* Farrar Straus Giroux, 1993.

L eyla Torres is an artist, writer, teacher, and storyteller. She was born in Bogotá, Colombia, the oldest of four children. Her interest in art began early in life with the strong support of her mother. After earning a bachelor of fine arts and education at the Universidad de la Sabana in Bogotá in 1982, she began her career as a painter and illustrator. She worked with Los Matachos, a talented group of puppeteers, designing puppets, developing scripts, and illustrating promotional materials. These experiences sparked Torres's interest in the art of storytelling.

Torres taught watercolor techniques at the Universidad de la Sabana for several years. During this time, she was commissioned to create a mural for Gustavo Restrepo High School in Bogotá, where she also taught art classes.

In 1985, Torres traveled to the United States with the desire to stay for one year. She writes, "During that time I saw new possibilities to further my career and I decided to stay" (personal communication). For the next three years, she studied printmaking at the Art Students League of New York. Since then, her art has been shown in various solo and group exhibits both in the United States and in Colombia.

Torres has worked as a Spanish language instructor and provided individual and group language instruction for children and adults. As a freelance interpreter and translator, she has facilitated pediatric basic life support workshops for Spanish-speaking audiences. She was a guest author at the Miami Book Fair International's tenth anniversary celebration in 1993 and a featured author at the International Reading Association annual convention in New Orleans in 1996.

One of Torres's dreams was to write and illustrate books for children. Her first picture book, *Subway Sparrow,* is based on a real-life event. It is the story of four people of different ages, different cultural backgrounds, and different languages, all working together to free a sparrow trapped in a New York City subway car. Published in both English and Spanish editions, *Subway Sparrow* was a remarkable debut, winning a *Parents' Choice* Award. The Bank Street School of New York honored it as a Selected Book of the Year in 1994. Torres's second book, *Saturday Sancocho,* is set in South America and is the story of a girl and her grandmother who barter with street merchants for the ingredients for their favorite Saturday meal. Also published in both Spanish and English editions, *Saturday Sancocho* is a beautifully illustrated tale about ingenuity and tradition.

Leyla Torres currently lives with her husband in Brooklyn, where she divides her time between painting, writing, and teaching the Spanish language and literature. She goes back to Colombia periodically, where most of her family lives. Despite the stresses of living in a large foreign city, New York has provided her with an opportunity to reaffirm and expand her identity as an artist. Children's literature enthusiasts look forward to more books written and illustrated by this talented artist and writer.

Saturday Sancocho

Leyla Torres has set her second book in her native Colombia. Every Saturday, Maria Lili looks forward to making *sancocho* with her grandparents, Mama Ana and Papa Angelino. But one Saturday morning they discover that there is no money to buy the ingredients for their special dish. All they have is a dozen eggs. Maria Lili is disappointed but Mama Ana is undaunted. As the day progresses, Maria Lili learns an important lesson about solving problems. Detailed, double-page watercolors enhance the mystery and provide a glimpse into Colombian culture. The engaging scenes at the outdoor market are abundant with green plaintains, thick cassava, fresh corn, tender carrots, onions, cilantro, and other tantalizing vegetables and fruits. Each person is portrayed as an individual with unique features; their subtle facial expressions and body language add to the humor of the story. As Mama Ana deftly bargains and Maria Lili assists, their playful canine companion finds plenty of mischief to keep herself occupied. When they return home with their mission accomplished, Maria Lili savors each spoonful of their culinary treat. This creative variation on the cumulative story ends with a recipe for the popular South American stew along with a reminder to have an adult help in the kitchen. Vegetarians can substitute tofu or gluten for the meat in the dish. After reading or listening to the story, readers of all ages will enjoy poring over the colorful pages, studying the patterns of the clothing, streets, and markets and following the antics of the dog. For some, this will be their first experience with bartering, siestas, hammocks, outdoor markets, and some of the fruits and vegetables. For others, the book will provide a satisfying visit with familiar activities and foods. Leyla Torres has written an engaging tale about a stereotype-defying grandmother and her adventurous granddaughter.

- Bartering
- Culinary Arts
- Grandmothers
- Ingenuity

Grades K–3

RELATED WORKS
Spanish Edition
El sancocho del sábado. Farrar Straus Giroux, 1995.

Culinary Arts

Green Corn Tamales/Tamales de elote by Gina Macaluso Rodríguez. Illustrated by Gary Shepard. Hispanic Books Distributors, 1994. See page 183.

Roses Sing on New Snow by Paul Yee. Illustrated by Harvey Chan. Macmillan, 1991.

Too Many Tamales by Gary Soto. Illustrated by Ed Martinez. Putnam, 1993. See page 164.

- Birds
- Cooperation
- Subways
- Kindness to Animals

Preschool–Grade 3

Subway Sparrow

Parents' Choice *Award*
Bank Street School Book of the Year

This is the engaging story of a sparrow trapped on a subway car in New York City along with four humans who speak three different languages. Will they be able to rescue the bird before the train reaches the next platform and a waiting crowd of people? Leyla Torres's first book will capture the hearts of readers of all ages. She skillfully combines her warm, appealing plot with detailed, vivid watercolors. Her use of unusual angles and perspectives extends and enriches the simple text. The inclusion of stark subway advertising and announcements contrasts with the human concern for the vulnerable sparrow. *Subway Sparrow* paints an optimistic urban scene, showing how four caring strangers working together can achieve a common goal in spite of the language, age, and cultural barriers that divide them. It is significant that Torres has chosen a young girl to lead them to break out of the anonymity induced by public transportation in a large city. Torres's heartwarming book will encourage readers to reevaluate their image of New York City as a cold, impersonal place. *Subway Sparrow* is a good choice to read aloud to children, with time and space provided for those who want to pore over the intriguing illustrations on their own. This may be the first time some youngsters have been given information about the importance of respecting all creatures, no matter how small and ordinary. Perhaps others will have rescue stories of their own to share through discussion, writing, or illustration.

RELATED WORKS

Spanish Edition: *Gorrión del metro.* Farrar Straus Giroux, 1993.

Animal Rescue: *The Rescue* by Rae Collins. Photographs by Craig Martin. Richard C. Owen Publishers, Inc., 1995.

Gloria Velásquez

Chicana (1949–)

Birthday: December 21
Address: California Polytechnic State University
Foreign Languages and Literatures Department
San Luis Obispo, CA 93407

"Educate, raza,
young Chicanitas
women warriors of Aztlán."

"I want to inspire people to believe you can dream and be anything
you want to be. Never forget your community."
(La Voz Hispana de Colorado, *May 31, 1995, 10*)

Books by Gloria Velásquez

I Used to Be a Superwoman. Santa Monica
College Press, 1994.

Juanita Fights the School Board. Arte
Público Press, 1994.

Maya's Divided World. Arte Público Press,
1995.

Tommy Stands Alone. Arte Público Press,
1995.

Gloria Velásquez, an award winning writer of poetry and fiction, graduated from Stanford University in California in 1985 with a Ph.D. in Latin American and Chicano literatures. Her short stories and poetry have been widely published in journals and anthologies. She has been a guest author at various universities in Europe, including France and Germany, where her fiction has been studied. She was the first Chicana writer to read her poetry and fiction at the University of Río Piedras in San Juan, Puerto Rico. She is currently a professor in the Foreign Languages and Literatures Department at California Polytechnic State University in San Luis Obispo, California.

Born in the small town of Loveland, Colorado, Velásquez grew up in Colorado and Texas. Her parents, Francisca Molinar-Velásquez and Juan Velásquez, were migrant workers until 1963. They traveled between Colorado and Texas working in the fields until they settled as factory and hospital workers in Johnstown, Colorado. Velásquez often writes about the experiences of growing up within the migrant cycle of backbreaking, low-paying work and constant change. She recalls that some of the restaurants in Loveland had signs that read NO MEXICANS ALLOWED. Childhood memories of work thinning sugar beets, prejudice against Latinos, and Eurocentric schools appear in a number of her poems. Her teachers and school counselors didn't recognize her strengths. "There wasn't a high school English teacher available to listen to a girl's poem of anguish written in 1968, upon the death of a brother in Vietnam. Pain was doubled, as their mother tried in vain to borrow funds to speed to his side" (*Denver Post,* August 1995, 18). Velásquez adds, "No one ever told me

I was smart—that I was going to be a well-known Latina author. In spite of that, I created my own vision" (*La Voz Hispana de Colorado,* May 31, 1995, 3).

After graduating from Roosevelt High School in Johnstown, Colorado, Velásquez attended college classes at night while she worked as a secretary in a local factory. She also worked as a teacher's aide at local primary and secondary schools until she received a full-time fellowship to study at the University of Northern Colorado in Greeley. She earned her B.A. in 1978, with a double major in Spanish and Chicano studies.

In the late seventies, Velásquez participated in "Canto al Pueblo" (Song of the People) festivals in Albuquerque, Milwaukee, and Corpus Christi, Texas. Her experiences at these festivals had a profound impact on her thinking and writing, and inspired her to pursue graduate studies in Latin American literature at Stanford University. Because of her academic achievement, she received a full scholarship. During her second year there, she won a literary prize in poetry from the Department of French and Italian. Her interest in women in Chicana literature from the early 1900s to the 1970s led to her doctoral dissertation on "Cultural Ambivalence in Early Chicana Prose Fiction." Subsequently, she received her Ph.D. in Latin American and Chicano literatures from Stanford in 1985.

Growing up in the sixties, Velásquez's role models were people like Delores Huerta and César Chávez, cofounders of the United Farm Workers, and Maya Angelou, African American poet and writer. She emphasizes the significance of having Latina/o role models, and after all her achievements, she has never forgotten her roots. She is proud of her heritage and wants to encourage all Chicano/as to be proud of who they are. "I came from the barrio and I will never change . . . It's important to make an effort to not distance yourself from the culture. I haven't changed in twenty years— I'm still a grass roots person" (*La Voz Hispana de Colorado,* May 31, 1995, 10). She feels that it is crucial to feature people of color in literature for young readers. Her Roosevelt High School series (named after her high school in Johnstown, Colorado) is about the pressures faced by young Chicana/os growing up in a society that does not value their heritage. The series has unlimited potential and Velásquez has a number of significant topics planned for future installments.

In 1989, Velásquez was the first Chicana to be inducted into the Hall of Fame at the University of Northern Colorado, where she was honored for her achievements in creative writing. Almost thirty years after her own graduation, Velásquez became the first Chicana to be invited to give the commencement address to graduating seniors at Roosevelt High School. She was also selected for inclusion in *Who's Who Among Hispanic Americans* in 1994. She attended the 1995 Women's World Conference in Beijing, where she participated in a panel discussion on writing. She keeps very busy with activities such as overseeing the first Chicana animated film, *Dog Town,* appearing on talk shows to discuss her work, and speaking at schools and bookstores.

In addition to her Roosevelt High School series, Velásquez is writing an autobiographical novel, *Toy Soldiers and Dolls,* which deals with the Vietnam War. (Her older brother, John, was killed in the war in 1968.) This book is slated to be published in 1997. Her famous "Superwoman" poem will appear in a Heinle and Heinle book on Spanish for Spanish speakers.

Gloria Velásquez tackles a number of significant issues in her writing. She uses irony, satire, humor, and symbolism in her poetry to challenge the marginalization and erasure of Chicana/o history, the roles of women, the plight of the farmworker, and the problems of poverty, ageism, and alcoholism. She writes about educational achievement, male dominance, incest, the desertion of single mothers, and much more.

In her compelling books for young adults, she incorporates important issues such as racism in schools, divorce, and the harassment and degradation of gay students into stories that are very readable, interesting, and well written. Each of the books in the series, while featuring the same group of multiracial high school students, focuses on one member of the group and the problems she or he is facing. Velásquez is adept at capturing teenage emotions and thought as well as the nuances of Latina/o culture. She hopes to inspire teamwork and a better understanding of diverse cultures. She notes, "I want to inspire social change and get people to care about human dignity. I want to educate our youth. I want to politicize them" (*Rocky Mountain News,* July 25, 1994).

More Information About Gloria Velásquez

Denver Post. August 16, 1995, 18.

Dictionary of Literary Biography. Volume 122, 302–305.

La Voz Hispana de Colorado. May 31, 1995, 3, 10.

Rocky Mountain News. July 25, 1994, and May 29, 1995, page numbers unavailable.

Who's Who Among Hispanic Americans, 856.

I Used to Be a Superwoman

• Poetry
• Bilingual

In this rich collection of bilingual poetry, Gloria Velásquez conveys a strong personal and political message that her voice as well as the Chicana/o voice will not be silenced. She takes us back to her childhood and then to Stanford, contrasting her early life with the present. From thinning sugar beets and picking potatoes to days locked up in a cold city, "surrounded by mediocrity," Velásquez searches for a better world among the limited choices. She contrasts a past of sugar factories, rundown shacks, baskets of food from the Salvation Army, scrubbing floors, picking strawberries, playing marbles, and borrowed houses with a present of useless theories, bourgeois words, cement walls, unfulfilled dreams, and "academic pimps." Drawing inspiration from Frida Kahlo, Crazy Horse, and other sung and unsung kin, she cries out for the freedom to run free like the wind on the mountaintops. "Wonderful Youth" is a poem that should be required reading for all teachers: it provides an excellent definition of "Eurocentric Curriculum." In several poems, she challenges the traditional role of the selfless woman who thinks only of her family: "I am the super-pendeja Chicana,/very, very tired,/oppressed and/fed up" (31). She eloquently expresses the universal needs to be valued, acknowledged, and to make a difference in "Self-Portrait 1991": "Will I die in obscurity? . . . Will society yearn for my lonely words?" (103). In "Letter to a Patroncito," Velásquez refers to a school board meeting that undoubtedly led her to write *Juanita Fights the School Board,* her first book in the Roosevelt High School series.

Velasquez's poems are about prejudice, poverty, survival, disillusionment, loneliness, solitude, violence, war, death, grieving, self-doubts, and despair. But they also ring with a hunger for social justice, a pride in her people, a search for human dignity, a hope for social equality, and a determination that the children of the sun will survive. Her heartfelt poems are illustrated by José Antonio Burciaga and her two children, Brandi Treviño and Robert John Velásquez Treviño. The poignant introduction was written by Margarita Luna Robles.

Grades 12–Adult

Juanita Fights the School Board

• Schools
• Discrimination

Juanita Fights the School Board is the first book in Gloria Velásquez's Roosevelt High School series. Fifteen-year-old Juanita "Johnny" Chávez is expelled from high school after a fight with a white classmate. The school district doesn't ask for Juanita's side of the story and doesn't punish Sheena

Martin, the young woman who started the fight and who has been taunting Juanita with racial slurs since school started. At first Juanita is devastated; her dreams of graduating from high school and continuing her education to become a Spanish teacher are shattered. But with the support of a counselor, a lawyer, and her family and friends, she sets about fighting for her rights.

Juanita lives with her parents and five siblings in the barrio. She is one of a handful of students of color in a predominantly white high school. Her father, who is very strict and sometimes abusive, works in the fields and her mother works hard to take care of the family, also working in the fields from time to time. They do not speak English so their children often translate for them.

Narration in the book alternates between Juanita and her counselor, Ms. Martínez, opening two perspectives on the story. Juanita's chapters show how prejudice impacts self-esteem. She suffers through the long weeks at home, helping with the housework and younger children, all the while longing to return to school. Her best friend, Maya, keeps her informed about the social events at school and a home tutor keeps her up to date in her studies. Ms. Martínez's chapters reveal that she endured similar humiliations when she was a child. The author skillfully juxtaposes the two viewpoints, one before and one after assimilation into the dominant culture of the United States. Velásquez fully develops Sandra Martínez's character, demonstrating the complexities faced by a Latina who struggled to escape her family and class background to find herself still searching for validation. Juanita and the discrimination case provide the bridge Sandy needs, and she finds herself feeling rejuvenated by the experience. She muses, "She reminded me so much of myself at that age, young, scared and angry. Angry at the whole world and not able to express it" (53).

This is an engrossing, accessible novel. Injustice, class differences, upward mobility, peer pressure, tradition and change, ageism, friendship, biculturalism, gender roles, institutionalized racism, assimilation, language differences, teenage emotions, intergenerational conflicts, civil rights, peaceful resistance, and the collision of cultures are just a few of the issues Velásquez skillfully weaves into this interesting, timely story. The multiracial cast of characters is rare in literature for young readers. Several fat-oppressive remarks made by the students are especially hurtful in a book that is about justice and fairness. A glossary translates terms such as *cholo/a, gabacho, m'ija,* and *¡Orale!* into English.

RELATED WORKS

Roosevelt High School Series

Maya's Divided World. See below.

Tommy Stands Alone. See pages 174–175.

Grades 7–11

• Divorce
• Mother/Daughter Relationship

Maya's Divided World

Maya's Divided World is the second book in Gloria Velásquez's Roosevelt High School series. Readers will recognize Maya as Juanita's best friend, who stood by her when she was expelled from school in *Juanita Fights the School Board*. Maya Gonzales is the only child in a middle-class family. Her mother, Sonia, has a Ph.D. from Stanford and is a college professor and her father, Armando, is an engineer. Life seems perfect for Maya with her gorgeous house, her position on the tennis team, and her success in school. But all this changes the summer before her junior year in high school. When she accompanies her mother on a trip to Santa Fe to visit relatives, Maya overhears her mother telling her grandmother that she is getting a divorce. Grandma blames Sonia for the problems in the marriage, saying she paid more attention to books than to her husband. She refuses to let her daughter stay in her house. Later, when school starts, Maya is ashamed to tell her friends about the divorce. When she tries to call her father, he is too busy to talk or to plan a time for them to get together. Becoming increasingly confused and disillusioned, Maya finds that tennis, school, and even her friends have lost their meaning. She starts hanging out with the heavy metal crowd, sneaking out at night to spend time with them. Finally, when she is arrested for shoplifting, her mother consults Sandra Martínez, the psychologist who helped Juanita with her battle against the school board. Sonia and Sandy are the only Chicana professionals in Laguna and have developed a friendship over the years. But Maya refuses to see a "shrink" and ends up running away from home. She turns to her old friend, Juanita, who convinces her to see Ms. Martínez. This is the turning point in the story, after which Maya gradually starts the long, difficult process of healing.

Velásquez again uses the double narration she employed in the first book, alternating between Maya and Ms. Martínez. This allows her to tell Maya's story from two perspectives and to add a fascinating subplot. Sandy's story parallels Maya's, not only helping her to empathize with her client but lending additional insights into Latina culture and family expectations and histories. At one point, Sandy realizes she has to follow her own advice and be honest, confronting her own problems. This subplot strengthens the story, enabling young readers to realize that adults do not always have everything worked out in their lives but are nevertheless able to offer support and guidance to others.

Velásquez's books are among the few in literature for young adults where the characters are multiracial; she shows African Americans, Puerto Ricans, and Chicano/as developing strong friendships and supporting each other. The glossary translates terms such as *compañeras, ¡Hijole!, raza,* and *¡sinverguenza!* into English. This second installment in the Roosevelt High School series is a welcome addition to literature for Latina/o readers as well as for young adults of all backgrounds.

Grades 7–11

RELATED WORKS

Roosevelt High School Series
Juanita Fights the School Board. See pages 171–172.

Tommy Stands Alone. See next page.

Divorce
Talk About a Family by Eloise Greenfield. HarperTrophy, 1993.

- Gay Males
- Homophobia
- Suicide (Attempted)

Tommy Stands Alone

Tommy Stands Alone is the third book in Gloria Velásquez's Roosevelt High School series. Readers will recognize Tommy as a friend of Juanita's and Maya's from the first two books in the series. Tomás Montoya is a quiet, light-skinned, green-eyed Chicano living with his working-class family in the same barrio in Laguna, California, where Juanita and several of their friends live. Tommy resents his father's machismo and the way he expects his hardworking wife to cater to his every wish. Although Tommy enjoys art class, he is becoming increasingly uncomfortable at school and with his friends' expectations that he date. But he finds himself going along with them to keep from being noticed. Trying to maintain his cool, he even goes so far as to laugh at their homophobic jokes. One day Rudy reads a note Tommy accidentally drops and Tyrone asks him point-blank in front of all their friends, "Are you a faggot or what, Tommy?" Angry and confused, Tommy runs away and tries to commit suicide. Luckily he calls Maya, who calls 911, and his life is saved; but his problems are far from over. Maya finally convinces him to see Ms. Martínez, the psychologist who helped both Maya and Juanita in Velásquez's earlier books. Ms. Martínez not only works with Tommy but also counsels his mother, who has convinced herself that it was an accident and told her husband that Tommy has pneumonia. When his father learns the truth, he kicks his son out of the house. As the story unfolds, Tommy struggles through the long painful coming-out process, which reveals not only his inner resources but who his real supporters are.

Passages narrated by Tommy are juxtaposed with those narrated by Ms. Martínez, who has just learned that her gay brother-in-law is HIV-positive. She also has painful memories of her brother's suicide years before and of her parents' subsequent denial. As she works with Tommy, she too learns from the process.

Gloria Velásquez's third installment in the series is especially important because, unfortunately, there are still very few books for young people about homosexuality. Homophobia oppresses at least one-tenth of our population; education should be a vehicle for counteracting *all* forms of oppression and for providing accurate, honest information about sexuality as well as other relevant topics. Our society is still appallingly misinformed about homosexuality; well-written books such as *Tommy Stands Alone* are desperately needed to support lesbian and gay youth in the process of coming to terms with their sexuality and to enable straight students to support their lesbian and gay friends.

Grades 7–11

RELATED WORKS

For Young Adults

Am I Blue? Coming Out from the Silence, edited by Marion Dane Bauer. HarperCollins, 1994.

Two Teenagers in Twenty: Writings by Gay and Lesbian Youth, edited by Ann Heron. Alyson Publications, 1993.

Young, Gay, and Proud! edited by Sasha Alyson. Alyson, 1991.

Who Framed Lorenzo Garcia? by R. J. Hamilton. Alycat Books, 1995. See page 202.

For Adults

Bridges of Respect: Creating Support for Lesbian and Gay Youth: A Resource Guide by Katherine Whitlick. American Friends Service Committee, 1989.

Death by Denial: Studies of Suicide in Gay and Lesbian Teenagers, edited by Gary Remafedi. Alyson Publications, 1994.

Helping Gay and Lesbian Youth: New Policies, New Programs, New Practice, edited by Teresa DeCrescenzio. Haworth, 1994.

The Last Closet: The Real Lives of Lesbian and Gay Teachers, by Rita M. Kissen. Heinemann, 1996.

One Teacher in Ten, edited by Kevin Jennings. Alyson Publications, 1995.

More Latina and Latino Voices

Manlio Argueta

Manlio Argueta is one of El Salvador's leading living authors. In 1977 he received Latin America's most prestigious literary award, the Casa de las Americas Prize, for *Caperucita en la Zona Roja*. He is also the author of *One Day of Life* and *Cuzcatlan Where the Southern Sea Beats*. Argueta is a supporter of projects aiding Salvadoran refugees. He was born in San Miguel, El Salvador, and has been dedicating himself to writing and the promotion of social and cultural activities from an early age. Argueta makes his home in San Jose, Costa Rica, and travels frequently throughout the Americas.

- Bilingual
- Folklore
- El Salvador
- Volcanoes
- Dogs

All Ages

Magic Dogs of the Volcanoes/Los perros mágicos de los volcanes. Illustrated by Elly Simmons. Children's Book Press, 1990.

Whenever Salvadoran people gather to tell stories, someone will always have a story about the magic dogs called *cadejos*. There are many tales about how the *cadejos* mysteriously appear at night to protect people from danger. *Magic Dogs of the Volcanoes/Los perros mágicos de los volcanes* is Manlio Argueta's original story about these famous wolflike animals. Land and labor issues, pacifism, magic, folklore, and art combine to create an engaging picture book.

Gioconda Belli

Gioconda Belli was born in Managua, Nicaragua, where she participated in the political struggle to overthrow the Somoza dictatorship. An internationally regarded poet, her work has been published in eight languages. She is heralded as one of the most gifted Central American writers to emerge in the last ten years. Belli currently lives in Santa Monica, California.

The Inhabited Woman. **Translated by Kathleen March. Curbstone Press, 1994; Warner Books, 1996.**

- Nicaragua
- Underground Movement
- Dictatorship

This exquisite and haunting story of a woman's tragic yet triumphant personal transformation is based on the author's own experiences in the guerrilla underground movement against a dictatorship. Belli has written a passionate novel about people whose lives are intertwined with the destiny of their country. Her internationally best-selling book has been praised for its melodic language, suspenseful plot, and sharply defined presentation of characters, as well as for being an intelligent and politically sophisticated adventure-romance.

Grades 12–Adult

RELATED WORK
See Isabel Allende's chapter, pages 28–37.

Pura Belpré (1899–1982)

Pura Belpré was born in Cidra, Puerto Rico. She attended the New York Public Library School program and Columbia University. She was the first Puerto Rican librarian in the New York City public library system. An expert in folklore, she established special programs emphasizing Puerto Rican culture at the Harlem branch of the public library and arranged storytelling hours in Spanish for neighborhood children. She became interested in designing puppets to enhance her stories and soon became known for her puppeteering skills. Her first book, *Perez and Martina: A Puerto Rican Folktale,* was published in 1932. Her books include: *Santiago, Dance of the Animals, The Tiger and the Rabbit and Other Tales, Juan Bobo and the Queen's Necklace, Ote: A Puerto Rican Folk Tale, Once in Puerto Rico,* and *The Rainbow Colored Horse* and a recent release, *Firefly Summer.* Belpré was recognized for her work with a number of awards including the Instituto de Puerto Rico, New York City, a citation for introducing the folklore of Puerto Rico in the United States.

- Folklore
- Puerto Rico
- Death
- Grieving

Grades K–3

Perez and Martina: A Puerto Rican Folktale. **Illustrated by Carlos Sanchez. Frederick Warne, 1932; Pura Belpre White, 1960.** *Perez y Martina,* **Viking, 1991.**

Pura Belpré based this book on a story her grandmother told her. It is an old Puerto Rican folktale which has been handed down by word of mouth for generations. As a student in library school in New York City, Belpré wrote *Perez y Martina* for a course in storytelling. The story of Martina and Perez forms the basis for another picture book, *Ricardo and the Puppets,* written and illustrated by Mary E. Little. Señorita Martina, a Spanish cockroach, marries Señor Perez, a mouse from Spain. When Martina cooks a tasty dish of rice, coconut juice, almonds, raisins, and sugar, Perez accidently falls into the boiling pot. Greatly saddened, Martina "took her guitar from off the wall, and sat in her chair playing and singing and weeping."

RELATED WORK
La tataranieta de Cucarachita Martina (Martina's Great-granddaughter) by Alma Flor Ada. Illustrated by Ana López Escrivá. Laredo, no date available. See page 24.

Ana Castillo

A na Castillo is a poet, novelist, essayist, editor, translator, and teacher. She was born in Chicago in 1953 and earned her Ph.D. degree from the University of Bremen in Germany. She has written several novels including *So Far from God, The Mixquiahuala Letters,* and *Sapogonia,* as well as poetry collections and chapbooks. In addition to her own published works, Castillo's writings have appeared in numerous anthologies in the United States and abroad, in English and in translation. Her work has won many awards and honors and has been the subject of scholarly investigations and publications in the United States, Mexico, Europe, and Asia. Castillo often appears as a keynote speaker at conferences and gives readings at conventions and book fairs.

- Magical Realism
- Women's Stories

Grades 12–Adult

So Far from God. **W. W. Norton, 1993.**
Mountains and Plains Booksellers Award
Carl Sandburg Literary Award in Fiction

So Far from God is the haunting, wacky story of two crowded decades in the life of a Chicana family. Sofia and her four daughters live in a small, out-wardly sleepy hamlet in central New Mexico. The book opens with the "death" and subsequent resurrection of the youngest daughter. As the story barrels forward, the past collides with the present, the miraculous is woven with the mundane, the modern is blended with the archaic, and the tragic is tempered with humor. Castillo's unique brand of magical realism is leavened with sly commentary, quirky characters, and zany, unpredictable cadences.

Denise Chávez

Denise Chávez is a playwright, novelist, poet, performer, and teacher. Her 1995 book, *Face of an Angel*, was awarded the American Book Award by the Before Columbus Foundation. Her plays have been produced throughout the United States and Europe. She has taken her one-woman show, *Women in the State of Grace*, throughout the United States, performing the roles of nine Latinas ages seven to seventy-eight. A native of New Mexico, she lives in the house where she grew up and writes in the room where she was born. Chávez has been a visiting professor of creative writing at New Mexico State University and has facilitated creative writing and theater workshops with students in elementary through high school.

The Last of the Menu Girls. Arte Público Press, 1986.

The seven interrelated stories in this first collection feature Rocío Esquibel, a young woman who pushes against the traditional roles society prescribes for women. As she comes to terms with the issues of her past, she emerges as a writer. Her mother counsels her to write the stories of their lives. In the title story, Rocío works in a hospital as a "menu girl," distributing and collecting menus from the patients. This story won the *Puerto del Sol* fiction award in 1985. *Library Journal* wrote, "These stories fairly shimmer with the warmth, tones, and language of the Southwest." In 1990, an adaptation of her story cycle, *The Last of the Menu Girls,* was produced as a play by Main Street Theater and the Teatro Bilingue de Houston.

- Short Stories
- Authorship

Grades 11–Adult

Maria Garcia

Maria Garcia was born in Kennedy, Texas, in 1944. When she was a little girl, her mother told her stories about her great-grandmother, stories of poverty, endurance, and dignity. A very proud woman, she set an example of never giving up. Her parents were Kiowa, Yaqui, Spanish, and French. Maria Garcia writes, "I am Chicana. I am Black. I am Native American. I am Asian. What does this mean? To children it can be very confusing." She writes about who she is and what she believes in. She feels that we are all human beings and we should be proud of who we are.

- Bilingual
- Prejudice
- Self-Acceptance

***The Adventures of Connie and Diego/Las aventuras de Connie y Diego*. Illustrated by Malaquias Montoya. Translated into Spanish by Alma Flor Ada. Children's Book Press, 1978; 1987.**

Connie and Diego were born with different colors all over their bodies. Everyone laughs at them until they decide to run away and find a place where they will be accepted. After a long journey, they finally understand where they truly belong. An eloquent story about learning to accept and love oneself, this beautifully illustrated book is part of the Fifth World Tales Series. A bilingual audiocassette is available through Children's Book Press.

All Ages

Richard García

Richard García was born in San Francisco to a Mexican American mother and a Puerto Rican father. He says, "The Puerto Rican and Mexican sides of my family are very different. . . . I grew up thinking of myself as a Mexican American, and am only recently beginning to think of myself as a Mexi-Rican. This seems like a good combination . . ." (*Aunt Otilia's Spirits,* 24). García is the author of a book of poetry, *The Flying Garcías,* and has been a poet-in-residence at Children's Hospital in Los Angeles.

- Bilingual
- Aunts
- Spiritualists

***My Aunt Otilia's Spirits/Los espíritus de mi Tía*. Illustrated by Robin Cherin and Roger I. Reyes. Children's Book Press, 1978; 1987.**

When Aunt Otilia comes to visit from Puerto Rico, her curious nephew finds out about her magical powers. One night, he watches in astonishment as her bones lift out of her body, float through the air, and fly through the window. The author writes that the story is based on a kernel of truth. Wherever his aunt went, she was accompanied by wall knocking and bed shakings. His family did not regard this as unusual or as a cause for concern: "The supernatural had a natural place in our life." This humorous story is accompanied by imaginative, bright illustrations. It is an excellent read-aloud and may also be used for storytelling.

Grades 2–Adult

Diane Gonzales Bertrand

D iane Gonzales Bertrand wrote her first novel in sixty-seven spiral notebooks when she was in junior high school. During high school and college, she continued to write and, when she became a teacher, she created plays for her students to perform. After receiving her master's degree in English in 1992, she began teaching creative writing and composition at St. Mary's University Writing Institute. She has written three novels and dozens of poems, which have been published in literary magazines. Recently, she has begun to write bilingual picture books for children. Her most recent book is *Alicia's Treasure*. Gonzales Bertrand continues to reside in her hometown, San Antonio, Texas.

Sweet Fifteen. Arte Público Press, 1995.

Preparations for the traditional quinceañera celebration marking Stephanie Bonilla's fifteenth birthday serve as a backdrop for this story about the place of ritual in modern families and communities. Stephanie feels that the quinceañera celebration is an outmoded tradition, an archaic custom. The unexpected death of her father and her mother's grief add to her reluctance to go through with the plans for her party. Can Rita, the seamstress selected to design Stephanie's quinceañera gown, help her develop an appreciation for the traditions and values of her culture? Both Latino/a and non-Latino/a readers will be drawn to this engaging examination of the stress felt by teenagers from traditional families caught up in the complex reality of modern life.

- Quinceañera
- Gender Roles
- Grieving
- Tradition and Change

Grades 6–10

RELATED WORK
"Bad Influence" in *An Island Like You* by Judith Ortiz Cofer. Orchard, 1995. See
    pages 90–91.

Juan Felipe Herrera

J uan Felipe Herrera, who was born in Fowler, California, is a prominent Mexican American poet. He has degrees in social anthropology from Stanford University and from the University of California at Los Angeles. He is the award-winning author of many books of poetry, including *Facegames*, which won a Before Columbus American Book Award; *Akrilica*, *Night Train to Tuxtla*, and *Days of Invasion*. His memoir, *Indian Journeys*, was published by Broken Moon Press. He is also an actor, a musician, and a professor at California State University at Fresno.

Calling the Doves/El canto de las palomas. Illustrated by Elly Simmons. Children's Book Press, 1995.

Hungry Mind Review *Children's Book of Distinction*

Juan Felipe Herrera tells the story of his childhood as the son of migrant farmworkers. He shares his experiences of eating breakfast under the open sky, listening to his mother recite poetry and sing songs, and hearing his father tell stories and call the doves. Rudolfo Anaya praised this beautiful book, saying it is "a sensitive story of a family who comes from Mexico to work in the fields of California. Juan Felipe's parents teach him a love for the land, and they give him the precious gift of poetry." Illustrator Elly Simmons dedicated her art to "the memory of Cesar Chavez and in honor of the work of the United Farmworkers Union."

All Ages

RELATED WORKS

La Causa: The Migrant Farm Workers' Story by De Ruiz, Dana Catherine, and Richard Larios. Illustrated by Rudy Gutierrez. Raintree/Steck-Vaughn, 1993. See page 202.

Voices from the Fields: Children of Migrant Farmworkers Tell Their Stories by Beth Atken. Little, Brown, 1993. See page 201.

. . . y no se lo tragó la tierra/ . . . And the Earth Did Not Devour Him by Tomás Rivera. Translated by Evangelina Vigil-Piñon. Arte Público Press, Third Edition, 1995. See pages 183–184.

See Gary Soto's chapter starting on page 149 for additional books about farmworkers.

Gina Macaluso Rodriguez

Gina Macaluso Rodriguez grew up in a bicultural family. Her mother, Sarah Torrez, is Mexican American and her father, Salvatore Macaluso, was born in Palermo, Sicily. Her maternal great-grandmother, Librada Marquez, was born in Tucson, Arizona, and married Manuel Flores of Magdalena, Texas. Her other maternal great-grandmother, Sarah Armendarez, was a Tarahumara Indian from Sonora, Mexico, and she married Guadalupe Torrez of Texas. Macaluso Rodriguez is married to Carlos Rodriguez and has three children, Nicholas, Cassandra, and Alejandro. She is a librarian with the Tucson-Pima Public Library System, having obtained her master of arts degree several years ago. *Green Corn Tamales* is her first book.

Green Corn Tamales/Tamales de elote. Illustrated by Gary Shepard. Hispanic Books Distributors, Inc., 1994.

Arroz con leche Award Winner

- Bilingual
- Culinary Arts
- Traditions

A Latino family gathers each Labor Day weekend at Grandmother's ranch to celebrate with a feast prepared by the whole family. In this engaging tale, Grandmother orchestrates and her young granddaughter participates in the traditional preparation of green corn tamales. This cheerful bilingual book ends with the author's mouthwatering recipe for green corn tamales and a glossary of words and phrases such as *capirotada, arroz,* and *toda la familia.*

Grades K–4

RELATED WORK

Too Many Tamales by Gary Soto. Illustrated by Ed Martinez. Putnam, 1993. See page 164.

Tomás Rivera (1935–1984)

Tomás Rivera was born to a family of migrant farmworkers in the south Texas town of Crystal City. From his early years until 1954, he traveled with his family, searching for farmwork as far north as Michigan and Minnesota. After earning a degree in English, Rivera taught in high schools, and later earned a Ph.D. in romance languages and literatures from the University of Oklahoma. In a short time, he became executive vice president of the University of Texas at El Paso, and then chancellor of the University of California at Riverside. He was a poet, novelist, short story writer, and literary critic. In his writing, Rivera documented the experiences he underwent and witnessed as a migrant worker.

. . . y no se lo tragó la tierra/ . . . And the Earth Did Not Devour Him. Translated by Evangelina Vigil-Piñon. Arte Público Press, Third Edition, 1995.

- Bilingual
- Migrant Farmworkers

Tomás Rivera's original novel won the first national award for Chicano literature in 1970 and has become a standard literary text for Latino literature classes around the country. The classic tells its stories through the eyes of a young boy, the child of migrant farmworkers. There are twelve chapters in the book, each one representing a month of the year, depicting the heartrending suffering of humiliation, deprivation, heat stroke, suicide, poverty, and backbreaking work. Rivera's groundbreaking novel immediately established itself as a major document of Chicano social and literary history.

RELATED WORKS

Tomás Rivera: The Complete Works, edited by Julián Olivares. Arte Público Press, 1992. This collection brings together the late author's entire literary production, including his classic novel, short fiction, poetry, and critical essays.

Tomás Rivera, 1935–1984: The Man and His Work, edited by Vernon E. Lattin, Rolando Hinojosa, and Gary D. Keller. Bilingual Press, no date available. (602) 965-3867. This volume features work by Rivera as well as poems written in his memory, drawings, photographs, and scholarly contributions.

For Younger Readers

Calling the Doves/El canto de las palomas by Juan Felipe Herrera. Illustrated by Elly Simmons. Children's Book Press, 1995. See page 182.

Voices from the Fields: Children of Migrant Farmworkers Tell Their Stories by Beth Aiken. Little, Brown, 1993. See page 201.

Abraham Rodriguez, Jr.

Abraham Rodriguez, Jr., was born and raised in the South Bronx in New York City, where he still lives. His work has appeared in *Story* and *Best Stories from New Writers.* In addition to *The Boy Without a Flag,* he is the author of *Spidertown,* an electrifying, gritty novel about the lives of young people of the South Bronx whose often reckless actions are propelled by an unquenchable yearning for a better life. Rodriguez has been proclaimed a major new voice in American fiction.

• Short Stories

The Boy Without a Flag: Tales of the South Bronx. Milkweed Editions, 1992.

The Village Voice described this collection as "the most nervy, anxious, and brilliant writing by a New York Puerto Rican author since Piri Thomas's *Down These Mean Streets.*" Rodriguez brings the South Bronx to life with bold, gut-wrenching stories that readers will long remember. The author says the stories are "about the rancid underbelly of the American Dream. These are the kids no one likes to talk about; they are seen as the enemy by most people. I want to show them as they are, not as society wishes them to be." Harshly realistic, spellbinding. The first story in the collection, "The Boy Without a Flag," is important reading for all educators.

Grades 12–Adult

Phyllis Tashlik

Phyllis Tashlik is a teacher in the New York City public schools. She divides her time between writing, editing, and working with teenage writers at Urban Academy, an alternative high school in New York City. She reports in the introduction to her book that her "students had gone through nine years of education and, although the NYC public school population is more than a third Hispanic, they had never been introduced to a single novel written by a Hispanic author and certainly not by a female Hispanic author." Determined to change this pattern, she applied for and received a grant and designed an elective class, "Las Mujeres Hispanas." This pioneer project introduced teenage Latinas to literature written by Latina authors. By selecting pieces by some of the best-known Latina writers and inviting her students to read and respond to them, she introduced them to their own potential as writers and as individuals.

Hispanic, Female and Young: An Anthology. Arte Público Press, 1994.

Books for the Teen Age
Quick Picks for Young Adults

• Collection of stories, poems, essays, and interviews

This innovative intergenerational dialogue combines the voices of young Latinas with those of such well-known writers as Lorna Dee Cervantes, Judith Ortiz Cofer, Nicholasa Mohr, Pat Mora, and others. Tashlik met with her students throughout the course of a year to read and discuss their reactions to the works of these writers. Individually and collectively, they went on to write a wide variety of engaging pieces. This groundbreaking anthology includes remembrances of childhood and family, the difficulties of growing up bicultural and bilingual, and what it is like to deal with both racism and misogyny. *Hispanic, Female and Young* is important reading for young Latina audiences on their road to discovery of themselves, their potential, and their culture. Readers of all backgrounds will enjoy and learn from this refreshing, one-of-a-kind book.

Grades 6–12

Victor Villaseñor

Victor Villaseñor grew up in North Country San Diego, California, on a ranch. School was difficult for him not only because he spoke only Spanish but because he had a learning disability: dyslexia. He eventually dropped out of school and became a laborer. However, his love of language combined with his family tradition of storytelling inspired his interest in writing. His work was rejected at first, but he was finally recognized as the gifted writer that he is. His autobiography, *Rain of Gold,* was a national best-seller and is now available in Spanish. He recently continued his family chronicle in the sequel, *Wild Steps of Heaven.* His 1973 novel, *Macho!,* was chosen by the New York Public Library for its distinguished list of Books for the Teenage and has recently been reissued by Arte Público Press. Villaseñor also wrote *Jury: The People vs. Juan Corona,* a nonfiction work that was published in 1976. In addition, he writes screenplays, most notably the award-winning *The Ballad of Gregorio Cortez.*

• Autobiographical Short Stories

Walking Stars: Stories of Magic and Power. Arte Público Press, 1994.

Américas *Children's and Young Adult Literature Award*

We are all "walking stars" if only we believe in ourselves and recognize the brilliance and power we each have as human beings. Villaseñor presents inspirational stories from his own family history, stories of his parents facing the ridicule of other children; developing the confidence to encounter the unknown; escaping from persecution by soldiers during the Mexican Revolution; and enduring hunger, thirst, and stress. In the preface, Villaseñor describes his first day of school, when he knew very little English, and his teacher yelled at him, "No Spanish!" She punished the students if they spoke one word of Spanish and hit them on the head if they continued. Villaseñor writes, "I'm not that smart or great, and I didn't become a writer because I did well in school and got A's. No, I became a writer because I had so much confusion and anguish inside of me . . ." (10). His stories, written from the heart, speak of pain and confusion and self-hate, and "then finally, that great 'real' magic of life that's sitting there, within each of us, waiting to erupt and help us overcome against all odds" (11).

Grades 6–12

Helena María Viramontes

*H*elena María Viramontes was born in East Los Angeles in 1954. She has been the coordinator of the Los Angeles Latino Writers Association and Literary Editor of *XismeArte Magazine.* She has won several literary awards, including the University of California, Irvine Chicano Literary Contest. Her work has been widely anthologized. Her first book of short stories, *The Moths and Other Stories,* explores women's struggles to overcome restrictions forced upon them by family, culture, and church. Her second book of short stories is titled *Paris Rats in East L.A.* Viramontes has taught in the Spanish Department at the University of California at Irvine and currently teaches creative writing at Cornell University in Ithaca, New York.

Under the Feet of Jesus. Dutton, 1995.

This extraordinary novel captures the conflict of cultures, the power of pride, and the dimensions of the human heart. The author dedicated the book to her parents, who met while picking cotton, and to the memory of César Chávez. At the center of the story is Estrella, whose mother has survived abandonment by her husband in a land that treats her as if she were invisible. As the story unfolds, Estrella crosses over the perilous border into womanhood. She learns to listen to her inner voice and to defy a system that would otherwise keep her down. Pushed to the margins of society, she learns to fight back and in so doing, discovers her own strength. Viramontes's novel is infused with wisdom, beauty, and imagination.

Grades 12–Adult

Additional Latina and Latino Authors

David T. Abalos
Edna Acosta-Belén
Iván Acosta
Oscar "Zeta" Acosta
Teresa Palomo Acosta
Marjorie Agosín
Kathleen Aguero
Jack Agueros
Eduardo Garcia Aguilar
Ricardo Aguilar
Jorge H. Aigla
Francisco X. Alarcon
Justo S. Alarcon
Norma Alarcon
Alicia Gaspar de Alba
Kathleen Alcalá
Ricardo Alcántara
Ciro Alegria
Claribel Alegría
Fernando Alegría
Felipe Alfau
Miguel Algarin
Dora Alonso
Fernando Alonso
Luis Ricardo Alonso
Francisca Altamirano
Joseph Alvarez
Lynn Alvarez
Jorge Amado
Alba Ambert

Luis Alberto Ambroggio
Mary Anchondo
George Ancona
Jorge Carrera Andrade
Marie Angel
Frances Aparicio
Helena Araujo
Electa Arenal
Reinaldo Arenas
José María Arguedas
Ivan Arguelles
Arturo Arias
M. Beatriz Arias
Ron Arias
Homero Aridjis
Roberto Arlt
José Armas
Carmen Armijo
Inés Arredondo
Juan José Arreola
Alfred Arteaga
Etelvina Astrada
Miguel Angel Asturias
Paulette Atencio
Alfred Avila
Kat Avila
Mariano Azuela
Jimmy Santiago Baca
Kathleen M. Baca
Beatriz Badikian

Miguel Barnet
José Barreiro
Raymond Barrio
Augusto Roa Bastos
Alberto Beltran
Alfredo H. Benavidas
Mario Bencastro
Mario Benedetti
Sandra Benitez
Abdelali Bentahila
Anilú Bernardo
Carmen T. Bernier-Grand
Mario Berrera
Jose Bianco
Adolfo Bioy Casares
Lygia Bojunga Nunes
María Luisa Bombal
Tomas Borge Martinez
Jorge Luis Borges
Irene Bordoy
María del Carmen Boza
Carmen Bravo-Villasante
Aristeo Brito
Yolanda Broyles-González
Juan Bruce-Novoa
Jose Antonio Burciaga
Tony Burciaga
Julia de Burgos
Elisabeth Burgos-Debray
Silvia Burunat

Guillermo Cabrera Infante
Caballero Calderón
Héctor Calderón
José Manual Calderón
Sara Levi Calderón
Rafael Campo
Julieta Campos
F. Isabel Campoy
Gonzalo Canal Ramirez
Cordelia Candelaria
Nash Candelaria
Daniel Cano
Burgos Cantor
Ernesto Cardenal
Alvaro Cardona-Hine
Alejo Carpentier
Angela L. Carrasquillo
Jaime Carrero
Elena Castedo
Rosario Castellanos
Otto Rene Castillo
Rafael Castillo
Ramón del Castillo
Sandra M. Castillo
Rosemary Catacalos
Marianne Celce-Murcia
Alex Cervantes
Lorna Dee Cervantes
Troy Cesáreo
Alfredo Chacón

Ricardo Cobian
Rubén Cobos
Francesca Colecchia
Francisco Coloane
Jesús Colón
Manuel Contreras
Eugenio Alberto Cano Correa
Lucha Corpi
Celia Correas de Zapata
Julio Cortázar
Rodolfo J. Cortina
Margarita Cota-Cardenas
Alejandro Cruz Martinez
Julia Cruz
Manuel Cruz
Migdalia Cruz
Ricardo Cortez Cruz
Ruth Cruz
Sor Juana Inés de la Cruz
Victor Hernandez Cruz
Pablo Antonio Cuadra
Gil Cuadros
Daisy Cubias
Barbara de la Cuesta
Carlos Cumpián
Verónica Cunningham
Rogue Dalton
Rubén Dario
Amparo Dávila
Abelardo B. Delgado
Abelardo Lalo Delgado
Marco Denevi
Dana Catherine De Ruiz
Tania Diaz Castro
José Donoso
Carlos Drummond de Andrade
Guadelupe Dueñas
Mile Durán
Roberto Durán
Paul Durand
Sergio Elizondo
Virgil P. Elizondo
Margarita Engle
Juan Armando Epple
Edna Escamill
David Escobar Galindo
Martín Espada
Rhina Espaillat
Paula María Espinosa
Herbert Espinoza
María Espinoza
María Virginia Estenssoro
Ramón Díaz Eterovic
Claudio Esteva Fagregat
Sandra María Esteves
Ezequiel Martinez Estrada
Liber Falco

Martín Favata
Nersys Felipe
Carole Fernández
Enrique Fernandez
José Fernández
Laura Fernández
Roberta Fernández
Roberto Fernández
Ronald Fernandez
Rosario Ferre
Renée Ferrer de Arréllaga
Linda Feyder
Carlos Nicolás Flores
Juan Flores
Maria Rosa Fort
Morella Fuenmayor
Carlos Fuentes
Gloria Fuertes
Ernesto Galarza
Benita Galeana
Eduardo Galeano
Mary Sue Galindo
Sergio Galindo
Edward Gallardo
Anamarie Garcia
Cristina García
Diana García
Guy García
Lionel G. García
Federico Garcia Lorca
Gabriel García Marquez
José Luis Garcia Sanchez
Magali García Ramis
Gustavo Alvarez Gardeazabal
Elena Garro
Beatriz de la Garza
Alicia Gaspar de Alba
Dagoberto Gilb
Lourdes Gil
Nora Glickman
Alma Gomez
Cruz Gomez
Guillermo Gomez-Pena
Ibis Gomez-Vega
Genaro Gonzales
Lucía M. González
Luisa Gonzalez
Ralfka Gonzalez
Ray González
Juan Goytisolo
Antonio Granados
Alejandro Gratten-Dominguez
Lucía Guerra
Jesus Guerrero Rea
Nicolás Guillén
Ramón Gutiérrez
Liliana Heker

Armand Hernandez
David Hernandez
Victor Hernández Cruz
Juan Hernandez-Senter
Leticia Herrera Alvarez
Floria Herrero Pinto
Oscar Hijuelos
Maria Hinojosa
Rolando Hinojosa
Carolina Hospital
Angela de Hoyos
Jorge Huerta
Vicente Huidobro
Jorge Ibargüengoitia
Arturo Islas
Iraida Iturralde
Ledo Ivo
Enrique Jaramillo Levi
Alfredo Jiménez
Francisco Jiménez
Juan Ramón Jiménez
Teresa de Jesus
Tina Juárez
Roberto Juarroz
Richard Larios
Tato Laviera
Graciela Limón
Maria Limon
Hugo Lindo
Clarice Lispector
María Elena Llano
Mario Vargas Llosa
Arcadio Lobato
Clara Lomás
Francisco Lomelí
Arcadia López
Blanca López de Mariscal
Jack López
Josefina López
Natashia López
Antonio Machado
Mary Machado
Eduardo Mallea
Jaime Manrique
E. A. Mares
Assumpta Margenat
Cruz Martel
Jose Marti
Patricia Preciado Martin
Demetria Martinez
Eliud Martinez
María Martinez
Max Martínez
Ruben Martínez
Victor Martínez
Magali Martinez Gamba
Hugo Martínez-Serros

Gerardo di Masso
Olga Elena Mattei
Pablo Medina
Rubén Medina
Cecilia Meireles
Carlos Mellizo
Miguel Mendez
Durango Mendoza
Pedro Mir
Gabriela Mistral
Berta G. Montalvo
Jesse G. Monteagudo
Carmen Monteflores
Victor Montejo
Julieta Montelongo
Mayra Montero
Matías Montes-Huidobro
Francisco X. Mora
Cherríe Moraga
Alejandro Morales
Aurora Levin Morales
Ed Morales
Rosario Morales
Cristina Moreno
Guadalupe Morfín
Barbara Mujica
Angelina Muniz
Elías Miguel Muñoz
Alejandro Murguia
Anna Muriá
Rosario Murillo
Carmen Naranjo
Aquiles Nazoa
Pablo Neruda
Amado Nervo
Bruce-Novoa
Guillermo Nunez
Achy Obejas
Silvina Ocampo
Victoria Ocampo
Manuel Zapata Olivella
Juan Carlos Onetti
José-Luis Orozco
Olga Orozco
Julio Ortega
Gilberto Rendón Ortiz
Rosalie Otero
Felix Padilla
Genaro Padilla
Heberto Padilla
Raymond Padilla
Antonio Palacios
Américo Paredes
Francisco Matos Paoli
Ambar Past
Ricardo Pau-Llosa
Octavio Paz

Ramón Paz Ipuana
Robert W. Pazmiñi
Ana Maria Pecannis
Narciso Peña
Sylvia Peña
Robert L. Perea
Hilda Perera
Gustavo Pérez Firmat
Loida Maritza Perez
Ramón "Tianguis" Pérez
Cristina Peri Rossi
Fernando Picó
Pedro Pietri
Miguel Piñero
Nélida Piñon
Beatrice Pita
Felix Pitre
Josefina Pla
Manuel Ponce
Mary Helen Ponce
Elena Poniatowska
Estela Portillo Trambley
Carmen de Posadas
Alex Prado de Lange
Delores Prida
Jorge Prieto
Catalina Prilick
Alfonso Quijada Urías
Naomi Quiñónez
Leroy V. Quintana
Horacio Quiroga
Claudia Quiróz
Charles Ramírez Berg
German Ramos
Manuel Ramos
Rodrigo Rey Rosa
Bessy Reyna
Julio Ricci
Albert Alvara Riós
Alberto Rios
Beatriz Rivera

Diana Rivera
Edward Rivera
Geraldo Miguel Rivera
Marina Rivera
Rick P. Rivera
Antonio Robles
Eduardo Robles Boza
Daniel Jácome Roca
Merce Rodoreda
Ana Rodriguez
Andres Rodriguez
Blanca Rodriguez
Joe Rodríguez
Richard Rodriguez
Victor Rodriguez
Danny Romero
Leo Romero
Javier Rondón
Alfonso Ruano
Moises Ruano
Jorge Ruffinelli
Leonel Rugama
Ronald Ruiz
María Amparo Ruiz de Burton
Benjamin Alire Saenz
Diana Sáenz
Floyd Salas
José David Saldívar
Luis Omar Salinas
Marta Salinas
Guillermo Samperio
Cepeda Samudio
Nidia Sanabria de Romero
Alberto Ruy Sanchez
Elba Rosario Sanchez
Ricardo Sánchez
Rosaura Sánchez
Trinidad Sánchez, Jr.
Virginia Sánchez Korrol
Moisés Sandoval
Jorge Sanjines

Francisco Santana
Danny Santiago
Esmeralda Santiago
Carmen Santiago Nodar
Yvonne Sapia
Severo Sarduy
James de Sauza
Isabel Schon
Manuel Scorza
María Laura Serrano
Nina Serrano
Beverly Silva
Antonio Skármeta
Maria Teresa Solari
Joseph Somoza
Roberto Sosa
Alfonsina Storni
Mario Suarez
Virgil Suárez
Caridad Svich
Carmen Tafolla
Karen T. Taha
Lygia Fagundes Telles
Susana Thenon
Piri Thomas
Omar Torres
J. L. Torres
Marta Traba
Ernesto Trejo
Jesús Salvador Treviño
Carla Trujillo
Charley Trujillo
Sabine Ulibarrí
Luz Maria Umpierre
Luis Alberto Urrea
Emilio Diaz Valcarcel
Gina Valdés
Guadalupe Valdés Fallis
Luis Valdez
Mercedes Valdivieso
Luisa Valenzuela

Rima de Vallbona
Victor Valle
César Vallejo
Mejía Vallejo
Antonio Valls
Gloria Vando
Félix Varela
Franklyn Varela
Kika Vargas
Zoraida Vásquez
Carmen Vazquez-Vigo
Anita Vélez Mitchell
Clemente Soto Velez
Diana Velez
Guillermo Verdecchia
Ana Lydia Vega
Ed Vega
E. J. Vega
Johanna Vega
Josfina Vicens
Sherezada "Chiqui" Vicioso
Cecilia Vicuña
Evangelina Vigil-Piñon
Eldin Villafañe
Javier Villafañe
Alma Luz Villanueva
Tino Villanueva
Alfredo Villanueva-Collado
José Antonio Villareal
Edit Villarreal
Xavier Villaurrutia
Leonor Villigas de Magnón
Marie Elise Wheatwind
Alicia Yáñez Cossío
Ricardo Yañez
Ricardo Means Ybarra
Berniece Zamora
Daisy Zamora
Iris Zaval
Rosalma Zubizarreta
Ahora Zurita

Optional Activities

These activities may be used with any of the author units. The major goal will be to enjoy fine literature; however, teachers, librarians, and parents might choose to extend the literary experience by selecting some of these activities. Many adults will invite individual youngsters or groups of youngsters to choose among the activities and to create some of their own.

The following resources are recommended for further exploration of the diverse roles literature may play in the classroom:

Lasting Impressions: Weaving Literature into the Writing Workshop by Shelley Harwayne. Heinemann, 1992.

Real Books for Reading: Learning to Read with Children's Literature by Linda Hart-Hewins and Jan Wells. Heinemann, 1990.

Talking About Books: Creating Literate Communities, edited by Kathy G. Short and Kathryn Mitchell Pierce. Heinemann, 1990.

1. SETTING THE STAGE: Set up an Author Center or Author Corner. Include a photograph of the author, a display of her/his books, posters, realia, maps, book jackets, a bulletin board, etc. Add student work as it is completed. Youngsters enjoy being involved in the planning of these author units. They might write to the publisher requesting materials such as posters featuring the author's books. Encourage them to take leadership roles in setting up the centers, creating the bulletin boards, and planning the activities.

2. COMPLETE WORKS: Provide an overview of the complete works of the author. As you read a book, discuss it within the context of the complete collection.

3. AUTHORS AS INDIVIDUAL PEOPLE AND AS WRITERS: Study the author's life. What experiences shaped their lives and thinking and led them to share their joys, struggles, defeats, and triumphs with their readers? What role does their cultural heritage play in their writing? Personal connections establish strong and long-lasting ties with the author. Even adults get excited when they have the same birthday or grew up in the same area as an author. Personalize the author units by focusing on the author's motivation for writing as a career and for writing each book. Why did the author write this particular book? Why did she or he choose this writing style? These words? How did the author's writing style or genre change from one book to the next?

4. LITERATURE LOGS/RESPONSE JOURNALS/WRITER'S NOTEBOOKS: Young readers may respond in writing to the selection read each day or week. These journals may be ongoing all year or semester long or shorter journals may be kept for each author or book. Encourage a wide variety of responses such as poems, letters, thoughts, feelings, illustrations, etc. Youngsters may choose to share these journals with partners, small groups, or the large group. These logs or journals may also be used for self-evaluation and/or teacher assessment.

5. POINT OF VIEW: Compare the points of view in books with similar themes. Discuss or rewrite the story from the points of view of selected characters. Perhaps each youngster or group of youngsters could choose a character and present the book(s) from a variety of points of view.

6. QUOTES: Select or encourage youngsters to select quotes from the books for discussion and/or written response. Use a quote from a book for the caption of a bulletin board or in a newsletter, essay, or story.

7. PREDICTIONS: Predict what will happen in the book, on the next page, in the next chapter, and/or in a sequel. These predictions may be written in the literature logs and/or discussed.

8. DEDICATION PAGE: Discuss and/or respond in writing to the dedication page. What additional information does it give us about the author? Encourage youngsters to create a dedication page for the next book they write.

9. CHARACTER LETTERS: Adults and youngsters might write a letter from one of the characters in the book to the class introducing, motivating, summarizing, embellishing, etc. Or one character could write to another character (within books or from book to book). For an engaging example of this idea, read *Dear Peter Rabbit* by Alma Flor Ada. See page s 13–14.

10. LETTERS: Some youngsters might be interested in writing letters to the authors. Addresses for most of the authors are included in the author units. Some authors are too busy to respond to each letter individually but might write a note to a class, school, or library.

11. AUTHOR VISITS: Invite the author to visit your class or school. Contact the publisher to arrange the visit. A resource that is helpful in planning and implementing an author visit is *Inviting Children's Authors and Illustrators: A How-to-Do-It Manual for School and Public Libraries,* written by Kathy East and published by Neal-Schuman Publishers. This practical manual explains all the steps including how, why, when, where, and who. Sample letters, advertising, bookmarks, budget forms, checklists, timelines, and photographs of some of the authors are included.

12. CONFERENCE CALLS: Arrange to make a conference call from your class to the author. Youngsters will enjoy reading the author's books and preparing questions in advance. This call might be taped and listened to again later.

13. INTERVIEWS: Role-play an imaginary interview with an author or character from a book. Or pretend that one character is interviewing another character.

14. RECIPES: Write individual or class recipes based on the book's message, such as "A Recipe for Friendship" or "A Recipe for Combating Prejudice." Display on the bulletin board featuring the author.

15. TRAVEL: Plan an imaginary or real trip to the places featured in the book. Write for travel brochures, study maps to plot your route, develop a budget, plan an itinerary, etc.

16. NEWSLETTERS: Include items from author units in your class, school, or library newsletter. Youngsters enjoy interviewing authors and writing about these intriguing discussions.

17. DRAMA: Youngsters love to create and perform in plays, puppet shows, pantomime, readers' theater, skits, dance, etc., based on a book or a collection of books. See Drama, page 205.

18. BOOK TALKS: Invite youngsters to prepare short Book Talks to introduce and inspire others to read the books they recommend. These may be done a few at a time whenever you have a few minutes or during an assigned time. Students may also do extra Book Talks for extra credit.

19. BOOK REPORTS: Find creative ways to make Book Reports more fun! *Book Report Forms* by Evan-Moor offers a number of innovative ideas.

20. BOOK BOXES: Combine art and book reports. Students cover a box with paper and then decorate it with words, drawings, cut-outs, etc., that represent the book. The Book Boxes may hold items or tasks related to the book. These items may be used to dramatize the book, or other students might write questions or comments about the book and put them in the boxes. Arrange for a Book Box Exhibit with boxes created by several individuals or groups displayed.

21. AUTHOR BOXES: Do the same as in #20 but with the focus on the author.

22. BOOK BUTTONS: Youngsters love designing buttons. These might be centered around themes from the books they have read. Directions: If you don't have a button maker, students may cut out a circle on construction paper and another on tagboard. Decorate with book title, author, illustrator, and pictures. Glue the construction paper to the cardboard. Tape a safety pin on the back. Wear these buttons during Book Talks, Book Reports, Books Fairs, etc.

23. BOOK RIBBONS: Young readers design ribbons to advertise their favorite books. Display on bulletin boards, around the room, halls, or library to encourage others to read the books.

24. CHARACTER BOARD: For each character in a book or series of books, make a five- to seven-inch-high paper figure. Place these figures on a chart or mural depicting the roles played in the book. Print their names above each. Below each write some of their personality traits.

25. CHARACTER GROWTH: To demonstrate the growth and changes in a character within a book or within a series, a student role-plays the character at each stage of her/his development. (Example: In Nicholasa Mohr's books, in what ways does the protagonist change from the beginning of the first book, *Felita,* to the end of the second book, *Going Home?*)

26. CHARACTER CUTOUTS: Enlarge pictures of characters onto a large piece of paper. Cut out and use to start a bulletin board. Youngsters might then add words describing the characters printed on colorful strips of paper and other creative illustrations depicting the setting of the story.

27. ART: Study the art techniques used in the book. Research. Then experiment with those techniques. Add the resulting creative efforts to the Author Center.

28. BOOKMARKS: Design bookmarks to go with selected books.

29. COLLAGE: Create individual or group collages portraying aspects from a book, a collection of books, and/or the author's life.

30. BOOK HUNT: Hide a book and create a coded message to help others find the book. Perhaps one youngster or group of youngsters could be in charge of this activity each day or week.

31. TIME LINE: Make a time line for the events in a book, a series of books, or the author's life.

32. SEQUENCE CARDS: (Created by youngsters and/or adults.) On each of four or five cards cut in a shape that symbolizes the story, write a word or sentence or draw a picture showing something that happened in the book. Youngsters may work individually or in groups to put the cards in order. Add these to the Author Center.

33. CLASS BOOKLET: Collect all the work done by the youngsters related to a book or author into a class booklet. Display.

34. BOARD GAMES: Youngsters might choose to create board games based on the events in a book. These may be used in a variety of ways including during free time and indoor recesses.

35. BIRTHDAYS: On an author's birthday, declare that day "_____ Day." For example, January 19 is Pat Mora Day. Have a readathon featuring the author's books. Youngsters might design cards and/or write letters to the authors. People of all ages are interested in which authors have birthdays on the same day as theirs or someone in their family. See the Birthday Chart in Appendix 3 on pages 196–197.

36. DIORAMAS: Youngsters might create dioramas based on the author's life, a book or a series of books.

37. POP-UP BOOKS: This is an optional activity for talented or older youngsters. Create a pop-up book based on the book being read.

38. MAPPING AND WEBBING: At first, make the character maps or semantic maps together as a group. Gradually, youngsters will be ready to create their own or to work together in groups. These might

be displayed at the Author Center or added to the Class Booklet.

39. CARTOONING: Create cartoons based on the events in a book or as a sequel to a book.

40. ADVICE BOX: Youngsters write letters from or to the characters in the books asking for advice. Periodically, the teacher or students read these letters to the class and they respond in writing, with discussion, or by role-playing. A fun example would be to write letters to Pip, the cat, in Gary Soto's book *The Cat's Meow,* asking advice on everything from the best ways to learn a new language to how to communicate with another species.

41. MOBILES: Design a mobile to introduce, promote, or represent a book or author.

42. RECOMMENDATIONS: Write a letter to the school media director recommending a book or series of books for purchase.

43. BOOK JACKETS: Youngsters might choose to design new book jackets for the books.

44. DIARY: Youngsters might pretend that they are one of the characters in a book. They prepare a diary that the character might have kept during the beginning, middle, end, and/or the most significant parts of the story. This activity enables them to "walk a mile in the shoes of the character," and to better understand the complexities and commonalities of the human experience.

45. SURVEY: Some youngsters might be interested in checking the public and/or school library to see which of the books by selected authors are included. Make a checklist or graph. They might want to check how many books about an ethnic group are included. Discuss the results and discuss ways to respond.

46. PLACE MATS: Pretend that an author or several authors are coming for lunch. Design place mats to honor your guests. Use fabric, yarn, etc. This would make a great culminating activity at the end of the year or semester to review all the authors studied. This idea was inspired by *The Dinner Party* by Judy Chicago, which

features a place setting for each of thirty-nine women from history.

47. AUTHOR QUILT OR MURAL: Quilts and murals make good culminating activities. A quilt might feature one square per author.

48. AUTHOR OR CHARACTER PARTY: At the end of the semester or year, each youngster might dress as their favorite character or author. They each give a short talk from the point of view of the author or character, using the voice, gestures, and props they think appropriate, avoiding stereotypes or caricatures. These talks could be videotaped. Later, they could watch the video and serve refreshments provided by the youngsters, inspired by the books represented. The video could also be used to introduce the author units to another group or shown at community events such as Parents' Night.

49. RIDDLES: Youngsters enjoy creating riddles based on the books or author studies. This activity is excellent for review. For example: "I'm thinking of a book about a girl who writes an essay that helps her teacher understand how she feels about her name." Answer: *My Name Is María Isabel* by Alma Flor Ada.

50. REVIEW BULLETIN BOARD: Invite youngsters to create and display cut-outs of all the characters from all the books read during the semester or year.

51. BOOK JAMBOREE: Invite youngsters to sit in a circle. Place all the books from a unit in the middle of the circle. Children select books for a final short browse and then they each share one or two comments about the book. This is an excellent review activity.

52. BOOK FAIR: This school-wide or library event is similar to the familiar Science Fair. Once a year, all the projects created by the youngsters are displayed. Parents, community members, and other youngsters will enjoy viewing the wide variety of projects.

53. ASSESSMENT: Youngsters might write tasks or questions that could be included in an evaluation instrument.

Encourage high-level questions that inspire critical thinking rather than recall of details. Example: Why was María Isabel's name so important to her? See pages 20–21.

54. ASSESSMENT: (Pre and Post) Invite individuals (any age) to make a list of all the authors that they can think of. Evaluate together as a group or individually. Did they include authors from diverse groups? Which groups were included? Excluded? Why? What recommendations do the members of the group have for improving this situation?

55. ASSESSMENT: Library Checkout: Are books available that represent diverse groups? Are youngsters requesting and checking out these books? What recommendations do youngsters have for books to be purchased?

Author Birthdays

People of all ages enjoy finding out which authors have birthdays on the same day as theirs or someone in their family. Personal connections such as this establish stronger and longer-lasting ties with the author and motivate youngsters to find out more about them by reading their books. On an author's birthday, declare that day "_____ Day." For example, January 19 is Pat Mora Day. Youngsters might choose to design cards and/or write letters to the authors on their birthdays. (Addresses for the authors are listed in the chapters.) The library or school could hold a readathon featuring the author's books or exhibit them in a display case in a prominent location.

!Feliz cumpleaños!
Happy birthday!

January

Alma Flor Ada 1-3-38
Pat Mora 1-19-42

February

Alberto Blanco 2-18-51
Judith Ortiz Cofer 2-24-52

March

Julia Alvarez 3-27-50

April

Irene Beltrán-Hernández 4-4-45
Gary Soto 4-12-52

May

María Cristina Brusca 5-4-50

July

Ofelia Dumas Lachtman 7-9-19
Luis J. Rodríguez 7-9-54

August

Isabel Allende 8-2-42

September

Omar Castañeda 9-6-54
Jan Romero Stevens 9-8-53
Carmen Lomas Garza 9-12-48
Michael Nava 9-16-54
Gloria Anzaldua 9-26-42

October

Leyla Torres 10-28-60
Rudolfo Anaya 10-30-37

November

Nicholasa Mohr 11-1-38

December

Sandra Cisneros 12-20-54
Lulu Delacre 12-20-57
Gloria Velásquez 12-21-49

Books and Stories About Birthdays

A Birthday Basket for Tía by Pat Mora. See page 125.

An Island Like You, "Bad Influence" by Judith Ortiz Cofer. See pages 90–91.

An Island Like You, "White Balloons" by Judith Ortiz Cofer. See pages 90–91.

Pablo's Tree by Pat Mora. See pages 129–130

Rituals of Survival, "Happy Birthday" by Nicholasa Mohr. See pages 119–120.

Sweet Fifteen by Diane Gonzales Bertrand. See page 181.

Uno, Dos, Tres: One, Two, Three by Pat Mora. See pages 130–131.

Woman Hollering Creek, "Eleven" by Sandra Cisneros. See pages 86–87.

Holidays and Special Days

The holidays and special days in this index include those that are unique to Latina and Latino cultures. For other holidays such as Thanksgiving, Christmas, and Easter, please see the Subject Index on page 223.

General

Ancona, George. *Fiesta U.S.A.* Lodestar Books, 1995.

Encuéntrame: fiestas populares de América Latina (Find Me: Popular Celebrations in Latin America) by various authors. Laredo, 1-800-547-5113.

Fitzjohn, Sue. *Festivals Together: A Guide to Multicultural Celebrations,* Hawthorn Press, 1993. A resource guide for celebrations and observations of special days and traditions of many different cultures. Includes stories, songs, crafts, activities, and recipes.

Garza-Lubeck, Maria, and Ana Maria Salinas. *Mexican Celebrations.* Institute of Latin American Studies, 1987.

Heath, Alan. *Windows on the World: Multicultural Festivals for Schools and Libraries.* Libraries Unlimited, 1991.

Silverthorne, Elizabeth. *Fiesta! Mexico's Great Celebrations,* illustrated by Jan Davey Ellis. Millbrook Press, 1992.

January 6

Epiphany: Three Kings' Day

A Puerto Rican holiday celebrating the coming of the Three Wise Men to honor the baby Jesus at Bethlehem. Epiphany is a very important holiday, surrounded by tradition. In Puerto Rico, children fill shoeboxes with grass cuttings and put them under their beds. The next morning, the boxes are filled with toys. The kings came and left the presents and the camels ate the grass.

Delacre, Lulu. *Las Navidades.* Scholastic, 1990. See page 98.

Zapatar, Beatriz McConnie. *Three Kings' Day.* Modern Curriculum Press, 1992.

May 5

Cinco de mayo (The Fifth of May)

This is the celebration of the day Benito Juárez and the Mexican army were victorious over the French army in the Battle of Puebla in 1862.

Ada, Alma Flor. *The Empty Piñata.* Spanish edition: *La piñata vacía.* Translated from the Spanish by Rosalma Zubizarreta. Illustrated by Vivi Escrivá. Santillana, 1993. See pages 14–15.

Behrens, June. *Fiesta! Cinco de mayo.* Children's Press, 1986.

Bradley, Mignon L. *Cinco de mayo: An Historical Play,* Luisa Productions, 1981.

Palacios, Argentina. *¡Viva México!: The Story of Benito Juarez and Cinco de mayo,* Steck-Vaughn, 1993.

Riehecky, Janet. *Cinco de mayo.* Children's Press, 1993.

September 16

El dia de independencia (Mexican Independence Day)

This is the celebration of independence from Spain, which was won in 1821, after three hundred years of Spanish rule.

Hispanic Heritage Month is September 15–October 15.

October 12

El día de la raza (Day of the Race)

This fall holiday is observed by many Spanish-speaking people all over the world, as a day to honor a common heritage in language and traditions.

November 1 and 2

Los días de muertos (Days of the Dead)

These special days honor relatives and friends who have died and celebrate their spiritual return to Earth to share a special feast with the living.

Ancona, George. *Pablo Remembers: The Fiesta of the Day of the Dead.* Lothrop, Lee and Shepard, 1993.

CUICA. *Día de los Muertos (All Souls' Day).* Illustrated by various artists. Laredo 1-800-547-5113.

Hoyt-Goldsmith, Diane. *Day of the Dead: A Mexican-American Celebration.* Holiday House, 1994.

Krull, Kathleen. *Maria Molina and the Days of the Dead.* Illustrated by Enrique O. Sanchez. Macmillan, 1994.

Lasky, Kathryn. *Days of the Dead.* Hyperion, 1994.

Levy, Janice. *The Spirit of Tio Fernando: A Day of the Dead Story.* Illustrated by Morella Fuenmayor. Albert Whitman and Company, 1995.

Salinas-Norman, Bobbi. *Folk Art Traditions: Volume II.* Pinata Publications, 1988. Available through Hampton-Brown 1-800-333-3510.

December 16–24

Las posadas (The Inns)

This festival re-creates the story of Mary and Joseph's search for lodging in Bethlehem.

Ets, Mary Hall, and Aurora Labastida. *Nine Days to Christmas.* Viking Press, 1956 (Caldecott Award Book); Spanish edition: *Nueve dias para Navidad.* Viking Press, 1991.

Mora, Pat, and Charles Ramirez Berg. *The Gift of the Poinsettia/El regalo de la flor de Nochebuena.* Piñata Books, 1995. See pages 127–128.

Resources for Children and Teenagers

Books

Aparicio, Frances R. (ed.). *Latino Voices.* Millbrook Press, 1994. Grades 4 to 10.

This excellent book is a collection of writings by Latino/a authors specially edited for young adult readers. The editor has done a beautiful job of introducing each section with background and historical information.

Atencio, Paulette. *Cuentos from My Childhood: Legends and Folktales of Northern New Mexico.* Museum of Northern New Mexico Press, 1991. Grades 3 to 8.

Storyteller Paulette Atencio presents twenty-six bilingual folktales, historical, religious, and supernatural legends, and humorous and cautionary stories she heard as a child growing up in New Mexico.

Atken, Beth. *Voices from the Fields: Children of Migrant Farmworkers Tell Their Stories.* Little, Brown, 1993. Grades 5 to 12.

Dedicated to César Chávez, these poignant oral histories feature nine young people who describe their experiences as children of migrant farmworkers. Illustrated with photographs by the author.

Augenbraum, Harold, and Ilan Stavans (eds.). *Growing up Latino: Memoirs and Stories: Reflections on Life in the United States.* Houghton Mifflin Company, 1993. Grades 6 to 12.

This diverse collection of classic and recent Latino/a writing shatters the myth of a singular U.S.-Latino/a experience, demonstrating the existence of

a rich tradition whose writers are finally being recognized by a rapidly growing audience. Includes contributions by Nicholasa Mohr, Gary Soto, Gloria Anzaldúa, Sandra Cisneros, and Rudolfo Anaya.

Buss, Fran Leeper, with Daisy Cubias. *Journey of the Sparrows.* Dutton, 1991; Dell Publishing, 1993. Grades 5 to 9.

Nailed into a crate in the back of a truck, fifteen-year-old Maria, her older sister, Julia, their little brother, Oscar, and a boy named Tomás endure a harrowing trip across the United States border and then north to Chicago. There they struggle to find work—cleaning, washing dishes—always careful to remain invisible so the authorities won't arrest and deport them. To lift the family's

spirits, Maria tells stories of a little sparrow who brings a rainbow. This moving story of the secret lives of political refugees from El Salvador who courageously triumph over incredible obstacles is an important contribution to juvenile literature.

Carlson, Lori M. (ed.). *Barrio Streets Carnival Dreams: Three Generations of Latino Artistry.* Holt, 1996.

An eclectic collection of poetry, essays, memoirs, sketches, paintings, and photographs.

Carlson, Lori M. *Cool Salsa: Bilingual Poems on Growing Up Latino in the United States.* Introduction by Oscar Hijuelos. Henry Holt, 1994. Grades 5 to 9.

Growing up Latino in the United States means learning the rules of two cultures, often speaking two languages and living two lives. These poems celebrate the glory and pain of that double life. Includes poems by Sandra Cisneros, Gary Soto, and Pat Mora. A *Horn Book Fanfare* Award Winner.

Carlson, Lori M., and Cynthia L. Ventura (eds.). *Where Angels Glide at Dawn: New Stories from Latin America.* Introduction by Isabel Allende. Illustrated by Jose Ortega. HarperCollins, 1990, Grades 5 to 10.

Ten short stories by writers from Argentina, Chile, Cuba, El Salvador, Mexico, Panama, Peru, Puerto Rico, and the Puerto Rican barrios of New York provide a glimpse into the diverse cultures of Latin America.

Cerar, K. Melissa. *Teenage Refugees from Nicaragua Speak Out.* Rosen Publishing Group, 1994. Grades 6 to 12.

Powerful oral histories by teenage refugees now living in the United States and Canada are set within the background of the history and politics of Nicaragua. Part of a series of nine books featuring teenage refugees from around the world.

Codye, Corinn. *Vilma Martinez.* Bilingual edition translated into Spanish by Alma Flor Ada. Illustrated by Susi Kilgore. Series: Hispanic Stories. Raintree, 1990. Grades 3 to 8.

A well-written biography of a woman who grew up to become a lawyer and to challenge before the highest courts in the country the laws that discriminated against her people.

Correas de Zapata, Celia. *Short Stories by Latin American Women: The Magic and the Real.* Arte Público Press, 1989. Grades 10 to Adult.

Thirty eloquent stories by women writers of Latin America such as Isabel Allende, Rosario Castellanos, Amparo Davila, Rosario Ferre, Clarice Lispector, Elena Poniatowska, and Luisa Valenzuela.

Cumpián, Carlos. *Latino Rainbow: Poems About Latino Americans.* Illustrated by Richard Leonard. Children's Press, 1994. Grades 4 to 8.

Twenty poems accompanied by rich paintings focus on Latino culture and history. The poems are about individuals and issues.

Davis, Marilyn. *Mexican Voices/American Dreams: An Oral History of Mexican Immigration.* Holt, 1990. Grades 8 to Adult.

This unique history of Mexican immigration to *el norte* is told from the perspective of the people who have lived it.

Delgado Votaw, Carmen. *Puerto Rican Women.* Lisboa Associates, 1995.

Biningual profiles and drawings of forty-three notable Puerto Rican women.

De Ruiz, Dana Catherine, and Richard Larios. *La Causa: The Migrant Farm Workers' Story.* Illustrated by Rudy Gutierrez. Raintree/Steck-Vaughn, 1993. Grades 3 to 7.

This readable book presents the origins of the United Farm Workers of America union and the efforts of César Chávez and Delores Huerta to organize migrant farmworkers in the 1960s.

Duberman, Martin (ed.). *Lives of Notable Gay Men and Lesbians.* Chelsea House, dates vary. Grades 6 to 12.

A unique series of thirty-three biographies, including *Gabriela Mistral—Guatemalan Poet* (forthcoming) and *Federico García Lorca—Spanish Dramatist and Poet,* written by Jaime Manrique. Call 1-800-848-BOOK for more information.

Frosch, Mary (ed.). *Coming of Age in America: A Multicultural Anthology.* New Press, 1994. Grades 6 to 12.

Foreword by Gary Soto. Short stories by Nicholasa Mohr, Durango Mendoza, Arturo Islas, Julia Alvarez, and many others.

Garza, Hedda. *Latinas: Hispanic Women in the United States.* Franklin Watts, 1994. Grades 9 to 12.

The important role played by Latina women in the history of the United States is documented in this inspiring, spirited book. There is much fascinating material here that has been hidden history for too long. Part of the Hispanic Experience in the Americas Series.

Gelman, Rita Golden. *Inside Nicaragua: Young People's Dreams and Fears.* Franklin Watts, 1988.

Rita Golden Gelman describes her experiences traveling through Nicaragua and the effects of the conflict on the lives of the young people of the country. Through personal narrative, she gives the reader not just the politicians and guerrillas, soldiers and saints, but a human story of the contrasts in Nicaragua, from the point of view of the young people she interviewed. Includes photographs, a glossary, bibliography, and index.

Hamilton, R. J. The Pride Pack #1: *Who Framed Lorenzo Garcia?* Alyson, 1995. Grades 6 to 12.

Kicked out of his house by his bigoted father, gay teen Ramon Torres has bounced from foster homes to the street and back again. Finding a safe haven has many roadblocks in this realistic, action-packed story. This title is the first in a series featuring gay and lesbian teens.

Hoobler, Dorothy and Thomas. *The Mexican American Family Album.* Oxford University Press, 1994. Grades 6 to 10.

Part of the series The American Family Album, this book presents the stories of Mexican American immigrants through historical photographs, diaries, letters, memoirs, and newspaper articles. The book provides a pictorial and written record of the country left behind, the journey to the new land, the life that the newcomers made for themselves in their adopted country, and the contributions made to the United States.

Kissinger, Katie. *All the Colors We Are/Todos los colores de nuestra piel.* Hampton-Brown, no date available. Grades 1 to 4.

This bilingual book frees children from the myths and stereotypes associated with skin color. It showcases the beautiful diversity of colors of humans. The outstanding full-color photographs support a simple, scientifically accurate explanation for skin tones.

McKissack, Patricia and Fredrick. *Taking a Stand Against Racism and Racial Discrimination*. Franklin Watts, 1990. Grades 4 to 10.

In this rare book the McKissacks outline the history of racism and the movements that have combatted it; they examine the different forms racism takes and analyze where it can lead if left unchallenged. They provide an overview of relevant court cases, boycotts, and protests.

Montejo, Victor. *The Bird Who Cleans the World*. Curbstone Press, 1991. All Ages.

A collection of Jakaltek Mayan folktales, first told to Montejo by his mother and the elders of his Guatemalan village. These tales examine the themes of nature, creation, mutual respect, and ethnic relations and conflicts.

Muse, Daphne (ed.). *Prejudice: Stories About Hate, Ignorance, Revelation, and Transformation*. Hyperion Books for Children, 1995, Grades 6 to 12.

This thought-provoking collection of short stories and excerpts from novels reveals many facets of prejudice. Readers will be inspired to join the struggle for a just and equitable society. Includes a story by Sandra Cisneros.

Nye, Naomi Shihab. *This Same Sky: A Collection of Poems*

from Around the World. Four Winds Press, 1992. All Ages.

From 68 countries worldwide come 129 voices of hope. Includes poems by Alberto Blanco, Octavio Paz, David Escobar Galindo, Jorge Carrera Andrade, Floria Herrero Pinto, Renée Ferrer de Arréllaga, and many others.

Nye, Naomi Shihab. *The Tree Is Older Than You Are: A Bilingual Gathering of Poems and Stories from Mexico with Paintings by Mexican Artists*. Simon & Schuster, 1995. All Ages.

This beautiful book features the work of sixty-four Mexican poets and painters including Alberto Blanco, Rodolfo Morales, Octavio Paz, Leticia Tarragó, Rosario Castellanos, Consuelo de Aerenlund, and Carmen Esquival. Best Books for Young Adults Award. *Hungry Mind Review* Children's Book of Distinction.

Ocampo, Silvina. *La Naranja Maravillosa (The Magic Orange)*. Santillana, no date available. 1-800-245-8584. Grades 5 to 8.

This book features a touching selection of short stories by the famous Argentinian author Silvina Ocampo. Some are joyful, others tragic; this is an engaging blend of fact and fantasy. In Spanish.

Ocampo, Silvina. *La Torre Sin Fin (The Tower of No End)*. Santillana, no date available. 1-800-245-8584. Grades 5 to 8.

Ocampo describes a young boy's adventure inside an enormous castle, where he makes a number of discoveries about life and himself. He learns to

paint and conquers his most secret fears. In Spanish.

Orozco, Jose-Luis (translator). *DeColores and Other Latin-American Folk Songs for Children*. Dutton Children's Books, 1995. 1-800-558-2110. Grades K to 3.

Twenty-seven bilingual songs, rhymes, and chants accompanied by bright collage illustrations. Arrangements for piano, guitar, and voice are included. An American Library Association Notable Book.

Parks, Marilyn, and Sharon Panik (retold by). *Quetzalcoatl Legends from Mexico and Central America Series*. Modern Curriculum Press, 1995. 1-800-321-3106.

This set of nine books includes a Spanish and English version and a teacher's guide for three stories: *A Quetzalcoatl Tale of Corn, A Quetzalcoatl Tale of the Ball Game,* and *A Quetzalcoatl Tale of Chocolate*.

Pena, Sylvia. *Tun-ta-ca-tun: More Stories and Poems in English and Spanish for Children*. Illustrated by Narciso Pena. Arte Público Press, 1986. Preschool to Young Adult.

This anthology realistically reflects the experience of Latina and Latino authors both in their country of origin and in the United States. This bilingual edition features fifteen poems and eight short stories by writers such as Nicholasa Mohr, Franklyn Varela, and Pat Mora.

Perera, Hilda. *Kiki: A Cuban Boy's Adventures in America*. Pickering Press, 1992. Grades 3 to 7.

Kiki Gómez, an eight-year-old Cuban boy, comes to the United States with his brother and cousins in the early 1960s. This book is based on Operation Peter Pan, which transported thousands of unaccompanied children from Cuba to the United States in 1960 and 1961.

Perez, Ramon Tianguis. *Diary of an Undocumented Immigrant*. Arte Público Press, 1991. 1-800-558-2110.

The author immerses readers in the world of the undocumented immigrant and the ordeals of crossing the border.

Santos, Richard G. *Origin of Spanish Names/Como te Llamas y Porque te Llamas Asi*. Illustrated by Humberto N. Cavazos. Photographs by Cynthia Ann Santos and Deborah A. Zamora. Richard G. Santos, 1981.

The author, a historian, provides a beginning etymology of Spanish names as well as a brief history of the Spanish language. Children and adults alike will be fascinated with this attractive bilingual volume.

Shields, Katrina. *In the Tiger's Mouth: An Empowerment Guide for Young Activists*. New Society Publishers, 1994.

Useful ideas and exercises for effective listening, speaking, facilitating, working cooperatively, forming support groups, self-renewal, and building bridges with the opposition. Insight into ways to overcome the inner obstacles to pursuing social change.

Singer, Bennett L. (ed.). *Growing Up Gay, Growing Up Lesbian: A Literary*

Anthology. New Press, 1994. Grades 6 to 12.

This valuable resource, geared specifically for lesbian and gay youth, includes over fifty poignant stories by established writers such as Gloria Anzaldúa, Jesse G. Monteagudo, Paula Gunn Allen, and Martina Navratilova.

Soto, Gary (ed.). *Pieces of the Heart: New Chicano Fiction.* Chronicle Books, 1993. Grades 9 to Adult.

This vibrant anthology of fifteen short stories by contemporary Chicano writers is united by the examination of cultural identity and family relationships. In his introductory essay, Soto describes writing as a brave act, one of utter loneliness and uncertainty. Writers include Sandra Cisneros, Mary

Helen Ponce, Ana Castillo, Jack Lopez, and Carlos Flores. Cover art is by Carmen Lomas Garza.

Sullivan, Charles (ed.). *Here Is My Kingdom: Hispanic-American Literature and Art for Young People.* Harry N. Abrams, Inc., 1994. Grades 3 to Adult.

The art and literature in this beautiful anthology work together to convey feelings of strength and pride.

Turner, Faythe (ed.). *Puerto Rican Writers at Home in the USA: An Anthology.* Open Hand, 1991. 1-800-558-2110.

The works of seventeen of America's foremost Puerto Rican writers reflect the influences of two cultures and two languages.

Verheyden-Hillard, Mary Ellen. *Scientist from Puerto Rico,*

Maria Cordero Hardy. Illustrated by Scarlet Biro. Series: American Women in Science Biography. The Equity Institute, 1985. Grades K to 4.

An inspiring fictionalized biography of a scientist who overcame numerous barriers to become head of a university department of medical technology.

Verheyden-Hillard, Mary Ellen. *Scientist with Determination, Elma Gonzales.* Illustrated by Marian Menzel. Series: American Women in Science Biography. The Equity Institute, 1985. Grades K to 4.

A fictionalized biography of a young girl whose curiosity and love of learning led to a career as a research scientist.

Westridge Young Writers Workshop. *Kids Explore America's Hispanic Heritage.* John Muir Publications, 1992. 1-800-558-2110.

Written by a group of students in Colorado, this book helps Latina and Latino children identify with their culture. Photographs and drawings.

Zapatar, Beatriz McConnie. *Fiesta!* Modern Curriculum Press, 1992. Grades 2 to 5.

Chucho, a young Colombian American boy, and his parents celebrate a fiesta like the ones in Colombia. Information about the history and traditions of the fiesta are provided. This book is part of Modern Curriculum's Multicultural Celebrations Series.

Magazines

Azul. Forthcoming. For more information contact Lori M. Carlson, c/o Henry Holt and Company, 115 West 18th Street, New York, NY 10011.

Chispa. This magazine is written in Spanish. Order from:

Innovacion y Comunicacion, S. A. de C. V. Tlacopac 6, Col. Campestre, C. P. 01040 Mexico, D. F. Tels. 662-60-46. Fax 662-77-81.

New Moon: The Magazine for Girls and Their Dreams.

New Moon Publishing, P.O. Box 3587, Duluth, MN 55803-3587.

This ad-free, bimonthly publication is edited by girls for girls ages 8 to 14. Featuring articles, fiction, poetry, cartoons, science

experiments, and art, this magazine is designed to encourage each girl to keep her voice and self-assurance as she moves from girl to woman. New Moon Publications also publishes *New Moon Parenting*, a bimonthly publication for parents of girls.

Audio

Ada, Alma Flor. *Aprender cantando I y II Cassettes (Learning Through Songs I and II Cassettes).* Laredo Publishing Company. 1-800-547-5113. All Ages.

In these cassettes in Spanish, Alma Flor Ada presents the multiple uses of songs in the

classroom: language and vocabulary development, reading instruction, literature and folklore enrichment, creative writing, development of identity, and cross-cultural appreciation. Examples of songs that can be used for each of these areas are sung by composer-singer Suni Paz. The lyrics for

all of the songs are provided on the inside cover.

Ada, Alma Flor. *Como una flor (Like a Flower).* Laredo Publishing Company. 1-800-547-5113. Grades 6 to 12.

Inspiring songs in Spanish for older student and adults.

Ada, Alma Flor. *Serie Cuéntame un Cuento (Tell Me a Story Series).* Laredo Publishing Company. 1-800-547-5113. Grades K to 4.

In this series of six cassettes, Alma Flor Ada reads contemporary versions of classic fairy tales on one side. On the other side,

Suni Paz sings them with a traditional Latin American folk beat.

Baker, Georgette. *Cantemos Chiquitos: Songs and Fingerplays from Mexico and South America.* The Talented, 1994. Grades K to 3.

_____. *Cantemos Chiquitos #2. More Traditional Songs from South of the Border.* The Talented, 1994. Grades K to 3.

These collections of bilingual songs and sayings feature the author singing and playing the guitar. Teachers and parents will find the tape and booklet format easy to use; children will enjoy the cheery music and be inspired to sing along.

Marimba Yalajon. *Chiapas! Heart of Wood Project,* 1994. All Ages.

This compact disc includes titles such as "Chiapas," "Guadalajara," "La Flora del Cafe," "La Marimba," and "Maria Bonita," which originate from the indigenous music of southern Mexico and Central America. Includes pleasing keyboard percussion music.

Vigil, Angel. *The Corn Woman.* Libraries Unlimited, 1995. Audio Stories and Legends of the Hispanic Southwest. Available in English or Spanish. 1-800-558-2110.

Drama

Feyder, Linda (ed.). *Shattering the Myth: Plays by Hispanic Women.* Selected by Denise Chávez. Arte Público Press, 1992. Grades 10 to Adult.

Compiled by renowned playwright and novelist Denise Chávez, the six plays in this collection battle the myths and stereotypes that continue to circumscribe the freedom of expression and life fulfillment for Latinas. The anthology contains *Shadow of a Man* by Cherríe Moraga, *Miriam's Flowers* by Migdalia Cruz, *Gleaning/Rebusca* by Caridad Svich, *Simply María or The American Dream* by Josefina López, *My Visits with MGM* by Edit Villarreal, and *A Dream of Canaries* by Diana Sáenz.

Hampton-Brown. *Plays and Puppetry Materials in Spanish.* 1-800-333-3510. Grades 3 to 5.

Three sets of materials: *La boda de la ratita y más teatro-cuentos (The Mouse's Wedding and Other Plays); El teatro del Escarabajo (Beetle Theatre);* and *¡Disfrázatel! (Dress Up).* Includes plays and information on masks, costumes, scenery, and how to make puppets.

Rosenberg, Joe. *¡Aplauso! Hispanic Children's Theater.* Pinata Books, 1995. All Ages.

This exciting collection of successfully staged and critically acclaimed Hispanic plays for young people of all ages includes diverse selections that run the gamut from social realism to fantasy. The plays are in English, Spanish, and bilingual formats. They offer excellent opportunities for audience participation.

Saldaña, Johnny. *Drama of Color: Improvisation with Multiethnic Folklore.* Heinemann, 1995. 1-800-541-2086. Elementary.

This unique resource is designed to promote the use of drama to enhance children's ethnic literacy by provoking personal insights into the multiethnic world of folklore. *Drama of Color* contains six chapters that cover such topics as the dramatization of stories in the classroom, reviews of literature that address the value of drama for children of color, and the use of stories from Latina/Latino, Native American, Asian and Pacific Islander, and African/African American folklore. Drama is an excellent avenue for examining worldviews and perspectives and dispelling stereotypes. Includes detailed lesson plans and additional resources.

Videos

¡A Bailar! The Journey of a Latin Dance Company. Cinema Guild, 1697 Broadway, #506, New York, NY 10019-5904. 1-800-723-5522.

This thirty-minute video presents the inspiring story of Eddie Torres's dream of recruiting club and street dancers, molding them into a professional dance troupe, and establishing a Latin dance company.

¡Adelante Mujeres! Women's History Project, 7738 Bell Road, Windsor, CA 95492-8518. (707) 838-6000.

Spanning almost five centuries, the major events, themes, organizations, and personalities are introduced chronologically to weave a powerful, affirmative story of the lives of Mexican American women.

American Tongues by Louis Alvarez and Andrew Kilker. New Day Films, 22D Hollywood Avenue, Hohokus, NJ 07434. (201) 652-6590.

Available with a study guide, this forty-minute video provides an excellent introduction to language diversity. The speech of people from a variety of United States locations provides an interesting study of dialects; excellent rebuttal for Standard English and English Only zealots.

Gary Soto Series: These videos are available directly from Gary Soto. Call (510) 845-4718 to order or for more information.

—*The Bike.* Rudy's odyssey around the neighborhood on his new bicycle. VHS 11 minutes.
—*Novio Boy.* Rudy's first date. VHS 30 minutes.
—*"The Pool Party."* 1993 Andrew Carnegie Medal winner. VHS 28 minutes. See

the review of the book on pages 160–161.

HISPANIC Magazine Guide to Hispanic Excellence. 98 San Jacinto Blvd., #1150, Austin, TX 78701.

A series of three videotapes: *The Leaders, Sports,* and *Arts and Entertainment.* The tapes feature John Leguizamo, Pablo Morales, Jackie Nespral, Antonio Novello, Paul Yzaguirre, and others sharing their experiences with overcoming difficulties in childhood and adult life. Designed to inspire young people. Guidebooks and a teacher's workbook are available.

Luis J. Rodriguez. Lannan Literary Video # 31. 1-800-869-7553.

Meeting an Author. Laredo Publishing Company. 1-800-547-5113.

Alma Flor Ada shares some of the experiences that led her to become an educational leader and an advocate of children's, parents', and teachers' rights. This video will inspire lively discussions at any grade level and will help motivate young people to discover their own potentials. Available in English.

Puerto Rico: Art and Identity. Cinema Guild, 1697 Broadway, #506, New York, NY 10019-5904. 1-800-723-5522.

This fifty-six-minute video provides an excellent survey of artists in Puerto Rico during the twentieth century as well as several earlier artists. The artists' creative expressions of national identity and culture are captured through interviews with contemporary artists and art critics interwoven with the works of art.

The Shadow of Hate: A History of Intolerance in America. Teaching Tolerance, 400 Washington Avenue, Montgomery, AL 36104.

Free to educators; limit one per school. Send your request on school letterhead to the address above. This is a complete teaching kit packaged in a permanent storage case. Included is a forty-minute video, 128-page text, and a teaching guide. Creative and critical thinking activities are emphasized along with group activities. Supplemental activities provide options for extending or modifying the units.

Teaching Peace. Resource Center for Redesigning Education. P. O. Box 298, Brandon, VT 05733-0298. 1-800-639-4122.

This thirty-minute video features Sister Anna McAnany in

the Hawaiian public schools explaining values of peace, love, and justice. Winner of second prize for documentaries at the 1992 Hawaii International Film Festival.

Writing from the Heart by Alma Flor Ada. Mariposa Transformative Educational Services, 1992. Available through Laredo Publishing Company. 1-800-547-5113.

This videotape, specifically developed for use with students, features noted author and educator Alma Flor Ada reading from her books and demystifying the writing process. The underlying message is that we can all be authors of our lives and of our own books. The sixty-seven-minute tape is divided into four segments that can be viewed individually. Available in English or Spanish.

Posters and Picture Sets

Commemorative Posters: Bilingual Press. (602) 965-3867.

Three posters are available: the official poster of the National Chicano Art Exhibition, a "Bilingualism in the Bicentennial and Beyond" poster, and an "America the Beautiful, América el Bilingüe" poster.

Hispanic Americans Poster Set: Knowledge Unlimited, 1992. 1-800-558-2110.

Set of five posters featuring Jaime Escalante, Gloria Estefan,

Nancy Lopez, Manuel Lujan, and Antonio Novello. The text on each poster describes background and accomplishments. Includes teacher's guide.

Hispanic Heritage Poster Set. Knowledge Unlimited, 1989. 1-800-558-2110.

Set of ten posters with portraits and background information on Simón Bolívar, Pablo Casals, César Chávez, Henry Cisneros, Roberto Clemente, Juan Ponce de León, Gabriel García Márquez, Rita Moreno,

Katherine Ortega, and Pablo Picasso.

Latina Women of Hope Posters. 1-800-558-2110.

Set of twelve posters with beautiful photographs, and a sixty-four-page guide with biographies and lesson ideas. Includes Julia Alvarez, Amalia Mesa Bains, Sandra Cisneros, Miriam Colon, Ana Sol Gutierrez, Antonia Hernandez, Delores Huerta, Tania Leon, Adriana Ocampo, Antonia Pantoja, Helen Rodriguez-Trias, and Nydia Velasquez. Also avail-

able through the Women's History Project: (707) 838-6000.

Mexican American/Chicana Women Photo Display: National Women's History Project, 7738 Bell Road, Windsor, CA 95492-8518. (707) 838-6000.

This photo display contains rare photographs gathered from archives and private collections throughout the nation. Each of the twenty black-and-white photographs is accompanied by a bilingual description in Spanish and English.

Resources for Educators, Librarians, and Parents

Books

Ada, Alma Flor, Violet J. Harris, and Lee Bennett Hopkins. *A Chorus of Cultures: Developing Literacy Through Multicultural Poetry.* Hampton-Brown Books, 1993.

This practical resource offers an instructional model for integrating poetry across the curriculum. The calendar format presents a poem for each day of the year along with related reading materials, song sheets, and optional activities for promoting self-esteem, exploring culture, and valuing diversity. Poets include Gary Soto, Eloise Greenfield, Lucille Clifton, Langston Hughes, Arnold Adoff, Paul Fleishman, Mitsuye Yamada, Joseph Bruchac, and many more diverse voices.

Ada, Alma Flor. *A Magical Encounter: Spanish-Language Children's Literature in the Classroom.* Santillana, 1990.

Using a literature-based approach to teaching, Ada provides a useful guide that is filled with exciting ideas and classroom-tested activities. Inspired by Paulo Freire's critical pedagogy, this is a state-of-the-art whole language resource that includes helpful guidelines designed to make each child's encounter with books meaningful.

Ada, Alma Flor, and Rosalma Zubizarreta. *Language Arts Through Children's Literature: Using Children's Book Press Multicultural, Bilingual Books to Develop Critical Thinking and Creative Expression.* Children's Book Press, 1989; update forthcoming. (415) 995-2200.

This excellent resource is useful for helping adults expand their thinking about multicultural literature for children. Part I presents Ada's educational philosophy; Part II is comprised of brief annotations of each book and suggestions for use.

Allen, Adela Artola. *Library Services for Hispanic Children: A Guide for Public and School Librarians.* Oryx Press, 1987.

This informative volume focuses on professional issues related to library services including information on how to evaluate materials and programs. The annotated lists include materials in Spanish and in English.

Allen, Judy, Earldena McNeill, and Velma Schmidt. *Cultural Awareness for Children.* Addison-Wesley Publishing Company, 1992.

This activity book includes recipes, art, games, drama, and resources.

Ambert, Alba N., and Maria D. Alvarez. *Puerto Rican Children on the Mainland: Interdisciplinary Perspectives.* Garland, 1991.

Anaya, Rudolfo. *The Anaya Reader.* Warner Books, 1995.

This collection contains four excellent essays about the omission of Chicano/a literature, history, and culture from the curriculum: "An American Chicano in King Arthur's Court," "Take the Tortillas Out of Your Poetry," "On the Education of Hispanic Children," and "The Censorship of Neglect." See review on pages 47–48.

Anzaldúa, Gloria (ed.). *Making Face, Making Soul/Haciendo Caras: Creative and Critical Perspectives by Women of Color*. Aunt Lute Foundation Books, 1990. See review on pages 58–59.

Arnberg, Lenore. *Raising Children Bilingually: The Pre-School Years*. Bilingual Press, no date available. (602) 965-3867.

This book answers many key questions parents have about their children's bilingual education, such as the effect of bilingualism on their intellectual, linguistic, and social development.

Baker, Colin. *A Parents' and Teachers' Guide to Bilingualism*. Bilingual Press, no date available. (602) 965-3867.

This readable book provides an introduction to questions concerning bilingualism that are of practical value to parents.

Beilke, Patricia F., and Frank J. Sciara. *Selecting Materials for and About Hispanic and East Asian Children and Young People*. Library Professional Publications/Shoestring Press, 1986.

Barrera, Mario. *Race and Class in the Southwest: A Theory of Racial Inequality*. Bilingual Press, no date available. (602) 965-3867.

Focuses on the economic foundations of inequality as they have affected Chicanos in the Southwest from the Mexican War to the present. Synthesizes class and colonial analyses.

Blicksilver, Edith (ed.). *The Ethnic American Woman: Problems, Protests, Lifestyles*. Kendall/Hunt, 1989.

Essays, poems, and stories by over ninety women including Nicholasa Mohr, La Verne González, Evangelina Vigil, Estela Portilla Trambley, Marina Rivera, Angela De Hoyos, Guadalupe Valdés Fallis, and Joan Baez.

Boyd, Alex. *Guide to Multicultural Resources*. Highsmith Press, 1995. 1-800-558-2110.

A concise directory, mediagraphy, and almanac of current information on multi-cultural organizations, services, and trends. Lists over 3,200 Hispanic, Asian, Native American, and African American associations, institutions, and organizations, as well as major local, state, and federal governmental organizations. Updated periodically.

California Department of Education. *Recommended Readings in Spanish Literature: Kindergarten through Grade 8*. California Department of Education, 1991.

An easy-to-use annotated bibliography of books in Spanish. Useful indexes.

Carrasquillo, Angela L. *Hispanic Children and Youth in the United States: A Resource Guide*. Bilingual Press, no date available. (602) 965-3867.

Discusses and analyzes from a variety of perspectives the complex problems facing Latina/o youth: oppressive poverty, rampant unemployment, and the general lack of economic opportunities.

Cordasco, Francesco, and Eugene Bucchioni (eds.) *Puerto Rican Community and Its Children on the Mainland: A Source Book for Teachers, Social Workers and Other Professionals*. Scarecrow, 1982.

Cortés, Eladio (ed.). *Dictionary of Mexican Literature*. Greenwood Press, 1992.

Derman-Sparks, Louise, and A.B.C. Task Force. *Anti-Bias Curriculum: Tools for Empowering Young Children*. National Association for the Education of Young Children, 1989. 1-800-424-2460.

East, Kathy. *Inviting Children's Authors and Illustrators: A How-to-Do-It Manual for School and Public Libraries*. Neal-Schuman Publishers, 1995.

This practical manual explains all the steps in planning and implementing an author visit including how, why, when, where, and who. Sample letters, advertising, bookmarks, budget forms, checklists, time lines, and photographs are included.

Escamilla, Kathy, Ana María Andrade, Amelia G. M. Basurte, and Olivia Ruiz, in collaboration with Marie M. Clay. *Instrumento de observación de los logros de la lecto-escritura inicial: Spanish Reconstruction of an Observation Survey: A Bilingual Text*. Heinemann, 1995. 1-800-541-2086.

The power of systematic observation to inform teachers and improve instruction is well documented. However, until now, this work has only supported English-language literacy, even though Spanish-speaking students constitute the fastest-growing group in American schools. Drawing on the theoretical framework that made Marie Clay's *An Observation Survey* such a success, a new team of authors has developed and applied these same tasks for Spanish-speaking students. This book considers how children who come into contact with two languages use those languages to make sense of their world, providing plenty of observation tasks to monitor their progress.

Fernández, Mayra. *Barrio Teacher*. Laredo, no date available.

Foreword by Alma Flor Ada. Multiple voices from the life experiences of this committed teacher, each poem is a vignette, a complete story. Deep, firm, and tender dedication and service.

Fernández, Roberta (ed.). *In Other Words: Literature by Latinas of the United States*. Arte Público Press, 1994.

Roberta Fernández has gathered representative examples of fiction, poetry, drama, and essay currently being written by Latinas in the United States. The work is arranged by genre, and the topics are as varied as the voices and styles of the writers: the challenge of two cultures; experiencing marginality as a result of class, ethnicity, and/or gender; Latina feminism; the celebration of one's culture and its people. Most of the pieces are in English; some are presented bilingually in English and Spanish. Included are Gloria Anzaldúa, Marjorie Agosín, Elena Castedo, Lorna Dee Cervantes, Lucha Corpi, Sandra María Esteves, Carolina Hospital, Aurora Levins Morales, Pat Mora, Cherríe Moraga, Nicholasa Mohr, Judith Ortiz Cofer, Estela Portillo, Delores Prida, Cecilia Vicuña, Evangelina Vigil-Piñon, Alma Villanueva, Berniece Zamora, and many others.

Fernández, Roberta. *Intaglio: A Novel in Six Stories*. Arte Público Press, 1990.

The winner of the Multicultural Publishers Exchange Best Book of Fiction, *Intaglio* presents sensitive portraits of six fascinating women of the Southwest as told through the admiring voices of young relatives. *Intaglio* is the process of being imprinted upon; each young woman tells how her older relative's example shaped her development. In "Andrea," the young narrator idealizes her aunt and takes dancing lessons hoping to follow in her footsteps. "Filomena" features a young woman who commemorates the Day of the Dead each year with her second mother. "Zulema" tells about a girl who learned to cope with the loss of her mother by becoming a storyteller; years later she elaborates on these *cuentos* for a young niece. "Amanda" is a story about a seamstress who captivates her young relative with her exquisite creations. In "Verónica," when a young woman is raped, the women in her family help her grieve by holding a wailing session in which they all cry together for the sorrows of all the women in the family. A beautiful old house is torn down in the name of progress in "Leonor." Years earlier in this house, a woman guided her granddaughters through the journey of their lives during a solstice ritual. The book includes several family trees and a glossary of Spanish words and phrases.

Fishman, Joshua, and Gary D. Keller. *Bilingual Education for Hispanic Students in the United States.* Bilingual Press, no date available.

An outstanding reference tool and text for teacher training courses. Gives a historical overview, defines the goals of bilingual education, reviews the research on instruction assessment, and more.

Fitzjohn, Sue. *Festivals Together: A Guide to Multicultural Celebrations.* 1993. Hawthorn

A resource guide for celebrations and observations of special days and traditions of many different cultures. Includes stories, songs, crafts, activities, and recipes.

Foster, David William. *Gay and Lesbian Themes in Latin American Writing.* Bilingual Press, no date available. (602) 965-3867.

Examines more than two dozen texts that deal with gay and lesbian topics, drawing

from them significant insights into the relationship between homosexuality and society in different Latin American countries and time periods.

Gibbons, Reginald (ed.). *New Writings from Mexico: A TriQuarterly Collection of Newly Translated Prose and Poetry.* Northwestern University, 1992.

This special issue of *TriQuarterly* includes writings by Alberto Blanco, Gloria Velásquez, and over fifty other examples of the vigorous and exciting new short fiction, poetry, and essays being written today.

Gonzalez, Ray (ed.). *Currents from the Dancing River: Contemporary Latino Fiction, Nonfiction and Poetry.* Harcourt Brace, 1994.

An extensive contemporary collection of the writings of some of the outstanding Latino/a writers in the United States today, including Gloria Anzaldúa, Gary Soto, Pat Mora, Rudolfo Anaya, and Nicholasa Mohr.

Hammond, Merryl, and Rob Collins. *One World, One Earth: Educating Children for Social Responsibility.* New Society Publishers, no date available.

Foreword by Rosalie Bertell. Featuring suggestions on how to educate, motivate, and activate young people, this is an excellent resource for parents and educators who want to help young people explore peace, environmental, and social justice issues. The authors offer learning activities, ice breakers, and lesson plans featuring music, games, drama, sample handouts, and useful resources. The book also includes suggestions for involving the wider community and creating a cooperative learning environment.

Hayden, Carla D. (ed.). *Venture into Cultures: A Resource Book of Multicultural Materials and Programs.* American Library Association, 1992.

An excellent annotated guide that presents basic titles and practical program ideas. The seven chapters include: African American, Arabic, Asian, Hispanic, Jewish, Native American, and Persian.

Heath, Alan. *Windows on the World: Multicultural Festivals for Schools and Libraries.* Libraries Unlimited, 1991.

Herrera-Sobek, María (ed.). *Beyond Stereotypes: The Critical Analysis of Chicana Literature.* Bilingual Review Press, no date available. (602) 965-3867.

This volume is the first collection of studies devoted exclusively to Chicana literature. It contains articles on the female hero in Chicano literature, the fictive voices of Chicana novelists, the prose of Gina Valdés and Sylvia Lizárraga, the short stories of Estela Portillo Trambley, the poetic "I" in Alma Villanueva's *Mother, May I?*, and humor in Chicana literature.

Heyck, Denis Lynn Daly (ed.). *Barrios and Borderlands: Cultures of Latinos and Latinas in the United States.* Routledge, 1994.

This anthology embraces a broad range of genres and disciplines; interviews, oral histories, poetry, essays, music, recipes, short stories, photographs, drama, and excerpts from novels make this a moving and original volume. Denis Lynn Daly Heyck is also the editor of *Life Stories of the Nicaraguan Revolution.*

Ioga, Cristina. *The Inner World of the Immigrant Child.* St. Martin's Press, 1995.

Foreword by Alma Flor Ada. "Dedicated to all immigrant children—may their voices be heard by teachers and administrators so that they reach their fullest potential and feel truly alive in school." Cristina Ioga has written an inspiring book that features the voices of immigrant children. It is designed to help educators understand the needs and feelings of immigrant children so that they can better facilitate their transition between two worlds.

Kanellos, Nicolás, and Claudio Esteva Fabregat (eds.). *Handbook of Hispanic Cultures of the United States.* Arte Público Press, 1994.

This award winning four-volume set includes: Literature and Art, History, Sociology, and Anthropology.

Knowledge Unlimited. *Bienvenidos!* A bilingual/bicultural teaching guide for introducing students to the customs, history, music, folklore, festivals, and language of Mexico. Grades K-6. 1-800-536-2303.

LaDuke, Betty. *Compañeras.* Davis Publications, no date.

This excellent resource features the role of Caribbean, Central American, and South American women in art and social change. Order #7515C3, Davis Publications, Inc., P.O. Box 15015, Worcester, MA 01615-9959. 1-800-533-2847.

Lomeli, Francisco A., and Carl R. Shirley (eds.). *Dictionary of Literary Biography: Chicano Writers.* First Series, Volume 82. Gale Research, 1989.

———. *Dictionary of Literary Biography: Chicano Writers.* Second Series, Volume 122. Gale Research, 1992.

Luis, William (ed.). *Dictionary of Literary Biography: Modern Latin-American Fiction Writers.* First Series, Volume 113. Gale Research, 1992.

Luis, William, and Ann Gonzales (eds.). *Dictionary of Literary Biography: Modern Latin-American Fiction Writers.* Second Series, Volume 145. Gale Research, 1994.

LaGuardia, Delores, and Hans P. Guth. *American Voices: Multicultural Literacy and Critical Thinking.* Mayfield Publishing, 1993.

This thematically organized multicultural anthology of essays, fiction, interviews, reviews, and poetry by writers of diverse backgrounds is designed as a college textbook but is also useful as a professional resource. Contributors include Lorna Dee Cervantes, Camilo Jose Vergara, Jose Luis, Rosa Maria Urbina, Arturo Madrid, and Rose del Castillo Guilbault.

Levine, David, Robert Lowe, Bob Peterson, and Rita Tenorio (eds.). *Rethinking Schools: An Agenda for Change.* New Press, 1995.

This book collects the best articles in eight years of *Rethinking Schools,* a leading education-reform journal. It includes an

excellent article by Elizabeth Martinez titled "Distorting Latino History: The California Textbook Controversy," in which she documents the inaccuracies, distortions, sanitizations, omissions, and outright racist accounts rampant in a Houghton Mifflin textbook series.

Lindgren, Merri V. (ed.). *The Multicolored Mirror: Cultural Substance in Literature for Children and Young Adults.* Cooperative Children's Book Center, 1991.

Teachers and librarians searching for materials on cultural authenticity will find bibliographies, resource lists, and articles by George Ancona, Rudine Sims Bishop, Tom Feelings, Phoebe Yeh, Doris Seale, Walter Dean Myers, and others in this reference book.

Loewen, J. W. *Lies My Teacher Told Me: Everything Your American History Textbook Got Wrong.* New Press, 1995.

An outstanding contribution to the literature that assesses contemporary United States history textbooks, this book documents distortions, omissions, and stereotypes as well as events that are presented without an analysis of the precipitating factors and with a striking lack of critical thinking.

López, Arcadia H. *Barrio Teacher.* Arte Público Press, 1992.

This is the inspiring autobiography of an outstanding educator who overcame the turmoil and dislocation of revolution and immigration, as well as the deprivation of growing up in a poor family during the Depression. Through hard work and ingenuity, López managed to gain a college education and return to her neighborhood to help other children of poverty and dislocation. A pioneer in urban education and bilingual education, López, now a retired teacher, made a significant contribution to her profession. A friend and colleague states in the introduction, "Her life is one of courage and determination in the face of hardships. This beautiful woman overcame a hearing impairment, poverty, and discrimination to become a dedicated teacher of highest distinction."

Magill, Frank N. (ed.). *Masterpieces of Latino Literature.* HarperCollins, 1994.

Descriptions, analyses, characters, plots, themes, critical evaluations, and significance of major works of fiction, nonfiction, drama, and poetry. Includes Rudolfo Anaya, Sandra Cisneros, Julia Alvarez, Judith Ortiz Cofer, and Gary Soto.

Martinez, Elizabeth (ed.). *500 Years of Chicano History/500 Años del Pueblo Chicano.* Southwest Organizing Project, 1991.

Through extensive use of historical photographs, period art, poetry, and text, this stirring Spanish/English bilingual reference work presents a dramatic history, one that does not avoid the realities of injustice and oppression. This important book speaks with grief and bitter truth but also joy and pride.

Martínez, Julio, and Francisco A. Lomeli (eds.). *Chicano Literature: A Reference Guide.* Greenwood Press, 1985.

These essays on Chicano literature include children's and young adult literature.

Mathias, Barbara, and Mary Ann French. *Forty Ways to Raise a Nonracist Child.* Harper Perennial, 1996.

Practical suggestions for all families.

Meyer, Doris (ed.). *Lives on the Line: The Testimony of Contemporary Latin American Authors.* University of California Press, 1988.

This extensive collection of writings by many of Latin America's finest authors acquaints the reader with the diversity of personal, social, and political experiences and perspectives among the writers. A bio-bibliographic note about the author precedes each selection. Includes contributions by Isabel Allende, Jorge Luis Borges, and Octavio Paz.

Muse, Daphne (ed.). *The New Press Guide to Multicultural Resources for Young Readers.* New Press, 1997.

Inspired by the *Whole Earth Catalogue,* this comprehensive reference guide provides educators, librarians, and parents with information about the growing body of multicultural educational materials. The first volume is intended for teaching and school programming related to students in grades K–8 with the subsequent volume for high school and college. Call (212) 629-8802 for more information.

Olivares, Rafael A. *Using the Newspaper to Teach ESL Learners.* International Reading Association. 1-800-336-READ.

This excellent book provides strategies and activities for teaching language arts, mathematics, science, and social studies.

Perez, Bertha, and Maria E. Torres-Guzman. *Learning in Two Worlds: An Integrated Spanish/English Biliteracy Approach.* Longman Publishing, 1992.

This excellent resource is significant for its coherent demonstration that children's cultural knowledge is the appropriate starting point for literacy and biliteracy development. The focus is on how teachers of Spanish-speaking students can facilitate literacy growth in both Spanish and English.

Pignatelli, Frank, and Susanna W. Pflaum (eds.). *Celebrating Diverse Voices: Progressive Education and Equity.* Resource Center for Redesigning Education, 1995. 1-800-639-4122.

This is the First Annual Yearbook of the Bank Street College of Education. Twelve strong chapters address the challenges of racial, cultural, and socioeconomic diversity and how public education can respond to the inequalities that divide people along these boundaries. This important book calls for a humane and compassionate education that is responsive to the life experiences of every child.

Ramirez, Gonzalo, and Jan Lee Ramirez. *Multiethnic Children's Literature.* Delmar Publishers, 1994.

A reference guide to K–8 multiethnic literature, this useful book includes chapters on the rationale for and history of multiethnic literature, guidelines for selecting multiethnic literature, activities for extending children's experience, addresses of publishers, and two indexes: author/title and subject.

Ramos, Juanita (comp. and ed.). *Compañeras: Latina Lesbians: An Anthology.* Latina Lesbian History Project, 1987; Routledge, 1994.

Compañeras is a collection of oral herstories, essays, poems, short stories, letters, journal entries, interviews, and artwork by and about Latina lesbians. In these pieces, some in Spanish, most in English, forty-seven Latinas of Argentinian, Brazilian, Chilean, Colombian, Cuban, Honduran, Mexican, Peruvian, Puerto Rican, and Nicaraguan descent address issues such as coming out as lesbians, relationships with family and friends, political organizing, and community building. The writers explore the process of commitment to a political struggle to end all forms of oppression. Includes a poem by Gloria Anzaldúa.

Rochman, Hazel. *Against Borders: Promoting Books for a Multicultural World.* American Library Association, 1993.

This award-winning book is designed to aid in directing students in grades 6–12 to reading materials that provide information about people from diverse cultural backgrounds. Beginning with her own immigrant experience, Rochman's essays focus on using books across cultures. The second section of the book consists of annotated bibliographies on specific ethnic groups and cultural issues. Useful indexes.

Ryan, Bryan (ed.). *Hispanic Writers: A Selection of Sketches from Contemporary Authors.* Gale Research, 1991.

Salazar, Norma. *Foolish Men! Sor Juana Inéz de la Cruz as Spiritual Protagonist, Educational Prism, and Symbol for Women.* LEPS Press, 1994.

This powerful book is framed within the field of educational historiography. It is the inspirational story of Sor Juana, the seventeenth-century literary genius, who symbolizes the right of women to participate and excel in intellectual and academic pursuits.

Schon, Isabel. *A Bicultural Heritage: Themes for the Exploration of Mexican and Mexican-American Culture in Books for Children and Adolescents.* Scarecrow Press, 1978.

Schon, Isabel (ed.). *Contemporary Spanish-Speaking Writers and Illustrators for Children and Young Adults: A Biographical Dictionary.* Greenwood Press, 1994.

This is the first worldwide guide to contemporary Spanish-speaking authors and illustrators for young readers. It features personal and professional information on more than two hundred contemporary Spanish-speaking authors and illustrators from Argentina, Austria, Bolivia, Brazil, Chile, Colombia, Costa Rica, Cuba, Great Britain, Italy, Mexico, Morocco, Peru, Romania, Spain, the United States, Uruguay, and Venezuela. (Only four authors are listed from the United States; the editor notes in the preface that she regrets the exclusion of those persons that time, geography, nonresponse, or unavailability at the time of compilation prevented from being included.)

Schon, Isabel. *A Hispanic Heritage: A Guide to Juvenile Books About Hispanic People and Cultures.* Scarecrow Press, 1980.

_____. *A Hispanic Heritage, Series II: A Guide to Juvenile Books About Hispanic People and Cultures.* Scarecrow Press, 1985.

_____. *A Hispanic Heritage, Series III: A Guide to Juvenile Books About Hispanic People and Cultures.* Scarecrow Press, 1988.

Isabel Schon's guides provide annotated bibliographies of children's and young adult books in English from Argentina, Bolivia, Chile, Colombia, Costa Rica, Dominican Republic, Ecuador, El Salvador, Guatemala, Honduras, Mexico, Nicaragua, Panama, Paraguay, Peru, Puerto Rico, Spain, United States, Uruguay, and Venezuela.

Telgen, Diane, and Jim Kamp (editors). *¡Latinas! Women of Achievement.* Visible Ink, 1996.

A 400-page biographical dictionary that includes information on seventy women, including Isabel Allende, Julia Alvarez, Ana Castillo, Denise Chávez, Sandra Cisneros, Judith Ortiz Cofer, Carmen Lomas Garza, and Pat Mora. Foreword by Nicholasa Mohr.

Telgen, Diane, and Jim Kamp (eds.). *Notable Hispanic American Women*. Gale Research, 1993.

A 448-page biographical dictionary that includes extensive information on over 275 women. Julia Alvarez, Sandra Cisneros, Carmen Lomas Garza, Nicholasa Mohr, and Pat Mora are included.

Trujillo, Carla (ed.). *Chicana Lesbians: The Girls Our Mothers Warned Us About*. Third Woman Press, 1991.

Composed of theoretical and creative writings and artwork by twenty-four Chicanas, this collection portrays the many differences in class, color, region, education, and language found in Latina lesbian literature. Distinctive styles and topics are featured, including fictional explorations of interracial relationships and critiques of gender bias and homophobia both in Latino and U.S. cultures. Writings by Gloria Anzaldúa, Cherríe Moraga, and Ana Castillo are included. Winner of the LAMBDA Book Award, Best Lesbian Anthology, the Out/Write Vanguard Award, Best Pioneering Contribution to the Field of Gay/Lesbian Lifestyle and Literature, this best-selling book has been praised as a testament to the power of unmasking, of reconfiguration.

Trotter, Tamara, and Joycelyn Allen. *Talking Justice: 602 Ways to Build and Promote Racial Harmony*. R and E Publishers, 1992. 1-800-558-2110.

A valuable handbook for all ages and all ethnic groups.

Urrea, L. A. *Across the Wire: Life and Hard Times on the Mexican Border*. Anchor WorldViews Press, 1993.

This engaging book provides us with insight into the human dimension of immigration. As a book for concerned educators, it provides a compelling vision of our mission to educate all children.

Zimmerman, Marc. *U.S. Latino Literature: An Essay and Annotated Bibliography*. March/Abrazo Press, 1992.

Journals and Magazines

America's Magazine
Organization of American States, 17th & Constitution Avenue NW, Ste. 300, Washington, DC 20006. (202) 458-3000. This magazine is designed to promote greater understanding among the peoples of the Western Hemisphere. Includes a focus on Latin American art, culture, history, literature, politics, and current events.

The Americas Review
Formerly *Revista Chicano-Riqueña*. A quarterly magazine of Latino/a literature, art, and thought that publishes the best in prose, poetry, essay, literary criticism, and book reviews. Call (800) 633-ARTE.

Aztlán
Chicano Studies Research Center, University of California–Los Angeles, 405 Hilgard Avenue, Los Angeles, CA 90024. (310) 825-2642. *A Journal of Chicano Studies* is a multidisciplinary journal devoted to the Mexican American experience in the United States.

The Bilingual Review/La Revista Bilingüe
Hispanic Research Center, Arizona State University, P.O. Box 872702, Tempe, AZ 85287-2702. (602) 965-3867. This journal provides coverage in all areas of bilingualism and bilingual education, ethnic scholarship, and the creative literature of Latino life in the United States. It also contains book reviews and annotated bibliographies as well as professional announcements and employment and training opportunities.

Hispania
Quarterly Journal of the American Association of Teachers of Spanish and Portuguese. Gunter Hall, Room 106, University of Northern Colorado, Greeley, CO 80639. (303) 351-1090.

HISPANIC Magazine
Hispanic Publishing Corporation, 98 San Jacinto Blvd, #1150, Austin, TX 78701. 1-800-251-2688. Information about business, arts, education, politics, current events, and lifestyles.

The Journal of Chicana Studies
Chicana/Latina Research Project, University of California at Davis, c/o Chicana Studies Program, Davis, CA 95616. (916) 752-2421.

Latin American Literary Review Press
121 Edgewood Avenue, Pittsburgh, PA 15218. (412) 371-9023. This scholarly publication provides a firsthand interpretation of Latin American literature for research and general readers.

The Latino Review of Books
Center for Latino, Latin American, and Caribbean Studies, University at Albany. State University of New York, Albany, NY 12222.

Multicultural Education: Magazine of the National Association of Multicultural Education
Caddo Gap Press, 3145 Geary Boulevard, #275, San Francisco, CA 94118. (415) 750-9978. FAX (415) 668-5450. $40.00 individual or $50.00 library/institution or with membership in the National Association of Multicultural Education. This excellent quarterly journal features articles, classroom practices, an extensive collection of reviews, and announcements of events and conferences. An example of a valuable article is "Mass Media as Multicultural

Curriculum: Public Competitor to School Education" by Carlos E. Cortés in the Spring 1995 issue.

MultiCultural Review

Greenwood Publishing Group, 88 Post Road W., P.O. Box 5007, Westport, CT 06881. $29.95 individual, $59 institutions. Dedicated to a better understanding of ethnic, racial, and religious diversity, this outstanding journal features reviews, articles, and information on current issues. An example of a valuable article is "Cesar Chavez and La Causa: Books for Children and Teenagers" by Oralia Garza de Cortes, featured in the March 1995 issue.

Radical Teacher

P. O. Box 102, Kendall Square Post Office, Cambridge, MA 02142. $8.00 employed, $4.00 unemployed and retired. A feminist and socialist journal on the theory and practice of teaching published by the Boston Women's Teachers' Group.

Review: Latin American Literature and Arts

680 Park Avenue, New York, NY 10021-5009. (212) 249-8950. One year, $18. A twice-yearly journal in English that features Latin American literature, film, sculpture, photography, theater, and dance.

Teaching Tolerance

400 Washington Avenue, Montgomery, AL. 36104. Fax (205) 264-3121. Published twice a year at no charge to educators by the Southern Poverty Law Center, a nonprofit legal and educational foundation based in Montgomery, Alabama.

Newsletters and Newspapers

Recovering the U.S. Hispanic Literary Heritage

E. Cullen Performance Hall, Room 256, Houston, TX 77204. This is a quarterly newsletter of information appropriate for teachers, scholars, and librarians.

Rethinking Schools

1001 E. Keefe Avenue, Milwaukee, WI 53212-9803. (414) 964-9646. Fax (414) 964-7220. $12.50 one-year subscription, $3.50 sample copy. *Rethinking Schools* is the country's leading grassroots voice for reform of our public schools. An independent quarterly journal written by teachers, parents, and activists, it analyzes educational policies and offers alternative teaching techniques and resources. Back issues and bibliographies are available. An example of an excellent article is "We Have Stories to Tell: A Case History of Puerto Ricans in Children's Books" by Sonia Nieto, featured in the Winter 1993 issue.

Catalogs

Arte Público Press

University of Houston, Houston, TX 77204-2090. 1-800-633-ARTE. AP is the oldest and largest publisher of U.S. Latina and Latino literature. The well-organized catalog includes fiction, poetry, drama, literary criticism, and art.

Bilingual Educational Services, Inc.

2514 South Grand Avenue, Los Angeles, CA 90007-9979. 1-800-448-6032. BES offers over one thousand titles for students from kindergarten through high school. They also offer a large line of filmstrips and videocassettes.

Bilingual Review Press

Hispanic Research Center, Arizona State University, P.O. Box 872702, Tempe, AZ 85287. (602) 965-3867. A nonprofit press that features professional resource books, masterworks of literature, novels, poetry, theater, folklore, and more.

Children's Book Press

246 1st Street, #101, San Francisco, CA 94105. (415) 995-2200. A nonprofit organization supported in part by grants from the California Arts Council. Publishes beautifully illustrated multicultural literature and audiocassettes, featuring both traditional and contemporary stories from minority and new immigrant cultures in the United States today. Many of the titles are bilingual.

De Colores, Inc.

P. O. Box 7487, Albuquerque, NM 87194. (502) 242-8075. Publisher of Chicano fiction, poetry, literature, history, art, and women's writing.

Great Ideas in Education Catalog

Resource Center for Redesigning Education, P.O. Box 298, Brandon, VT 05733-0298. 1-800-639-4122. Founded in 1993 to facilitate a deeper thinking about the role of schooling in the emerging post-industrial world.

Hampton-Brown Books

P.O. Box 369, Marina, CA 93933. 1-800-333-3510. Many cultures, many languages, many possibilities. Child-centered materials for ESL/ELD, multicultural education, balanced bilingual literacy, Spanish phonics, home-school connections, dual-language programs, and Head Start–Title I programs. Features theme packs, staff development materials, plays and puppetry, make-and-take-home books, and take-home parent packs. A number of Alma Flor Ada's books and her author videos are available through HBB.

Hispanic Book Distributors (HBD), Inc.

1665 West Grant Road, Tucson, AZ 85745. 1-800-634-2124. HBD is committed to providing quality Spanish-language informational and educational materials (books, periodicals, cassettes, and videos) to schools, libraries, and other institutions working with the Spanish-speaking population. Their objective is to promote the use and the development of the Spanish language as a vehicle for fostering long-lasting bonds of understanding between Hispanics and non-Hispanics.

Laredo Publishing Company

8907 Wilshire Blvd., Beverly Hills, CA 90211. 1-800-547-5113. By carefully selecting and publishing books and programs of high quality content, Laredo is a strong advocate for excellence in bilingual/multicultural education. Their titles provide students with literature designed to help youngsters become better readers, better writers, and above all, successful and proud of their heritage. Most of their titles are in Spanish but some are also in English. Laredo carries many of Alma Flor Ada's books.

Latino/Latina Books

Small Press Distribution, 1814 San Pablo Avenue, Berkeley, CA 94702. 1-800-869-7553. Features many titles for the mature reader, some appropriate for high school. An extensive selection of works translated from Spanish into English. SPD carries books from over three hundred literary small presses. Poetry, fiction, and cultural studies by Latina and Latino writers from throughout North, South, and Central America, Cuba, Puerto Rico, Spain, and Mexico.

Mariuccia Iaconi Book Imports

970 Tennessee Street, San Francisco, CA 94107 (415) 821-1216, 1-800-955-9577. Features a wide variety of materials in Spanish and some bilingual titles. Includes storybooks, multimedia, literature kits, reference books, textbooks, and more. The catalog is very well organized and attractively designed. Dedicated to children—to firing their imaginations, stimulating their minds, and enrapturing them with love for life.

Multicultural Catalog

American Econo•Clad Services, P.O. Box 1777, Topeka, KS 66601. 1-800-255-3502. This extensive, easy-to-use catalog includes multicultural, bilingual, and Spanish titles for readers K–12 as well as resources for educators. Thousands of fully annotated titles organized by grade level and ethnic group. Spanish titles are paired with the English edition when both are available.

New Society Publishers

New Society Educational Foundation, 4527 Springfield Avenue, Philadelphia, PA 19143. 1-800-333-9093. Featuring books to build a new society, NSP is a not-for-profit, worker-controlled publishing house dedicated to promoting fundamental changes through nonviolent action. Materials address the needs identified by a growing global network of social and economic justice, antiracist, human rights, feminist, and environmental movements.

Santillana

"Literature and Textbook Catalog." 2105 86th Avenue, Miami, FL 33122. 1-800-245-8584. K–12 materials in Spanish. Picture books, videos, fiction, reference, and text materials. Includes many of Alma Flor Ada's books.

Third Woman Press

Chicana Studies, University of California, 3412 Dwinelle Hall, Berkeley, CA 94720. (510) 642-0240. Third Woman Press publishes works by and about Latinas.

Women's History Catalog

National Women's History Project, 7738 Bell Road, Windsor, CA 95492-8518. (707) 838-6000. Includes biography, reference books, picture sets, videos, posters, curriculum units, calendars etc.

Organizations and Centers

Afro-Hispanic Institute (AHI)

3306 Ross Pl. NW, Washington, DC 20008. (202) 966-7783. The AHI promotes the study of Afro-Hispanic literature and culture, including the publishing of books and the distribution of materials.

American Association of Teachers of Spanish and Portuguese

Gunter Hall, Room 106, University of Northern Colorado, Greeley, Colorado 80639. (303) 351-1090. Promotes the teaching of Spanish and Portuguese. Annual meeting, student awards, national Spanish examination, and placement bureau. Quarterly journal.

Association of Hispanic Arts

173 East 116th Street, Second Floor, New York, NY 10029. (212) 860-5445. Nonprofit, dedicated to strengthening Latino/a cultural institutions and to bringing the work of Latino/a artists to the public. Provides a clearinghouse of information about Latino/a arts and culture, publications, technical assistance to artists and art organizations and special projects.

Association of Mexican American Educators

634 South Spring Street #1010, Los Angeles, CA 90014. (213) 892-9901.

Association of Teachers of Latin American Studies

252-58 63 Avenue, Flushing, NY 11362-2406. (718) 428-1237. Promotes the teaching of Latin American studies in U.S. schools and colleges. Offers conferences, workshops, and curricular materials.

Center for the Study of Books in Spanish for Children and Adolescents

California State University, San Marcos, CA 92096-0001. (619) 752-4070. Headed by Dr. Isabel Schon, the center collects and evaluates books in Spanish from around the world. An annual conference is held.

Chicana/Latina Research Project

University of California at Davis, c/o Chicana Studies Program, Davis, CA 95616. (916) 752-2421. Nonprofit organization devoted to faculty development and research support. Workshops, seminars, publications. Publishes *The Journal of Chicana Studies.*

Chicana Studies Research Center

University of California, 405 Higard Avenue, Los Angeles, CA 90024.

ERIC Clearinghouse on Urban Education

Publication: *A Directory of Anti-Bias Education Resources and Services.* Order from: ERIC Clearinghouse on Urban Education, Box 40, Teachers College, Columbia University, New York, NY 10027.

Institute for Puerto Rican Affairs

606 18th Street, NW, Washington, DC 20006. (202) 371-8111. Dedicated to creating an appreciation for the history, arts, literature, and other forms of cultural expression of Puerto Rican people. Provides public forums, exhibitions, and workshops.

Latin American Writers Institute (LAWI)

c/o Hostos Community College, 500 Grand Concourse, Bronx, NY 10451. (718) 518-4195. LAWI is a literary and service organization for the promotion and dissemination of the work of Latino/a writers writing in English or Spanish and residing in the United States. Provides workshops, conferences, and awards.

Mexican American Legal Defense and Education Fund

634 S. Spring Street, 11th Fl., Los Angeles, CA 90014. (213) 629-2512. Works to protect civil rights of Hispanics. Has an education litigation department.

Mexican American Women's National Association

1101 17th Street NW, #803, Washington, DC 20036-4704. (202) 833-0060. Provides resource information on national issues affecting Mexican American women.

Mexican Heritage Society

P.O. Box 2723, Port Arthur, TX 77643. (409) 962-3147. Dedicated to promoting Mexican culture through cultural events and a scholarship program.

Multicultural Publishing and Education Council

2280 Grass Valley Highway #181, Auburn, CA 95603-2536. (916) 889-4438. A national networking and support organization for independent publishers of multicultural books and materials.

National Alliance of Spanish-Speaking People for Equality

1701 16th Street NW, #601, Washington, DC 20009. (202) 234-8198. This human rights group is concerned with ending discrimination against Latinos, Latinas, and others. Provides a referral information service and participates in literacy programs.

National Association for Chicano Studies (NACS)

c/o Dr. Carlos S. Maldonado, Eastern Washington University, Chicano Education Program, Monroe Hall 198, MS-170, Cheney, WA 99004. (509) 359-2404. A research and information organization providing educational, cultural, and political materials.

National Association of Cuban American Women USA, Inc.

2119 South Webster Street, Fort Wayne, IN 46802. (219) 745-5421. National support group devoted to improving education, job training, and benefits for Cuban American women.

National Clearinghouse for Bilingual Education

1118 22nd Street NW, Washington, DC 20037. 1-800-321-6223 or (202) 467-0867. Free mini-bibliographies, digests, information packets, bimonthly newletter, program information, referrals, publications. Nonprofit.

National Conference of Puerto Rican Women

5 Thomas Circle, NW, Washington, DC 20005. (202) 387-4716. Promotes the equal participation of Puerto Rican women and other Latinas in social, economic, and political life in the United States.

National Organization for Multicultural Education

Membership information: Donna Gollnick, NCATE, 2029 K Street N.W., #500, Washington, DC 20006. Publication: *Multicultural Education.* See Journals on pages 212–213

Resource Center of the Americas (RCTA)

317 17th Avenue SE, Minneapolis, MN 55414. (612) 627-9445. RCTA provides information to people of all ages about social, cultural, political, and economic conditions of Latin America, believing it is the responsibility of all U.S. citizens to be informed about their country's relationship with other nations and peoples.

Title Index

Illustrator Index

Awards and Honors Index

This index includes the awards and honors won by the books included in this volume. For information about the awards, honors, fellowships, and grants won by individual authors, please refer to the biographical sketch in each chapter.

Subject Index